# Creativity and Innovation in the Fashion Business

T0309229

*Creativity and Innovation in the Fashion Business* explores the ways in which creativity and innovation play a central role across the fashion industry, paying particular attention to design and technical perspectives. This topic is examined through careful theoretical analysis, incorporating the perspectives of multiple contributors who together possess a wealth of combined experience in creative and technical roles in the fashion business.

Broad in scope, this textbook first provides a wide overview of creativity and innovative developments across the industry, before considering technical and digital innovation in production and product development, as well as trend forecasting. The final part of the book then consists of an exploration of sustainable innovation in design for fashion brands and retailers. Each chapter includes aims and summaries to structure learning and highlight key points, academic insights from thought leaders and interviews from industry and academia.

A vital introductory textbook, *Creativity and Innovation in the Fashion Industry* is well-suited to undergraduate and postgraduate modules across subjects such as Fashion Business, Fashion Design and Manufacturing, Product Development, Innovation Management, and Buying and Merchandising. Online resources include PowerPoint slides and a test bank.

**Helen Goworek** PhD is Professor in Marketing and MSc Marketing Programme Director at Durham University, UK. Helen's prior experience of working in the fashion industry in buying and design for retailers and manufacturers for several years influences her research in the fields of product development, retailing and sustainability.

**Fiona Bailey** is Programme leader in Fashion Management at De Montfort University, UK. Fiona's research focuses on Gen Z's online search behaviour and UX design strategies for fashion retailers. She has over 20 years experience in the fashion industry, as a buyer for one of the UK's biggest retailers, Next, and as an entrepreneur, jointly setting up the award-winning, sustainable, girlswear brand Kingdom of Origin. She regularly contributes to BBC radio as a retail business expert and holds a BA in Business Management with languages from Edinburgh Napier University, UK and a MA in Design Management from De Montfort University, UK.

## Mastering Fashion Management

The fashion industry is dynamic, constantly evolving and worth billions worldwide: it's no wonder that Fashion Business Management has come to occupy a central position within the Business School globally. This series meets the need for rigorous yet practical and accessible textbooks that cover the full spectrum of the fashion industry and its management.

Collectively, *Mastering Fashion Management* is a valuable resource for advanced undergraduate and postgraduate students of Fashion Management, helping them gain an in-depth understanding of contemporary concepts and the realities of practice across the entire fashion chain – from design development and product sourcing, to buying and merchandising, sustainability, and sales and marketing. Individually, each text provides essential reading for a core topic. A range of consistent pedagogical features are used throughout the texts, including international case studies, highlighting the practical importance of theoretical concepts.

Postgraduate students studying for a Masters in Fashion Management in particular will find each text invaluable reading, providing the knowledge and tools to approach a future career in fashion with confidence.

**Sustainable Fashion Management**
*Claudia E. Henninger, Kirsi Niinimäki, Marta Blazquez Cano and Celina Jones*

**Fashion Supply Chain Management**
*Virginia Grose and Nicola Mansfield*

**Celebrity Fashion Marketing**
Developing a Human Fashion Brand
*Fykaa Caan and Angela Lee*

**Luxury Fashion Brand Management**
Unifying Fashion With Sustainability
*Olga Mitterfellner*

**Fashion Business and Digital Transformation**
Technology and Innovation across the Fashion Industry
*Charlene Gallery and Jo Conlon*

**Customer Experience in Fashion Retailing**
Merging Theory and Practice
*Bethan Alexander*

**Luxury Fashion Marketing and Branding**
A Strategic Approach
*Alice Dallabona*

**Creativity and Innovation in the Fashion Business**
Contemporary Issues in Fashion Design and Product Development
*Helen Goworek and Fiona Bailey*

For more information about the series, please visit https://www.routledge.com/Mastering-Fashion-Management/book-series/FM

# Creativity and Innovation in the Fashion Business

## Contemporary Issues in Fashion Design and Product Development

Helen Goworek and Fiona Bailey

Routledge
Taylor & Francis Group

LONDON AND NEW YORK

Designed cover image: toos / Getty Images

First published 2025
by Routledge
4 Park Square, Milton Park, Abingdon, Oxon OX14 4RN

and by Routledge
605 Third Avenue, New York, NY 10158

*Routledge is an imprint of the Taylor & Francis Group, an informa business*

*British Library Cataloguing-in-Publication Data*
A catalogue record for this book is available from the British Library

ISBN: 9781032365824 (hbk)
ISBN: 9781032365800 (pbk)
ISBN: 9781003332749 (ebk)

DOI: 10.4324/9781003332749

Typeset in Bembo
by Deanta Global Publishing Services, Chennai, India

Access the Support Material: www.routledge.com/9781032365800

# Contents

# Author's Note

*Helen Goworek*

Creativity and innovation are two closely related concepts which are explored in detail in this book in the context of the fashion business, to which they are so vital. The ways in which creativity and innovation operate in theory and practice are explored, focusing primarily on fashion products, illustrated by interviews with over 20 specialist practitioners and academics. The topics covered comprise sources of creative inspiration; technical aspects of innovation and creativity; applying innovation theory to practice; fashion forecasting and sustainable fashion, as well as innovation in branded and mass market fashion. The book is aimed mainly at undergraduate or postgraduate students and lecturers on fashion or business programmes, as well as designers and their colleagues working in fashion product development.

My involvement in writing this book stemmed from completing a review for Routledge of another book in their *Mastering Fashion Management* series. After spotting "Creativity and Innovation in the Fashion Business" on the list of potential publications in this series, I was keen to submit a proposal. I hadn't seen another title specifically investigating this interesting topic before, despite it being at the heart of the fashion sector. I was particularly interested in taking the opportunity to discuss creativity and innovation with new and existing contacts in the fashion business and academia. Fiona Bailey and I have worked in some of the same organisations (at different times) and I was very pleased when she offered to write one of the chapters. As Fiona lectures in fashion innovation and has numerous industry contacts, she agreed to take on a larger role as co-author to help inform and shape other content throughout the book, conducting several of the interviews. Chapter authors Erica Charles, Carol Cloughton and Ruth Kelly, whom I've previously collaborated with in organisations and in research projects, bring extensive experience in creative, marketing and technical roles in the fashion business to their content in the book.

# Acknowledgements

We would like to thank the many people who have supported the development and content of this book over the last two years. Every contribution has been invaluable. We would like to thank Rupert Spurrier, Sophia Levine, Emma Morley and Kirsty Hardwick from Routledge who have provided excellent advice and support to bring the book to fruition; academics Steve Conway, David Smith, Alison Gwilt and Michael Beverland for providing advice above and beyond their interviews; Bettina Becker, George Bouvier, Claudia Henninger, Alana James, Lee Martin, Mike Saren and Stephanie Scott for their thoughts on creativity and innovation; Jos Berry, CLO-3D (Fernanda and Vera), Caroline Gration, Karen Purdy, Gemma Shiel and Helen Tarratt for kindly offering a wide range of their fashion images; Anil Raja for his feedback and incredible knowledge of Intellectual Property law; and Kirstie Alexander, Lesley Herrington, Sarah-Jane King, Jessica Apps and Eve Hanson for graciously giving their expert opinions.

A huge thank you to all of the interview participants and contributors from industry for their expertise and being so generous with their time: Jos Berry, Abigail Bourne, Jonathan Chippindale, Angélique Dietz, Harriet Eccleston, Joanna Feeley, Jo Gooding, Caroline Gration, Zoe Hinton, Tom Holmes, Bradley Lane, Jade McSorley, Simon Platts, Richard Price, Karen Purdy, Yiva Wu, Fran Sheldon, Gemma Shiel, Craig Smith, Elizabeth Stiles and Helen Tarratt.

Helen Goworek would like to thank Deborah, Fiona, Helen, Julia, Karen, Kathy and Ruth for the many conversations that have kept her updated with the fashion industry over the years.

Fiona Bailey would like to thank her wonderful colleagues Karen Hickinbotham and Siobhan Merrall for their feedback, friendship and encouragement. Fiona would also like to thank her husband Mike, and children Will, Louis and Bea for their constant love and support.

# List of Figures

# List of Tables

# List of Contributors

**Erica Charles** is Programme Leader for MSc Sustainable Fashion Business at the British School of Fashion – Glasgow Caledonian University, UK. Having previously managed branding and design projects for global brands, her research interests include fashion brand management and marketing communications, responsible business and social sustainability in fashion supply chains.

**Carol Cloughton** is a Senior Lecturer and Programme Leader in Fashion Marketing at York St John University, UK. She has over 20 years' experience developing and managing successful product categories for multiple global fashion and sportswear brands. Her research focuses on identifying trends, their meanings and how they could transform a brand's or retailer's future strategy.

Prior to founding Weft x Warp Fabric Consultancy Ltd, **Ruth Kelly** directed fabric development at renowned athletic apparel brand Lululemon. Passionate about materials, she's a creative fabric innovator and entrepreneur, connecting startups, manufacturers, mills and brands worldwide. Ruth holds a BSc in Textile Technology from the University of Manchester, UK.

# Introduction

*Helen Goworek*

Creativity and innovation are closely intertwined concepts which will be defined and explored in this book, with a specific focus on the context of the fashion business. Fashion has numerous definitions, and in this study it will be confined largely to the clothing and footwear sector. The creative economy has become increasingly important in Western countries, rising to 4.3 million jobs in the UK in 2022, constituting 12.9% of jobs in the UK, having expanded at twice the speed of the UK economy in general during 2011 to 2019 (DCMS, 2022). Designer fashion is considered to be one of nine subsectors of the creative industries by the UK government. Wilson (2009) presciently discussed the growing importance of the creative economy, addressing the potential clash between creativity and commerce and questioning whether the education system was sufficiently prepared at the time for this burgeoning sector. Martin and Wilson (2018:ix) describe creativity as "a universal human capacity", stating that "commercially motivated interest in creativity has mushroomed, and there is now a global industry dedicated to enhancing, fostering, enabling, and developing creativity in the workplace". This book largely addresses creativity within the context of being employed within this industry, but may also have relevance for those engaged in being creative as a leisure pursuit.

Clothing is a key sector of the economy, valued at £63.5 billion per year in the UK at the time of writing (Mintel, 2023a), second only to the food sector in many countries, since both of these markets are vital to the population. Fashion intersects with innovation by its very nature, which involves continuous development of new concepts. Omari et al. (2022) state that "a product-innovating organisation is one that is focused on creating new and value-creating end-user experiences". Innovation in the fashion sector is not limited to products, but also relates to connected areas, such as packaging, services and business models. This chapter discusses the central role played by creativity and innovation in the fashion business, beginning by defining creativity and innovation. Creativity and innovation-related

DOI: 10.4324/9781003332749-1

roles in the fashion business will be discussed throughout the book – e.g., fashion designers, textile designers, garment technologists, textile technologists, fashion marketers and fashion buyers – brought to life by interviews providing insights from experienced specialists in these fields. Key themes raised frequently in the interviews include sustainability (see Chapter 6) and the impact of artificial intelligence (AI) on innovation. Indeed, market research experts Mintel (2023b) predict that AI will become even further integrated with shoppers' customised interactions with fashion brands online.

## Defining and Examining Creativity and Innovation in the Context of Fashion

Creativity and innovation both indicate a sense of newness or novelty in products, services or concepts. Within the fashion business, creativity and innovation primarily relate to the development and integration of new ideas within processes or products. Such ideas may not always be brand new, but they may be implemented effectively for the first time within a particular product or process in order to be classed as innovative. Innovation may be a more prevalent approach in certain parts of an organisation, with some focusing more on novelty, whilst others prefer stability, according to Conway and Steward (2009:2), who state that "the management of innovation can be seen as the capability to handle such tensions creatively". Conway and Steward (2009:10) define innovation as a combination of invention and "bringing into common usage", incorporating novelty, processes of development and commercialisation. They also note that there is a distinction between innovation and similar terms such as design, diffusion and discovery (Conway & Steward, 2009). Tidd and Bessant (2021:19) define innovation succinctly as "creating value from ideas" and they propose that innovation is concerned not only with the creation of commercial value, but also social value in areas such as education, health and the alleviation of poverty. Smith (2024) is in agreement that innovation is not limited to technological developments, but can relate to concepts that are for the benefit of society. Innovation is generally considered to intersect with business and White (2023) proposes that innovation and entrepreneurship are complementary in nature. Innovation goes beyond the instigation of an idea to comprise the development and subsequent commercialisation of the idea. Innovation therefore requires the generation of an initial idea, which is followed by developing variations on the idea to make the concept's features more viable for production, to ultimately deliver value to customers at an appropriate quality standard and price. Innovation can refer to a process (or multiple, interconnected processes) or the output that results from the process.

The literature on innovation focuses largely on products, services and processes. However, innovation is not limited to these areas as it can also be applied to business models – e.g., a business moving from selling new products to a rental system. Innovations can include, but are not limited to, inventions which are entirely new to the world. Innovations are more often incremental in nature rather than radical, building on the features of existing products, thus making consumers feel that less risk is involved and potentially making them more inclined to purchase such products. Similarly, companies in the fashion sector may feel that incremental changes are safer for them, with less investment risk and a potentially higher level of profitability if similar products have a track record of appealing to their customers. New products or services may therefore be considered as innovations if they are new to the company which offers them or are serving new markets such as a different geographic location or if they are serving a new purpose. However, being overly cautious with innovation can limit a company's profitability if their competitors are able to steal a march on them with more innovative merchandise. Fashion brands and retailers therefore need to devise a relevant market strategy, deciding where to position themselves in terms of the extent of innovation they require to maintain or improve their market share, and therefore specifying to their designers to what extent they can be creative in their design development.

Martin and Wilson (2017:423) have explored the relevance of novelty, value and recognition, leading them to incorporate "the discovery and bringing into being of new possibility" within their definition of creativity. Creative inspiration for fashion (see Chapter 2) can lead to the development of new products on a spectrum that ranges from radical, "new-to-the-world" innovations to product types that are novel to the company or are additional products in a firm's existing ranges through to simply slightly amended replacements for existing products (Jobber and Ellis-Chadwick, 2023). New fashion products can therefore span from inventions or brand new combinations of styling and materials at one end of this spectrum through to very minor, incremental changes at the other. Whilst the phrase "New Product Development" (see Chapter 4) implies the launch of a new concept for a retailer, fashion product development is more likely to involve the introduction of new styles into an existing range or minor amendments to existing styles within a range – e.g., updating colours or improving comfort. When fashion retailers or brands develop product ranges that are new to the organisation, in doing so they are likely to complete a justification of a new product sector launch, assessing key competitors, potential market share, target customers, product value, pricing, set-up costs, manufacturing and selling locations, and overall timescale. Employees within creative roles will need to incorporate such factors into their creative thinking, requiring an understanding of the organisation within which they operate and the customers who will buy or use their products.

The creative fashion ideas that receive publicity are occasionally of the new-to-the-world type, but in practical terms, much of a fashion designer's work is based on creating more incremental changes to appeal to customers' tastes. The term "innovative" is often applied to the more *avant-garde* ready-to-wear designers' collections, often linked with being "conceptual", denoting that the specific combination of elements is novel, developed via intellectual and intuitive styling, more so than being an invention or a new technical development. London is often perceived as an influential hub for innovative design, particularly in connection with graduates from the creative degree courses offered in the city, such as Ingrid Kraftchenko and Masha Popova (see London Fashion Week, 2024). Men's wear brand Rhyzem was launched at London Fashion Week in 2022 by alumni of London College of Fashion and Central St Martins respectively, Yiva Wu and Boqun Huang, incorporating transparent fabrics and fluid styling (see Figure 1.1 and Chapter 7). In tandem with its edgy image, the UK has also seen the continued success of classic design houses such as Paul Smith and Margaret Howell. Other cities have been perceived as creating cutting-edge fashion at various times, including Tokyo and Antwerp, whereas the long-established fashion capitals of Paris, Milan and New York have tended to retain a reputation for more classic and sophisticated luxury.

The relationship between creativity and innovation can vary, dependent upon the product or service sector in which they take place. Creativity may be considered to be a component of innovation, or vice versa. Creativity can be considered a crucial element within business and society overall, as Wilson (2009: 179) states: "our ability to manage creativity is pivotal to future economic prosperity and social welfare". However, tension may sometimes exist between the more finance- and sales-orientated departments within a business and the creative, design-related employees, despite their collaboration being mutually beneficial and essential for a company's successful performance. Fashion companies have tended to move from a production orientation towards a market orientation, where customer demand can take priority over production issues (Goworek et al., 2016). Applying the term "commercial" to fashion design would usually be regarded as a compliment in the mass market, meaning that designs have wide appeal, but the same word can be considered somewhat derogatory in the ready-to-wear sector, where the output of certain designers may be viewed as more of an art form. Martin and Wilson (2018: ix) state that "human creativity has undoubtedly brought progress, but not without cost, especially to the natural environment", and there is consequently a growing need to consider sustainability within creative work.

This book uses the definition of branded fashion companies as those which primarily engage in the design and marketing of products using their own brand name and mainly sold by other companies' retail outlets or websites (although occasionally brands such as Nike or Adidas and well-known designers have a few of their own stores too). However, "own-label" retailers can be defined as companies which are predominantly involved in distribution of products directly to customers (who sometimes also work with manufacturers to develop products under their own label). Manufacturers and suppliers are companies responsible for producing

**FIGURE 1.1** Innovative men's wear designs by Rhyzem at London Fashion Week, emphasising craftsmanship and sustainability. *Photos with permission from Yiva Wu*

or supplying the goods which are sold by brands and retailers. A variety of roles are essential for creativity within the fashion business. Most notably, designers of garments and textiles play central roles in developing the products that provide the sector's sales and income in many companies. Design roles are offered technical support by garment technologists and textile technologists who also require creative skills to innovate in fabrics and garments, largely through developing new techniques, technologies, components and processes which are incorporated into garment design. Marketers, buyers and visual merchandisers are amongst the many roles where creativity is an essential approach in the fashion retail sector, in that they are concerned primarily with the visual appearance of promotion or products. Indeed, marketers involved in the development of concepts for advertising campaigns often have the formal job title of "creative". However, creativity and innovation are not exclusively in the domain of visually or technically orientated staff, with employees in any role having the capacity to develop and implement new ideas that innovate in business processes or which facilitate their colleagues' creativity.

> Professor Mike Saren has compiled the following academic definitions for this book, which he has adapted from his 2018 book *Marketing Graffiti: The Writing on the Wall*:
>
> Innovation: the realisation of new possibilities by transforming an original idea or concept to produce a new technology, design, process, system, style or other product or service which has some practical use. The degree of "newness" can vary from an incremental development of an existing innovation to a radical advance resulting in something completely new.
> Creativity: the ability to think of something new, involving a combination of vision, inspiration, originality, imagination, ingenuity, insight, and inventiveness. Creativity is normally a characteristic of an individual (although historically attributed to Gods and, more controversially, some now ascribe to machines, e.g. AI). A creative idea may appear by chance or serendipity (a Eureka moment), but it is more often the result of purposeful activity, even if the result was not expected.

Experts from business and academic fields, including interviewees from the other chapters within this book, were asked to define creativity and innovation, based on their own experience, as expressed in Tables 1.1–1.4. Most of the interviewees have expanded further on their definitions in later chapters. The purpose of acquiring these definitions is to view whether there is a consensus on interpretations of creativity and innovation amongst fashion practitioners and academics. The responses showed limited commonality in the definition of creativity and innovation amongst those selected, even from those within the same field of work. However, newness was the most frequent word used within their definitions. Several included thinking or thought processes, with a few mentioning innovation and creativity as value-adding, problem-solving or seeking solutions, and some discussing change

**TABLE 1.1** Definitions of creativity and innovation by practitioners and academics

| Design and product specialists in the fashion sector | Definitions |
| --- | --- |
| Jos Berry, CEO of Concepts Paris forecasting agency | Creativity is a sum of deep knowledge, because it's a very technical area, and that spark of something which is unquantifiable, very emotional and instinctive. Creativity is always based on being aware of what is happening and all that information and data processing plus emotion. |
| Abigail Bourne, Senior Buyer at Joules | For me, as a Buyer, innovation within fashion is constantly thriving to offer the customer the best possible product, be that through design, fit, fabric innovation or cost. Being creative drives innovation in itself – offering newness and re-thinking product keeps the industry fresh and moving. |
| Helen Tarratt, Fashion Consultant | Creativity is creating something that someone buys and they're happy with, that's fit for purpose .... It's creating something that the company's buyer likes .... For me it's about the retail buyer liking and selecting my design, which gives me a real sense of achievement. I think innovation is coming up with something that is very new ... coming up with something new that no one's really doing .... That's how I define innovation, more invention than creative. |
| Yiva Wu, Designer for ready-to-wear label Rhyzem | I always define creativity and innovation in fashion as telling a story through your own fashion language. I don't think creativity and innovation is only about inventing something extremely new or creating something that's never seen before in this entire world, I always believe that a good designer with creativity and innovation is someone who could use regular things to create their own system, dissolving inherent rules and thinking in design. |
| Angélique Dietz, Product Creation and Advanced Manufacturing Executive | Creativity and innovation for me are a natural output of behaviours and a way of being, such as being curious; being open; interested to keep learning; humility; asking questions ... experiencing new things. It's a way to approach life. |
| Karen Purdy, CEO of Purdy Creative design studio | Anything that sparks an idea in my head is creativity and I can find it personally in all walks of life ... if you're a creative person, your eyes are open and one idea leads to another ... it's taking it and putting your own spin onto something that makes you a creative person. I think there's a crossover between creativity and innovation because if you close your mind to innovation, you're not open to creativity. |
| Elizabeth Stiles, fashion coach and consultant | Creativity is a task to make sense of what's going on inside your mind. |
| Gemma Shiel, CEO of fashion brand Lazy Oaf | You have to decide how to prioritise innovation, and you can sometimes get so preoccupied with it being fresh and new and doing something different that it inhibits what you're producing or executing. At the same time, it's got to be a driver for you to achieve and create something that feels new and exciting and that you need in your life. |

| Creativity and innovation specialists in the fashion business | Definitions |
|---|---|
| Bradley Lane, former Senior Digital Leader at John Lewis | Creativity for me is about generating ideas, concepts or solutions that assist the customer/user. You can achieve this by using your past knowledge, experiences and your creative imagination. To be creative you need to try to think outside of the box, finding innovative ways to solve problems or do things differently. Innovation is about applying creative ideas or solutions that bring about meaningful change or improvement. |
| Richard Price, Managing Director for Clothing, Home and Beauty at Marks and Spencer | Innovation is creating something that nobody else has thought of that is new and ground-breaking and makes a difference. There's no point in doing innovation for innovation's sake. It has to have positive impact on the desirability or sustainability or longevity of a product or service. The important thing is it has to provide a solution or make a product better, more durable, cheaper or less harmful to the environment. It has to have a purpose. |
| Craig Smith, formerly Global Director for Innovation at PANGAIA | Innovation is a term that has become ubiquitous within business and often tends to have an air of mystery around but in essence is a form of problem-solving. Innovation or innovative thinking can be utilised in any form of business and is intended to lead to new products, processes, services or the improvements in those that already exist within a company. Innovation should be seen as a spectrum where solutions can be incredibly complex leading to disruptive solutions or more simplistic leading to incremental improvements. The type of innovation that is pursued is contingent on the business appetite for it, the resources that are allocated to it and the patience that exists to create change. |
| Jonathan Chippindale, CEO of Holition Consultancy | Creativity for me is searching into the unknown… The notion of being creative is doing something different that people notice. |
| Dr Jo Gooding, co-founder and Research Director of StyleAbility | Creativity gives the opportunity to create new ideas, solutions or approaches. Creativity happens on the borders of the usual– and occurs when we ask the question "Why?" When creativity is seen in a business context it is often called innovation. |
| Simon Platts, CEO Recomme | By definition, creativity creates innovation …. I think people are looking outside of our industry for creativity but we should be talking as a fashion industry. |
| **Academics in fashion education** | **Definitions** |
| Zoe Hinton, Senior Lecturer in Fashion, London College of Fashion | Creativity and innovation are about generating new and original ideas and then implementing those to create value in whatever you're doing … being able to discover newness and also empowering people to develop the ideas. |
| Professor Alison Gwilt, Professor in Design, University of New South Wales, Sydney | If your customers are telling you that sustainability matters, surely that is how you do something innovative as a designer? For designers and businesses this means speaking to your consumers in a way that moves beyond understanding what colours or styles they like and instead gathering real information that could drive innovation within the sector so much more. |

| | |
|---|---|
| Caroline Gration, Founder and Director, the Fashion School London | Innovation has an intelligence behind it that I wouldn't say creativity needs. Innovation is taking something that's already there and then moving it along. I think they are quite different, although they're absolutely intertwined and innovation is about the execution. I think there's more clarity of thought with innovation and you work out a route through to get to the product at the end … you're far more successful in fashion if you're innovative as opposed to just creative. Creativity comes from the heart, from inside, and innovation uses your brain more. |
| Jade McSorley, Digital Fashion Researcher, University of the Arts, London | Creativity is taking risks and problem-solving, like being able to be creative in the face of adversity or when you feel like you can't find a solution to something, then being creative in your approach. I think innovation is part of being creative; it's essential and exciting and can be rewarding, but I still always have this air of caution where I think we need to not just innovate for the sake of innovation … we need to responsibly innovate. |
| George Bouvier, Executive Director of Academia Cerebra, Milan – a multidisciplinary education consultancy for the luxury, fashion and creative industries | Successful innovations in Luxury Fashion occur when a creator (normally a designer or creative director) conceives of a totally new design configuration or concept, often through lateral thinking, that creates an entirely new category in the consumers' crowded mental space that is deep, intimate and powerful enough to transform into actionable desire … innovations in luxury do not come often and, when they do, they are normally hidden from view because the primary purpose of luxury is not the pursuit of innovation *per se* but rather the delivery of continuity, heritage, craftsmanship, scarcity, high value, collectability etc. that luxury customers expect. |
| Dr Alana James, Assistant Professor in Fashion, Northumbria University | Applied creativity and innovation can challenge "business-as-usual" approaches, catalysing responsible action to move away from linear methods of production, use and disposal across the sector. |
| **Academics in Innovation Management** | **Definitions** |
| Dr Steve Conway, Associate Professor in Innovation, University of Leicester | Innovation is the combination of the new idea plus commercialisation or bringing it into use. |
| Professor David Smith, Emeritus Professor in Innovation Management, Nottingham Trent University | There are broadly three ways in which innovation can arise, firstly, simply from ideas …. The second source is mainly the idea of scientific discovery or the development of science …. The third one is technology … that for the most part usually already exists, but somebody applies it and uses it in some way to create an innovation. |
| Professor Michael Beverland, University of Sussex | I would think of innovation as some type of novelty that makes an impact on a particular stakeholder audience that involves primarily a shift or a change in meaning or the communication of meaning … [for] the fashion industry, I think of symbolism and meaning, which means that it may not be classically new, but could just be a reimagining of something else that's relevant for the time. |
| Professor Mike Saren, Emeritus Professor in Marketing, University of Leicester | Innovation is the realisation of new possibilities by transforming an original idea or concept to produce a new technology, design, process, system, style or other product or service which has some practical use. Creativity is the ability to think of something new, involving a combination of vision, inspiration, originality, imagination, ingenuity, insight and inventiveness. |

or improvement in relation to innovation. Abigail Bourne, Senior Buyer for Joules women's wear, provides the concise definition shown in Table 1.1 which is compatible with many of the others: "Being creative drives innovation in itself – offering newness and re-thinking product keeps the industry fresh and moving." Overall, taking into account the definitions from existing publications and interviews for this book, in the context of the fashion business, creativity can be defined as conceiving new possibilitiess in original combinations which become innovations when they are developed into novel concepts or products that offer value by meeting consumers' needs responsibly. Creative work can be precarious in nature (McRobbie, 2017), but in order to secure a sufficiently reliable income to spend time in this type of career, it is important to implement creativity in a commercial way, taking into account the target customer.

The overall aim of this book is to understand ways in which creativity and innovation connect to theory and practice in the context of the fashion business. The book explores the practical application of creative thought processes at various levels in the fashion business. Additionally, leading innovation theories, largely derived from the business and management discipline, are applied to this creative product sector. Practical examples are used throughout the book to demonstrate to readers the relevance and application of existing theory. Content in the chapters is interconnected, in a similar way to the connections between organisations in the industry, since the same core development and production processes form a fundamental framework across different sectors of the fashion business. The content of this book incorporates the following topics, supplemented by relevant interviews from practitioners and academics.

## Chapter 2: Key Sources of Creative Inspiration in the Fashion Business

This chapter explores a range of sources typically used by fashion creatives to inspire ideas. Key areas covered include fashion history, art, ethnic clothing, contemporary culture (music, media and sport) and technological developments. Methods of finding this information will also be assessed.

## Chapter 3: Technical Aspects of Innovation in the Fashion Business

Innovative technology for fashion and textile development and production can incorporate new methods for product development or production of garments or componentry. This chapter considers a variety of digital and mechanical technological aspects and how they can potentially interconnect to drive innovation. The main aspects covered comprise textile innovations and smart textiles, garment production innovations and virtual fashion design.

## Chapter 4: Applying Innovation Theory to the Fashion Business

This chapter assesses theories on systems of innovation which can be applied to the fashion business and proposes new theoretical models for fashion product development. Stage-gate New Product Development (NPD) theories, the front end of innovation, linear models of innovation, the product life cycle, Rogers's diffusion of innovations, social innovation and co-creation are examples of the key theories which will be examined.

## Chapter 5: Creativity and Innovation in Fashion Forecasting

This chapter explores the role and structure of the fashion forecasting sector and its integration within the fashion business. The organisation of forecasting consultancies and prediction packages will be considered, alongside the distribution of trend information via international fashion and fabric trade fairs. The integration of consumer ideas into companies' innovation processes will also be discussed.

## Chapter 6: Sustainability and Innovation in the Fashion Business

This chapter assesses the significance of environmental and social sustainability in the contemporary fashion business. Key topics will include fashion and the circular economy, how sustainability can be embedded in fashion and textile design processes and sustainable brands and retailers. The emphasis will be placed on ways in which the product development stage influences how resources are used and New Product Development's impact on sustainability throughout the garment life cycle.

## Chapter 7: Innovation in the Fashion Business for Branded and Ready-to-Wear Fashion

This chapter examines innovation sources and processes used in the development of branded fashion (typically mid-priced product ranges which focus on designing and promoting garments and which are not primarily retailers) and "designer" ready-to-wear collections (which are ordinarily at the top end of the price range and usually present their collections on the catwalk). The differences between branded and designer collections will be explored, alongside discussion of how the organisational structure of these market levels affects innovation processes.

## Chapter 8: Innovation in the Mass Market Fashion Business

This chapter investigates innovations in fabric and fashion product development and production for the mass market and how they differ from branded products. The influence of price, production volume and product accessibility within this large-scale market will be considered, as well as key constraints on innovation and solutions used in the industry to overcome these constraints. Key drivers of innovation are explored, including trends, intuition, competitive advantage and supplier-driven innovation. The different stages of the design process for the mass market are also examined in context.

## References

Conway, S. and Steward, F. (2009) *Managing and Shaping Innovation*. Oxford: Oxford University Press.

DCMS (2022) *DCMS Sector Economic Estimates*, available online at: https://www.gov.uk/government/statistics/dcms-sector-economic-estimates-employment-july-2021-june-2022

Jobber, D. and Ellis-Chadwick, F.E. (2023) *Principles and Practice of Marketing. 10th edition*, Maidenhead: McGraw Hill.

London Fashion Week (2024) *Designers*, available online at: https://londonfashionweek.co.uk/designers

Martin, L. and Wilson, N. (2017) Defining creativity with discovery, *Creativity Research Journal*, 29(4), 417–425. https://doi:10.1080/10400419.2017.1376543

Martin, L. and Wilson, N. (eds.) (2018) *The Palgrave Handbook of Creativity at Work*, London: Palgrave Macmillan.

McRobbie, A. (2017) *Be Creative: Making a Living in the New Culture Industries*, London: Polity.

Mintel (2023a) *Clothing Retailing UK*, London: Mintel, available from www.mintel.com

Mintel (2023b) *Fashion Technology and Innovation UK*, London: Mintel, available from www.mintel.com

Omari, D., Scott, S., and Tsinopoulos, C. (2022) 'The Relationship between Quality Management and Product Innovation: A Systematic Review', *29th Innovation and Product Development Management Conference*, Hamburg, July 2022.

Saren, M. (2018) *Marketing Graffiti: The Writing on the Wall*, Abingdon on Thames: Routledge. (For more detail see 'creating solutions' pp. 165–169.)

Smith, D. (2024) *Exploring Innovation, 4th edition*, Maidenhead: McGraw Hill.

Tidd, J. and Bessant, J. (2021) *Managing Innovation: Integrating Technological, Market and Organizational Change, 7th edition*, Chichester: Wiley.

White, J.C. (2023) *Innovation in the Arts: Concepts, Theories, and Practices*, New York: Routledge.

Wilson, N. (2009) Learning to manage creativity: An occupational hazard for the UK's creative industries, *Creative Industries Journal*, 2(2), 179–190.

# Key Sources of Creative Inspiration in the Fashion Business

*Helen Goworek*

## Introduction

Seeking inspiration is the starting point for fulfilling a design brief, alongside an understanding of the requirements of the customers for whom the products are intended. Creative inspiration often takes the form of visual and written information obtained from a variety of sources. This information could simply be recalled from memory, or more often the information can be collated and presented to be shared with colleagues collaborating in creative processes. Creative inspiration is most frequently taken from looking at historical, current or predicted sources of inspiration – in other words, being influenced by the past, present or future (see Figure 2.1). Financial implications can also play a part in the direction of creativity to be explored – e.g., being inspired by products that have been profitable for the company previously or product types that are predicted to rise in sales in the future.

This chapter explores a range of sources typically used by fashion creatives to inspire ideas, fashion trends, fashion history, art, contemporary culture, ethnic clothing and technical developments being the main elements. Methods of finding and utilising this information will also be assessed, from web searches to directional shopping trips and gallery visits. The chapter will also introduce technical developments in the fashion business to link through to a more in-depth exploration in Chapter 3.

DOI: 10.4324/9781003332749-2

**FIGURE 2.1** The three Ps of inspiration for fashion products.

## Fashion Trends

Innovation in clothing design is influenced significantly by prevailing fashion trends (see also Chapter 5). Identifying the point at which a particular look becomes a trend is not an exact science, but undoubtedly relates to its adoption by increasing numbers of people. Fashion looks may be considered as trends depending on whether they meet some or all of the following criteria: featuring in various branded ranges or numerous designers' runway collections in the same season, being worn by several celebrities or influencers, being worn by multiple fashionable consumers or being identified explicitly as trends in fashion magazines, websites, newspapers, fashion forecasting publications (see Chapter 5) or trade journals. Trends can take the form of garment silhouettes, design details, colour, surface decoration (such as print or embroidery), fastenings or accessories, for example. Researching to gather trend information forms a significant part of the role of those involved in designing or selecting garments. This research may be collected by viewing images from runway shows online or travelling to visit stores that sell leading fashion brands, known in the business as "directional shopping", to make notes, photograph or buy relevant garments. Despite being widespread within the sector, this approach has implications for the ownership of Intellectual Property (IP) within product designs, and consequently fashion companies are frequently involved in litigation, many of the larger firms employing legal teams on a permanent basis for this reason (see below).

Streetwear and sportswear brands may take a different approach to creative inspiration – e.g., by interviewing some of their more forward-thinking potential customers to identify their current style influences, seeking out trends in a process first labelled in the 1990s as "coolhunting" (Pedroni, 2019). Alternatively, fashion businesses can invest in trend publications which are available online or as hard copies, purchased from companies which specialise in forecasting fashion trends, typically from one to two years in advance of the season when the products will be sold to the public, such as Promostyl, WGSN and Concepts Paris (see Chapter 5). Fashion forecasting agencies can produce customised trends and colour palettes which are exclusive to an individual organisation, or they can offer standard trend publications with multiple copies produced by the agencies, which are more economical, but are also available to competing fashion companies within the same markets.

Making decisions on which of the various trends to follow requires retailers' or brands' careful consideration of which styles will appeal to their target customers, achieving a balance between the existing contents of consumers' wardrobes and a degree of innovation which is novel yet acceptable enough not to alienate them. After identifying appropriate trends, designers then interpret them creatively – e.g. by using lengths of hemlines, shapes of sleeves or prints on similar themes. Fashion trends for garments and footwear are often derived from the factors discussed below.

## Fashion History and Art

Fashion history is a rich source of creative inspiration for fashion designers. Some time after clothing styles have gone out of fashion, they may enjoy a renewed resurgence in popularity in an ongoing cycle. This often happens 20 years or more after the garments were originally fashionable and their supply has become limited, their consequent rarity thus refreshing consumers' interest in these looks. Fashion history publications, websites, vintage stores, charity shops and the entertainment industry sell or provide resources regarding historical fashion themes, supplying consumers with inspiration for styles which they can choose to adopt. UK clothing brands Joanie, a B Corporation (or "B Corp", see Chapter 6) and Collectif are examples of current garment ranges which are largely inspired by eras from the 1940s to the 1970s.

The late fashion designer Vivienne Westwood stated that she gained much of her inspiration for her fashion by visiting the Wallace Collection, a museum in Marylebone, London (www.wallacecollection.org), demonstrated by the similarity of her eponymous brand's corsets to the garments in the gallery's 18th-century portraiture. Art has a wide-ranging influence on fashion, as a popular source of information regarding fashions from history or via the application of imagery from art movements on clothing. Imagery related to art movements or specific artists' work can be applied to clothing, particularly through print patterns on fabric. Images within fabric designs may be inspired by the style of an art movement by using similar types of shape, art media and colouration. Aspects of more than one art movement may be combined by the designer to configure a new and innovative style of print. Whereas prints are applied to fabric after it has been constructed, images can be integrated within the construction of the material itself – e.g., within the structure of lace or knitwear. Patterns can be incorporated within knitted garments with different coloured yarns, using practical techniques such as intarsia or Fair Isle. Designers in the field of fashion and textiles may gather inspiration for their work by viewing art history books, visiting art galleries and exhibitions or searching online (see Figure 2.2). Alternatively, print images on clothing may directly reproduce artists' work, in which case the artist would need to be acknowledged in line

**FIGURE 2.2** Fashion history galleries at Bowes Museum, County Durham (left) and the former Snibston Discovery Museum, Leicestershire (right). Author's own photos

with the IP rights legislation in the region/s in which the products are sold, such as copyright law in the UK (see patents, trade marks, copyright and designs in the section on Intellectual Property below). For example, the graphic street art style of the late artist Keith Haring has inspired prints on clothing and footwear since the 1980s, with the artist being credited by brands and retailers that have used his artwork, most notably the streetwear brand Stüssy.

## Intellectual Property

By Fiona Bailey

### What Is Intellectual Property?

Intellectual property arises out of human intellectual effort. This refers to "creations of the mind", and includes inventions, literary and artistic works and symbols, brand or trading names, images and designs (Intellectual Property Office, 2023). Intellectual property rights allow creators to be identified as the originator of a work, protecting creative output by controlling the copying, use and commercial exploitation of works (Intellectual Property Office, 2023). Innovation is essential for the growth of business, but there is significant time, effort and expense involved in innovation. The resulting Intellectual Property is one of the most valuable business assets. Strong IP protection is necessary within the fashion industry to encourage and reward innovation and to protect designers' brand creativity and originality (Intellectual Property Office, 2023) and to prevent competitors taking unfair advantage of work created by someone else. A fashion business delivering innovative products which are not properly protected will inevitably be quickly copied (infringed) by their competitors, resulting in loss of sales and a lower than planned return on investment (ROI) of their innovation. The UK's IP laws provide a basis for creators to safeguard their original works and maintain competitive advantage in the global fashion market.

### Types of IP Rights

There are four main types of IP rights recognised under English law. These are all relevant to the fashion industry and will be explored in the sections below.

### Trademarks

Trademarks are critical to protect brand identity, such as words, names, logos, slogans or other signs which can distinguish the goods or services of one brand from another. Creating a solid trademark helps build customer loyalty through brand recognition and reputation. A trademark will protect against the mark being used by others without the consent of the trademark owner. This is important as the brand's identity is arguably its most valuable asset and main marketing tool which must be protected. When a trademark owner's rights have been exploited without the consent of the trademark owner, those trademark rights are said to have been infringed. There are two types of trademarks, registered ® or unregistered ™. A registered trademark gives brands stronger legal brand protection. If the trademark is not registered, there is a risk that competitors will register and gain the trademark rights before the original brand does. It could also be more challenging to enforce unregistered trademarks. When a trademark remains unregistered, this is denoted by ™ instead of ®. Unregistered trademarks may be protected under the law of "passing off", and passing off may occur if a business or individual is trying to pass off its products as originating from or endorsed by the original brand, and therefore benefiting from the associated increase in sales that may result. In order to succeed in a claim for passing off, the claimant would have to show: (a) that its brand has goodwill or a reputation, (b) there has been a misrepresentation by the infringer which is likely to lead the public to believe that the infringing goods are those of the true brand owner and (c) the claimant has suffered damage as a result. Within the fashion industry, it is common for brand logos or signs to be used within designs and patterns, and these may be protected trademarks – e.g., the Louis Vuitton LV monogram used on its bags and accessories and the Gucci logo used as a belt buckle. Patterns can also be trademarked, like Burberry's distinctive check and Adidas's three stripes.

## Design Rights

Design rights can be unregistered or registered. Unregistered design rights protect the shape and configuration of 3D objects, and if certain criteria are met, the shape, colours, texture, materials and ornamentation (the decorative elements) of the design may also be protected. Registered design rights protect the distinctive look of a novel product or object, and will not be granted unless the design is new or novel, and original. "New or novel" means that no identical, or very similar design is known to have existed, and "original means that the design has been created with effort and is not an imitation of an existing design. Due to the nature of the fashion industry, very few designs can claim to be truly original, with most being heavily influenced by previous or existing designs. Design rights protect 3D shapes and configuration, and registration will ensure that the product cannot be manufactured, sold or imported.

## Copyright

Copyright applies to artistic works or written words, such as books, films, music, broadcasts and photographs. The right to copy or reproduce the work is protected by copyright. In the fashion industry, designers and brands can seek IP rights for all their original works of art such as fabric designs and prints, garment drawings, representations and even artistic components within the overall design. Copyright is an automatic right and is freely assigned to the owner without the need to register with the UK Intellectual Property Office (IPO). As with trademarks and design rights, to be eligible for copyright protection, artists must ensure their creations are original. Copyright protection exists throughout the UK and much of the world, and protects the work from being copied or reproduced without the copyright owner's consent. Copyright protection can be identified by a © symbol, and the following words are also often included: "All Rights Reserved", signifying to others that the copyright owner is asserting their rights.

## Patents

Patents are perhaps the most valuable type of Intellectual Property right. They are certainly the most difficult to register and attain, and there is a strict criterion for patentability. The novelty of the idea is critical. According to the UK IPO:

> "An invention must not be known or disclosed anywhere in the world prior to the filing or priority date." When a fashion business is looking to patent an innovative idea, they will usually ask the supplier of the product to sign a confidentiality agreement (or NDA which refers to a non-disclosure agreement) to ensure confidentiality and prevent the patented idea being leaked before it is registered. Patents are only applicable to new inventions which provide a new way of doing something, never seen before. This is called the "Inventive Step", and refers to "where an invention is not obvious to experts in the field and does not already exist in prior art".
>
> (Intellectual Property Office, 2023)

It is not just products which can be patented, the apparatus and process for producing the product and the use of the product can all be patented. A patent granted would protect against the idea being used, sold or manufactured by anyone other than the owner.

*Summary*

According to Bruce and Bessant (2005:27), "if the design has novel and inventive qualities, then a patent may be feasible, if the features of the design configuration are novel, then these may be subject to copyright. If articles are being sold under a particular trade name, or sign, then they may be protected by a registered trademark". Ultimately, Intellectual Property is one of the most valuable assets for a fashion business. The importance of recognising these rights and protecting them appropriately in order to prevent others from profiteering cannot be understated. It is also important for designers to be aware of these rights so that when they create their own designs, they are aware of the rights of others.

## References

Bruce, M. and Bessant, J. (2005) *Design in Business: Strategic Innovation through Design*, Harlow: Financial Times Prentice Hall.

Intellectual Property Office. (2023) *Intellectual Property: Types and Uses of Intellectual Property*, GOV.UK. Available at: https://www.gov.uk/government/collections/intellectual-property -types-and-uses-of-intellectual-property

# Contemporary Culture

Contemporary trends in popular culture, such as music, media and sport, can also provide a wide range of inspiration for innovative fashion products. There has long been a close relationship between music and personal image, with musical genres often becoming synonymous with specific fashion looks. Fashion designers themselves may influence these looks by working in collaboration with music artists or their stylists to develop outfits that are compatible with their recordings and listeners. Conversely, at the mass market level, designers may derive inspiration from singers and bands, who are often viewed as innovators or early adopters of fashion trends (see Chapter 4). Many other aspects of the media may also inspire clothing design, traditionally from film and TV shows, and now more widely from social media influencers (SMIs). For example, SMIs can discuss the brands of clothing they're wearing (often for payment from the brands) or produce unboxing videos where they open packages of new items of clothing. Sport is another major source of inspiration, clothing originally developed for sport being a prevalent trend in Western cultures since the 1980s, with the roots of its influence starting in the 1960s and 1970s. Items that were previously used almost solely in professional or amateur sporting contexts, such as training shoes, became adopted as part of mainstream fashion. Key assets of such products were association with the success of sports stars and aspects of comfort, resulting in their repurposing as leisurewear in a new consumer market which achieved a rapid rate of expansion. The popularity of certain sports in themselves has risen or diminished over the years; basketball, skateboarding and surfing having been major influences on fashion in the 1980s and 1990s, for example.

## Ethnic Styling

Clothing from different cultures globally has long been an extensive source of inspiration for fashion designers. Different types of fabric, colours, silhouettes, styling details, surface decoration and components have offered a cornucopia of ideas to influence product development. Overseas travel, books on national dress and museum exhibits are key sources of inspiration that designers can use in this respect. Retailers may purchase original ethnic products for their customers directly from the relevant countries or may simply derive aspects of styling in their own label ranges from ethnic garments. The term "ethnic" has traditionally been used in the fashion industry to denote styles that have been influenced overtly by the clothing of a specific culture, have a traditional "folk" style more generally or perhaps combine elements of clothing from different cultures. However, in recent years brands which have produced garments that are clearly identifiable as reproducing features or complete looks within their fashion collections from certain cultures have understandably been widely criticised in the press and on social media for relying on cultural appropriation. Some of the main points of contention are the brands' adoption of such styles to gain financial profit without reference, payment or acknowledgment for the originators of the ideas, further complicated by potential difficulty in identifying owners of the Intellectual Property of historical and traditional clothing. Alternatively, brands could avoid becoming embroiled in such problematic ethical issues by reducing or eliminating reliance on ethnic themes and developing their own unique and innovative styles instead. Actions have begun to be taken to address cultural appropriation, including consumers voicing their views on this on social media and music festivals banning stalls from selling such items (Petter, 2020; Saunders, 2023).

## Technological Developments

Within the field of fashion design, innovative technology can incorporate new techniques to produce or develop existing product types, or can offer the potential to use new methods for designing or producing garments or their components. During the 1990s, opportunities began to arise for designers to use Computer-Aided Design (CAD) to develop garment design ideas, which has since become standard practice for many companies as the technology has become progressively more economical and accessible due to improved economies of scale. One of the most beneficial aspects of CAD technology for designers of fabric or garments is the ability to instantly render new colourways (colour variants of the products) digitally, which had previously usually been carried out via designers' painstaking and time-consuming mixing of physical paint colours or using flat-tip pens such as Pantone™. The ability to present designs in a range of colours via CAD therefore enhances the efficiency of the product development process, with the digitisation of the designs also meaning they can be sent online to clients, rather than waiting for artwork to be posted by mail or courier. CAD systems such as CLO-3D (see Figures 2.3 and 2.4) or Optitex can also be used to enhance the visualisations of garments, giving a 3D appearance of the product on a model in a 2D file or print-out to show clients how the finished product could look, before taking the time and expense of producing the fabric and sewing a physical sample. Figure 2.3 demonstrates how realistic CLO-3D images can look in comparison to photographs of physical samples of the same designs. This 3D-effect form of virtual fashion design is similar to that used within video games.

CAD can also be used to connect to a specialist fabric printer to place a selected image or pattern directly onto a plain piece of fabric, enabling a sample garment to be made that allows the client to see a close representation of how the item will look when it is later mass-produced, or to be photographed for a website before it is made in bulk. This saves investing in the full printing process, which can involve extensive costs in the manufacturing and tooling of metal print cylinders for specific prints, for example. CAD is generally used for 2D work, and the more

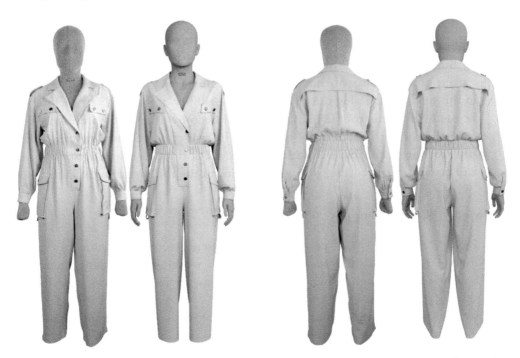

**FIGURE 2.3** 3D images of a garment by CLO (from left to right, figures 2 and 4) in comparison with photographs of the finished garment (figures 1 and 3). Image with permission from CLO

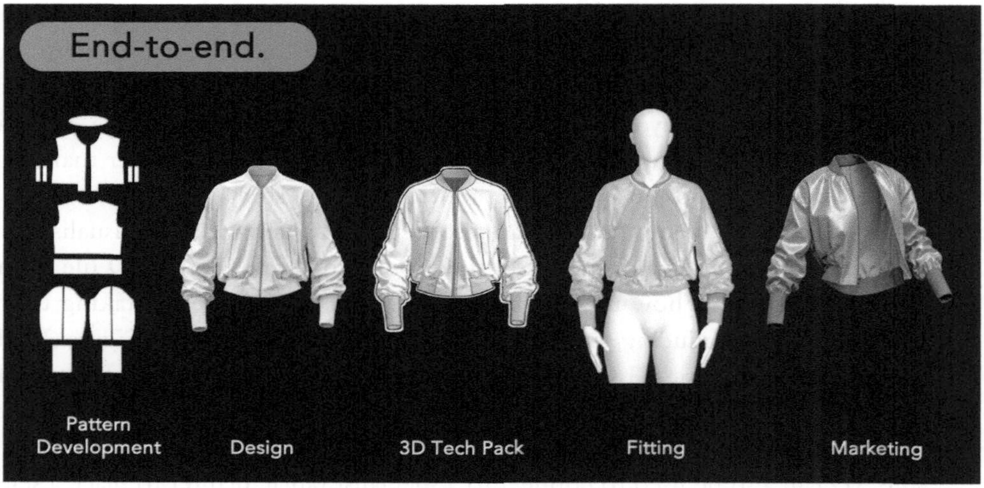

**FIGURE 2.4** Garment services offered by CLO. Image with permission from CLO

recent development of 3D printing, using layers of synthetic materials to build up a selected shape that has been designed digitally, has had a similar level of impact on the work of designers (see Chapter 3). Within the fashion industry, 3D printers are not directly relevant to making complete garments at the time of writing, but they could be used to make rapid prototypes of 3D components such as buttons. New technology can also offer companies the opportunity to use innovative techniques within fashion and textiles product development to produce new and inventive aspects of fabric or garments. A key area for innovative technological development in this field is increasing the degree of sustainability of fabrics. New techniques can be used where environmental sustainability becomes a priority in the fibre content and construction of fabrics, for example. The reduction of waste material is another key area for sustainable innovation by designers, through selecting styles or details and using pattern–cutting software that aids in the minimisation of fabric usage.

## Competitive Intelligence

In the fashion business, competitive intelligence refers to companies gathering information about their competitors' ways of working, particularly their products and prices. Stephanie Kitchen, a fashion designer for Berghaus, describes comp shopping as "(going) to a variety of shops and boutiques to look at products, gauge what's already been done by other brands, look at the layout of stores and see how items have been merchandised" (Sibley, 2014). Typically, fashion buyers, designers and merchandisers who are employed by fashion brands, retailers or manufacturers undertake "comp shopping", an abbreviation of "comparative shopping" or "competitor shopping". For firms which are less quick to adopt fashion trends than their competitors, comp shopping may provide a level of creative inspiration. However, it is important that their ideas are not too close to the original source as there is a fine line between taking inspiration and infringing Intellectual Property laws (see above). Comp shopping is more frequently used for companies to keep updated on the products their competitors are offering so that they are aware of the full range of items available in the market for their target consumers. Comp shopping may be carried out by visiting stores and recording information as sketches, photos or written notes, and it may also be done online. Whilst it's useful to see garments in person, especially to feel the tactile qualities of the fabric, one of the advantages of doing comp shopping online instead is that there may be additional information available from competitors' websites such as their best-selling products or details of items that have been reduced in the sale, implying that they have not sold well. Comp shopping may be conducted informally, without being recorded, or it may be documented in a report and shared with colleagues.

Fashion designers may also participate in directional shopping, which usually involves researching into trends at designer/ready-to-wear level. Directional shopping is not usually aimed at direct competitors in the fashion market, but is primarily to gain inspiration from products that are more exclusive and at a higher price level. This can involve researching in magazines (see Figure 2.5) and visits to retailers that sell a selection of designer brands, such as Selfridges (UK), Galeries Lafayette (Paris) or Saks Fifth Avenue (New York), or areas of major cities where designer stores are clustered together, such as Via Montenapoleone in Milan. Increasingly, however, directional shopping can be carried out online without requiring the

**FIGURE 2.5**  Specialist fashion magazines on sale in a London store. Author's own photo

expense of a trip. Photos of designers' merchandise are often available online, and fashion forecasting websites offer images from shop windows in various cities to their customers. Ready-to-wear collections are even made accessible to the public well in advance of the products being available to purchase, as their runway shows take place months beforehand and are widely reported in the media – e.g., on www.vogue.com. Certain fashion capitals may be known for distinctive styles of design adopted by designers showing their collections on the runway in the same location – e.g., the UK is renowned for innovative designs which are often inspired by street fashion, several Belgian designers are known for their *avant-garde* "deconstructed" clothing which challenges conventional notions of garment construction, and Japanese designers have become famous for artistic folding and draping which is not confined to the shape of the body.

## Applying Creative Inspiration in the Fashion Business

Having located sources of creative inspiration, those involved in fashion product development, such as fashion buyers or designers, need to store, collate and assess this information prior to embarking on the design process. The inspirational information may be solely for use by the designer who collected it, therefore a high quality of presentation may not be essential. More frequently, however, it may be shared with clients, suppliers or in-house colleagues, in which case clarity and standard of presentation will be more important. Collation of creative inspiration can typically take a visual format – e.g., physical photos and magazine cuttings combined in a collage or a digital folder or some may be compiled in the form of written notes. Photoshop® and other design-related programs or apps are useful for combining scans, photos and sketches of inspiration materials to be presented as "mood boards", "concept boards" or "story boards" that can sum up a creative theme by combining content such as garment styling and fabric swatches or yarn (see Figure 2.6). Images of scenery, for example, may also be added to evoke a mood for creative inspiration, as well as a colour story – i.e., small blocks of co-ordinating shades. Compiling mood boards is usually part of the fashion designer's role, and they may be distributed or displayed so that members of the design team within a fashion brand, retailer or manufacturer can all be inspired by the same sources, thereby enabling them to follow a similar theme in the development of product ideas. Within the fashion business, garment design is frequently undertaken by fashion designers who are employed directly by fashion brands or who work for firms which supply garments to retailers.

Own-label fashion retailers (i.e., those that mostly sell garments featuring the retailer's own name on the label) can sometimes employ their own in-house design teams to conduct the full design process for the garments that they offer – e.g., Next and Zara – leading to a highly co-ordinated and complementary product

MEMORY LANE

The Boho mood is not going away. This mix of retro, craft and cultural elements influences the world of style and is spreading even in Asia.

Le phénomène Boho n'a pas disparu. L'alliance d'artisanat, de rétro et de touches culturelles continue d'influencer l'univers du style, y compris en Asie.

PANTONE: 25/ 18-5616 TCX  26/ 19-3536 TCX  27/ 17-0840 TCX  28/ 16-1350 TCX  29/ 18-4247 TCX  30/ 18-2027 TCX

**FIGURE 2.6** Example of a mood board from Concepts Paris. Image with permission from Jos Berry

range. Alternatively, certain own–label fashion retailers employ a small–scale design team which is largely responsible for compiling creative trend inspirations, such as mood boards and colour stories, to be briefed to the fashion designers who work for their suppliers. This enables the retailers to sell clothing within consistent themes despite those who design the garments being employed by various suppliers, often in different locations around the world. Fashion designers whose jobs focus solely on compiling creative inspiration do not design the final details of garments that are sold in stores, but they benefit from understanding how clothing is designed and constructed in order to effectively select suitable sources of inspiration. In the UK, many of the fashion designers who design the clothing consumers buy from the mass market are employed by the suppliers who produce the garments bought by the retailers. The suppliers may be manufacturers which own clothing factories, or they may be companies that essentially provide a design service and act as interme-diaries with factories (see Figure 2.7). Clothing factories usually manufacture gar-ments for several different brands or retail clients, since supplying only one fashion brand would be a higher risk. However, the suppliers themselves and the designers who work for them, are rarely if ever visible to the public since their names don't feature directly on garment labels.

RI3645
LAYERING RACER VEST

RI2996
PANELLED SPORTS BRA

PHONE
POCKET

RI3584
LONGLINE RAIN JACKET

RI3654
SLEEK SEAM
PHONE TIGHT

**FIGURE 2.7** Working drawings of designs by a supplier for a client. Image with permission from Karen Purdy

Designers can often implement creative inspiration by initially gathering further information on the themes that have been identified in mood boards. The themes usually have titles and a short description which enables designers to seek further relevant visual information – e.g., from books, exhibitions or online. Designers may require suitable space to accommodate their research, equipment and materials, and often work in studio spaces with large desks or tables and wall space to display creative inspiration, which can necessitate them working in a separate location to other company functions such as sales, buying or marketing. The creative process for fashion design can involve designers laying out the inspiration in front of them or viewing it on a digital screen, then sketching a range of ideas that uses elements from the themes in a vast range of combinations. Garment features such as skirt

**TABLE 2.1** Aspects of garment design decision-making

| Design aspect | Examples |
| --- | --- |
| Fabric fibre content | *Cotton, silk, viscose, mixed fibres* |
| Fabric weave or knit | *Woven fabric types: satin, sateen, twill, tulle*<br>*Knitting techniques: intarsia, Fair Isle, seed stitch, cable* |
| Fabric pattern | *Woven: colour-woven (coloured pattern woven within the fabric such as gingham, tartan, dogtooth or Madras checks), two-tone (warp and weft threads of different colours), jacquard (self-coloured woven pattern), brocade (embossed-effect woven pattern)*<br>*printed: all-over print, placement print, border print in patterns such as florals* |
| Fabric weight (measured in grams per square metre) | *Fine (e.g., georgette), medium (e.g., poplin), heavy (e.g., melton)* |
| Fabric decoration | *Embroidery, broderie anglaise, cornelli, applique* |
| Dyeing techniques | *Ombre (dip-dye), tie-dye, all-over dyeing, garment dyeing* |
| Silhouette | *A-line, puffball, bodycon, fishtail* |
| Sleeve shapes | *Set-in, raglan, bell, leg o' mutton* |
| Trouser shapes | *Flared, bootcut, drainpipe, tapered* |
| Pleats and gathers | *Knife pleats, box pleats, ruffles, pintucks* |
| Stitching techniques | *Shirring, blanket stitch, saddle stitch, flatseam* |
| Darts | *Princess line, French darts, armhole darts, godets* |
| Trims | *Lace, ribbon, bows, ric rac* |
| Edging | *Binding, piping, blind hemming, facing* |
| Fastenings | *Buttons, zips, hooks and eyes, velcro* |
| Internal components | *Shoulder pads, interfacing, elastic, wadding* |

lengths, collars, sleeves and lapels can be designed in various shapes and dimensions. Selecting from various options of stitching, construction, fastenings, materials and colours results in almost innumerable potential design permutations (see Table 2.1). The design creation process can therefore sometimes be formulaic and almost mathematical in nature, running through variations of shapes, widths, lengths before arriving at appropriate styles that the designer feels could be most appropriate for their customers. However, the process is not scientific, in that the notion of which are the most suitable designs can be highly subjective.

Drawing skills can be very useful to enable designers to effectively translate inspirational themes into 2D designs, although having strong drawing ability is no guarantee of being an effective designer, and vice versa. Therefore, drawing and design skills can constitute two different creative talents. Drawings of garments usually require sufficient clarity for colleagues to be able to interpret them, therefore a clear and basic style of illustration, known as a working drawing or "flat" is used to show a selected garment as if it had been laid flat on a table, to remove some of the artistic flourishes which can sometimes detract from a garment's features (see Figure 2.7). Computer-generated garment templates can also be the starting point for design ideas (see Figure 2.8). After evaluating the sketches or CAD images of products that are most suitable for the target customer, the strongest design ideas can then be selected by the designer or their colleagues to be presented to managers or clients, so sketching ability is often helpful in order to represent the concepts from the designer's mind clearly on paper or screen. The translation of inspiration into cognitive ideas that can then be transferred onto paper by hand can be one of the most enjoyable and creative aspects of the job for many designers.

The preferred designs from a selection of initial ideas may then be transformed into fashion illustrations with more of a 3D appearance via the designer's own drawing skills or (if the company can afford it) using computer-aided design, such as CLO-3D, or making physical garment samples. Fashion illustrations may be used to present specific garment designs or to demonstrate a certain look for a fashion trend (see Figure 2.9), with many different styles of illustration being available, employing various media or CAD. Illustration offers fashion designers or freelance illustrators the opportunity to produce creative artwork with a commercial purpose, and is sometimes incorporated into advertising or other types of promotion for fashion brands.

Sample garments are individual prototypes which can offer the company's employees or their clients a realistic view of how the items may look in production. In a micro-scale company, the designer may personally make the sample garment, but it is more likely that a specialist sample machinist with expert sewing skills may work within a supplier or manufacturer's design studio or factory to produce samples. Pattern-cutting is an essential stage in the transition from 2D concepts to 3D garments. The designer or a pattern-cutter interprets the style from the drawing into flat paper or card for each piece of the garment (see Figure 2.10), representing the shapes of the component pieces that will be cut out of fabric and sewn together to create an item of clothing. The prototype garment may sometimes be referred to as a "toile " (pronounced "twahl"), derived from a French word for "cloth". Toiles were traditionally made from calico or muslin – i.e., basic weave undyed cotton fabrics which are available in different thicknesses and can therefore be used as more economical substitutes for the various materials in which the final garments are intended to be produced in bulk. (The calico fabric itself may also be referred to as "toile".)

The prototype is fitted onto a mannequin or a live model of a suitable size to check that it fits effectively to allow sufficient movement and to see, for example, whether the hem is correctly balanced. If the fit of the garment is not as the designer

**FIGURE 2.8** Monochrome garment design image using CAD. Image with permission from CLO

# 10 LONGING FOR THE FRENCH LINGERIE STYLE

" Desire for
something
beautiful.

*Désir de quelque
chose de beau.*
"

**FIGURE 2.9** Examples of fashion illustrations by fashion forecasting company Concepts Paris. Image with permission from Jos Berry

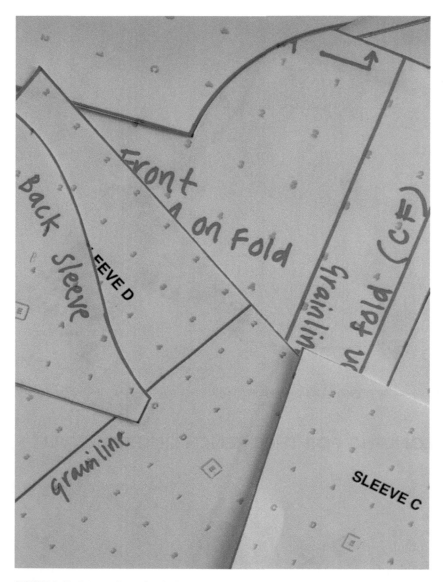

**FIGURE 2.10** Pattern pieces for clothing. Photograph with permission from Caroline Gration

intended, then amendments can be made, such as making the item fit more tightly or adding more length to the pattern. Further samples can be made by amending the patterns and the garment refitted on a model until the designer or the client is satisfied with how it fits. Pattern-cutting can be considered a creative process, with pattern-cutters having the skills to interpret verbal or 2D ideas into three dimensions. This job is therefore sometimes advertised as "creative pattern-cutter", and this process can sometimes be part of the designer's role, especially in small organisations. The prototyping element of the creative process enhances the fit and therefore the quality of a garment, but it can also add time and expense to the product development phase.

Another creative option for realising design ideas in three dimensions is to model fabric directly onto the mannequin (dress stand) in a procedure known as "draping", thus eliminating the requirement for sketching. Designers can drape cloth such as calico onto a mannequin, manipulating the way in which it folds and gathers, securing it onto the stand with pins. The fabric can be drawn on with pen or chalk to indicate where folds are located before being dismantled and transformed into a 2D paper or card pattern so that the design can be reconstructed, with fastenings and seams to hold it in place when worn. Initially developed in the 1930s, this highly creative and instinctive form of dress design was popularised by Japanese and Belgian designers in the 1980s and 1990s, denoting luxury through its use of larger than average volumes of flowing fabric. Draping has elements in common with traditional forms of garment-making from single lengths of fabric, as used in rectangular saris in South Asia and semi-circular Ancient Roman togas.

The creative process can be psychologically exhausting at times due to the amount of cognitive effort and concentration required in drawing concepts from deep within the designer's memory bank to be deployed in novel combinations. This is reflected in Conway and Steward's (2009) description of innovation as an emotional process, thus reflecting the interjection of aspects of the designer's emotions and personality within product development. This emotional connection with creativity and innovation is illustrated by those involved in product development using terms linked to childbirth, sometimes referring to products that they have developed as "my baby" and discussing how products are "conceived" and "nurtured". Designers may sometimes take a strongly protective approach to design, feeling a sense of the product ideas being interconnected with their personal identity and signature style, which can consequently make them reluctant to amend the products.

## Summary

This chapter demonstrates how the creative process for the same garment can connect from one person to another, and how those involved in the process therefore require visual and verbal communication, technical and social skills to collaborate effectively to achieve the tangible representation of conceptual ideas. The key sources of creative inspiration for fashion design can be represented by a funnel of ingredients from the past (fashion history and art or ethnic styling), present (contemporary culture and competitive intelligence) and/or future (fashion trends and technological developments), which the designer blends in varying proportions to form the ideas for new fashion products which meet the needs of a brand or retailer's target customers (see Figure 2.11).

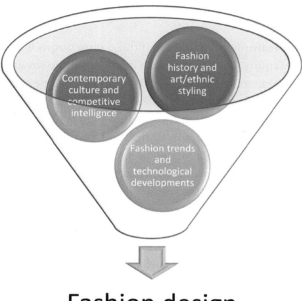

# Fashion design

**FIGURE 2.11**   The fashion funnel: key ingredients for creative inspiration for fashion design.

## Interviews with Fashion Specialists and Educators

**Caroline Gration is Director of the Fashion School in London and Brighton, UK, a not-for-profit community interest company offering short courses in fashion for 6 to 19 year olds and adults. Caroline gained an MA from the Royal College of Art before pursuing a career as a designer for ready-to-wear labels, then as a Senior Lecturer in Fashion at UK universities prior to founding her business in 2012.**

*How would you sum up the creative and innovative aspects of the work that you do?*

After working as a fashion designer then as a Senior Lecturer in Fashion, I set up the London Fashion School in Brighton in 2012, with the aim of enabling students to realise their creative potential in a caring environment. We later expanded to open a studio near the King's Road in Chelsea, and we've also offered our courses in Manchester. We aim to instil confidence in children by positive encouragement and promoting a healthy love of fashion. I wanted to encourage students to realise the value not only of creative design, but also technical skills of sewing, pattern-cutting, drawing, styling and photographic skills. We offer our students a knowledge of the fashion industry and tell them about the range of career possibilities, encouraging their individual fashion aspirations, whether that's wanting to be the next Dior or sewing their own sustainable garments to wear. Our philosophy is to also create an understanding of the ecological impact of fashion and to foster ethical awareness. For example, we're supported by fashion designers who repurpose their surplus fabrics, instead of disposing of them, by offering them to our Fashion School students to use in their designs.

**FIGURE 2.12** Caroline Gration, left, and the Fashion School, right. Photos with permission from Caroline Gration

Creativity in fashion is based on another way of looking at the known and not searching for approval. I think to be creative with fashion you have to totally own your creativity. You have to have another angle of looking at things, and creativity doesn't always mean the short route. To be creative, to immerse yourself in something, may be a very long route, so creativity has to come with a sense of self-belief, whether that is slightly off-kilter because of another way of thinking. Within fashion, and probably the same with creativity within any field, it is often an afterthought now, but if we think about people who move things forward, they just have another way of thinking. They're not accepting what's there, they're thinking "How can I turn this around?" It doesn't always cost money to be creative, which is one of the wonderful things about it. If you need to be taught how to be creative, it's not going to work. You can be guided, but it has to be within you. In fashion media, the word "'creative" just doesn't come up very often now. Employers say they're going to try and promote a creative atmosphere, but it's still quite formulaic. I suppose creativity is part of that trio. You've got to be creative, but you've also got to be committed and to be able to network. Nobody's going to come to you. You need to get out there and show people who you are. Creativity on its own is a bit of a bubble. I think fashion is changing so much now, and it's absolutely unrecognisable from when we were young. Fashion is getting worse in terms of sustainability, and because business is so important in fashion now, and finance, it quashes creativity and free thought about that. It's all about what we're selling.

With young people and with ourselves, we buy second-hand clothes, but that's not really what magazines or media are promoting. Maybe creativity is defined in a completely different way from when we were young. I think creativity is always the same, I don't think it changes. I think things change around it, but the bubble of being creative stays the same. I feel we've moved back in a lot of ways to the 1950s in terms of mainstream fashion and the way we all dressed the same. I think that education makes it really hard for children to understand the value of their own creativity because they're led by modules and they learn to pass this exam. I think it's freedom of thought, it's another way of looking at things and having that whole fire inside you, of just pushing all the time, and sometimes also part of creativity is the knowledge that you may end up with absolutely nothing at the end of it, it's not a surefire win. If you think that, you're going to start the most wonderful idea, and actually that's all it is, a brilliant idea.

*Do you think innovation is separate from creativity, or is there some crossover?*

I see them quite separately because I think innovation is much more realistic. Innovation has an intelligence behind it that I wouldn't say creativity needs. Innovation is the execution of your idea, and that's really important. So innovation doesn't even necessarily have to be that creative. Innovation can be taking something that's already there and then moving it along. Creativity is much more raw and visceral, so for me I think they are quite different, although they're absolutely intertwined, and innovation is about the execution. I think there's more clarity of thought with innovation, and you work out a route through to get to the product at the end. It's maybe taking an understanding or an idea or even a design that's already there. So, for example, you've take the basis of a trend and you'll flip it over and do something amazing with that and you execute it. So I think you're far more successful in fashion if you're innovative as opposed to just creative. Creativity comes from the heart, from inside, and innovation uses your brain more. When I think of innovation, I think of the trio of creativity, commitment and networking. I think if you're creative, sometimes you just have them. There are many people who are really creative who just didn't get the chance to develop it, so for me they're different things, but they are very much linked.

When the kids arrive [at the Fashion School], if they're creative I get them to follow their own thing. Because of social media, when children are taught, they're always looking for approval and don't want do anything if they don't think they're going to get approval for it. Everyone that's come through here and is going to do something [creative] really well, has been so involved in their own thing and they wouldn't look for approval.

*How do you incorporate creativity and innovation into the teaching at the Fashion School?*

I think the best way to promote it is to have an absolutely free agenda and you're just there to discuss and help push their ideas through. We're really lucky because we don't assess anything formally. We'll have a conversation and I suppose it's assessment about how you can improve something, but we don't mark work, so people feel that they're allowed to make mistakes and we'd rather be there talking with them at the time to say "try this or try that". It's immediate, so it's not that they try something and then we write something and give it to them at the end. We're there with them, so we're very careful that we don't put our own aesthetic onto anybody. I think when you're not assessing, you just go in with the idea that you're going to help bring them to their best potential. We always tutor closely and we always persuade them to try things they're not comfortable with. We might say, "Try it for two hours, then come back and tell me what you think."

**FIGURE 2.13**  The Fashion School London. Photos with permission from Caroline Gration

I make it quite clear to our students. that when they're with me, because I'm so skills-based, it isn't going to get you into a degree that you're a good pattern-cutter, but if you have an understanding of construction and about how to realise garments when you go to a degree course and you've got a superpower that comes out of your pocket, and then it's really relevant. People who study with us get into the university they want, and everybody is primed to do well through that university process.

*Do you think are there any particularly important recent innovations or creative processes in the fashion industry that you think are particularly important?*

I think AI has such potential, and I know people are very nervous about it, but I think it's going to be incredible, and that's really exciting. I like the idea of digital fashion being worn by your persona online. There's a whole new direction, for good or bad, and I'd be delighted to see where that's going. I think that's where I see people who just got into fashion and are now getting really interested in that innovation that I view as being important. There are also things that haven't really happened, that we spoke about at least 20 years ago, like clothes that had properties within them that were health benefits, and that's never fully developed, so there are things that haven't happened in terms of a trend.

I recently wrote to Primark and said, "I have to say from the beginning that I'm anti-fast fashion, but can I do a customisation 'no buy' workshop in the window and you put the clothes the kids have made on mannequin stands in the windows. I think there's another way and you have this massive influence, good or bad, over these kids and I know that there's something positive in there as well." So that's what we did. We put them in Westfields in London and some other places, and then they said "Would you be interested in using the basement of Primark in Manchester?" So I started a Fashion School demonstration there. My aim is for kids to realise that there's value in working with what you've already got rather than what you buy, so that seems to have worked really well.

*Do you think there are any current brands or people who you feel are really innovative and creative?*

I see a lot of really talented and creative young designers at London Fashion Week, and they have such great ideas, like Helen Kirkum's trainers. Trainers are such polluting products, we've all got a pair and they go in the bin. I work with a guy called Rerun who was saying the same, about giving further life to your trainers or buying ones that are hybrid, made from other ones. Chopova Lowena, two fashion graduates based in London, are doing well, and they support us at the Fashion School. You see people who are totally into fashion and they really believe in it, and that's what they do until 2:00 in the morning, but then their ideas are not getting picked up because now you're measured whether you're successful by the numbers on your post on Instagram, rather than how talented you are. I think the idea that it's easy to be successful in fashion and you don't actually have to be talented is a real shame.

*Interview by Helen Goworek*

## References

Sustainable Sewing Classes & Workshops, available online at: https://www.thefashionschool
    -uk.com/
Benson, S. (2021) *AnOther Magazine*, September 2021 Helen Kirkum, the Designer Giving New
    Life to Waste Trainers, available online at: https://www.anothermag.com/fashion-beauty
    /13562/helen-kirkum-footwear-designer-interview-sustainable-fashion-brands
Chopova Lowena. (2024) chopovalowena.com
Rerun. (2024) RERUN rerunstreetwear.com

**Zoe Hinton is Course Leader for BA (Hons) Fashion Buying and Merchandising at London College of Fashion (LCF), University of the Arts. After graduating with a Fashion Design degree from De Montfort University, Zoe worked as a fashion buyer for major retailers for 15 years before beginning her academic career.**

*How would you sum up the creative and innovative work that you do in education and have done in industry?*

For me, it's all about empowering the students and allowing them to be creative and innovative. I think a lot of the time that is allowing people confidence to be able to explore and develop their ideas. I think discovering newness is another big one. In terms of working in industry, innovation was all about staying ahead of what was happening, so having to

**FIGURE 2.14**   Zoe Hinton. Photo with permission from Zoe Hinton

keep up with what the innovations were and what you could deliver as an innovation. For instance, working in maternity wear, which I did for quite a long time, we had to be really clear that it was an area of the market which wouldn't necessarily be very innovative in the classical sense. However, there were lots of things we did within that brand that were innovative because they were different to what had been done before. I think a lot of the time innovation is doing something new and different that can deliver.

There were two times where I worked on things that I would say were probably the most innovative I've been in industry. One of them was the maternity wear brand, which was at New Look, and for me to go in there and change things was probably quite challenging. The other time when I was able to do that was at House of Fraser when I was responsible for their young fashion brand Therapy, and it was very much the start of fast fashion and what that could deliver. That area wasn't something that necessarily House of Fraser was particularly famous for, but they were good at delivering branded product and we were an own-label young fashion brand under their umbrella. We had to go against the grain and do something different, and I think that was probably the most exciting time I found in my buying career. It was keeping abreast of everything that was happening, and I think we were very lucky in that the people working on the team at the time were all of one mind. I think it's about having the creativity yourself and the confidence to go out there, but I think there's a lot to be said for strength in numbers and the fact that we were all in it together.

*Could you explain the process of innovation or creativity in the companies that you've worked in or the sector overall from your experience?*

For the companies I worked with in industry, it's a similar process, sometimes it just involves different things. For us, the process of innovation involved things like idea generation and brainstorming and working really closely with the design teams as a buyer and a merchandiser. There was a lot of research, analysis of market trends and testing out ideas. Also there was a lot of data analysis, so I was looking at what the data was telling us and then making changes accordingly. I think that's something that's massively changed in terms of the industry, that there is so much more data out there and it makes the job probably more challenging in some ways than it than it ever has been. We did a lot of testing of ideas, and when I was at New Look it was right at the beginning of using social media, so there was a lot of testing things like Facebook to get consumer feedback. There was also the prototyping and testing of garments, which now has been sped up by digital technology and there are platforms such as CLO-3D or Browzwear where you can see what the product's going to look like before it even goes through the sampling and manufacturing process, so retailers can test it out and get a customer reaction. COVID got people out of their comfort zone because we had to find new ways of doing things, testing things and moving forward, and I think lots of retailers who I've spoken to started to ramp it up during that period, but now their ways seem to have gone back to normal.

Idea generation for us would be all about finding out what was going on. The design team were brilliant at going out there and finding macro trends that would be used, and we as a buying and merchandising team would then look at what the competition were doing to come up with ideas. We would be constantly reviewing the range and thinking, "Okay, what could we do better?", and then the design team would say in response, "This is happening here." House of Fraser was historically a branded business; however, they had implemented an in-house design team for the whole of their private label offer to support the buying and merchandising (B&M) teams. There was also an in-house design team at New Look.

One of the directors I had was very aware that you learn from failure. I think you can never have a brand that's on 100% full-price sales really. It's unlikely that that would happen, so you almost need those failures to be able to learn from them and move on. I think data is changing that somewhat, because from what I'm hearing from contacts within industry, it's not so much about history any more. Although its still important, it's now not solely about looking at what's sold last year because you've got so much up-to-speed data that can tell you in real time what's going to happen, so you don't have to be so risk-averse when making decisions.

*What do you think are the most important recent innovations in the fashion industry from your perspective?*

From an industry perspective, the most important innovations are use of things like 3D and being able to customise products through artificial intelligence. I think important recent innovations are advancements in 3D design and printing, and there are digital fabric files that retailers can use, so on CLO, for instance, you can see how fabrics work because there's a 3D file for it, so you can show how a chiffon would react as opposed to a satin or a cotton [in a garment]. I think innovations in terms of sustainable fabrics and sustainable fashion practices are really interesting. We find at LCF that lots of the students' final projects focus on things like this, and I'm really excited by how things are developing. Also there are innovations in things like product life cycle management systems and how retailers are going to manage contacts from a digital perspective.

*In what ways do you incorporate creativity and innovation into your teaching, in the ways in which you teach and also the content?*

I think just reading and asking, saying you don't understand everything, and to have the confidence to just ask questions and have open-mindedness and be curious with everything. I'm really encouraged when students ask questions because I think you're not going to get anywhere without doing that. From a lecturing and an education point of view, I encourage them to be able to do that. We have visiting lecturers that come in to give industry sessions. We've also implemented for our final year students a mentoring process, so we have a set of industry experts who are within the industry at the moment, generally within B&M roles or sustainability and they offer some of their time to be able to support students. I was speaking to some of the students about it and they were really positive. It gives them so much more confidence to have a conversation with someone who's actually in the industry at the moment, and it not only empowers them to think more creatively and strategically, but also gives them connections for the future post-graduation.

*How would you define creativity and innovation based on your own experience?*

I think it's hard to define it, but for me the obvious answer is creativity and innovation would be about generating new and original ideas and then implementing those to create value in whatever you're doing. Within that, the really important things to me are being able to discover newness and also empowering the people to develop the ideas, because I think sometimes people struggle with having confidence in exploration. There are various retailers I know of, for instance, that are using reverse mentoring, so they're bringing in people at entry level that act as mentors to managers, so management can mentor you, but also you can mentor upwards, which I think is really valuable.

*Are there any particular theories of creativity or innovation that either influence your work or you incorporate into your teaching?*

There are many theories we use throughout our teaching across the Fashion Business School at LCF, from the classic ones such as Rogers's diffusion of innovations to the more recent and contemporary. To complement this, we also ensure that we support and scaffold student projects by encouraging use of models like the Business Model Canvas. This allows them to be able to be creative and innovative, however at the same time effectively formulate their ideas and cement what it is that they want to do.

*Who do you consider to be the most innovative and creative fashion retailers, brands or companies in the fashion business currently?*

It's difficult to pin down a particular brand. I think it's how [the companies] deal with their brands, and a lot of it is about the kindness and the empathy as well. Although every brand obviously needs to be profitable, there is now more awareness of how many things contribute to this profitability, from the product and the supply chain to the staff themselves. I think that's its therefore really difficult for the retailers to think, "How are we going to change this from a from a just profit point of view to a more inclusive, diverse and responsible environment?" People such as Patagonia, for instance, considered sustainability at a very early stage and changed things immeasurably in the clothing market, leading the way for many more. However, when ASOS first came into being, it was a revelation in terms of them doing things differently (selling fast fashion online), and it was difficult at the time to be able to keep up with what these people were doing. It was also a revelation in the retail world in terms of fast fashion, and it was a huge lesson in how important it was to change and adapt quickly to what was happening.

I think a lot of retailers out there now are being more innovative. Sometimes it's the smaller brands that can be classed as being more innovative than anybody else, like Nobody's Child, for instance, who recently did a project with our students. In terms of both sustainability and positive mindset, they are a great voice in retail, and when working with them it was so good to see that they pride themselves not only their product, but also their company ethos and the fact that kind is king. It's really refreshing to see that, and it makes me reflect that is an innovation in itself, because it's a novelty in the tough fashion business to think about things that way. The first place I worked for within B&M was Arcadia, where the focus was primarily the profitability of the business with little thought given to people, which is why it's really refreshing to see brands that are focusing on kindness, supporting people to think big and allowing them time to research and realise their ideas.

*Interview by Helen Goworek*

**Karen Purdy is CEO of Purdy Creative, a sportswear and leisurewear fashion design agency based in Leicester. Since graduating with a Contour Design degree, Karen worked as a fashion designer and consultant for manufacturers and retailers before launching her current business in 2018.**

**FIGURE 2.15** Karen Purdy in her studio, left, and artwork from Purdy Creative, right. Author's own photo, image on right with permission from Karen Purdy

*How would you sum up the creative and innovative work that you do as part of your business currently?*

Primarily we are a design consultancy, we focus on the design of fashion products and specialise in the sports and lifestyle market. We are researching the market by extensively visiting trade shows, sourcing fabrics and constantly staying aware of important trends. This is an essential part of making sure that the product design is fresh visually, exciting and offering newness. As a business, the way we promote our Unique Selling Proposition (USP) is that we are more circular in development and can do this mainly because I've been in this industry for 35 years with experience in all angles of the industry, including design, manufacture and retail. This means we do not just visualise design, but consider the full lifecycle of a product and always consider where it's going to get made, where it's going to get sold, how it's marketed and what that customer would look like. By circular, I mean that if a customer asked me to design a twist on a denim jacket, I'd consider where my inspiration comes from right through to the manufacture and where it could be sold, covering all aspects of the possible lifecycle of that garment. The design initially is the most important thing for a customer, making it visually exciting and new to fit in with the DNA of their brand. However, I can't design without considering its next process, how that product is made and where that product finally fits into the marketplace. I am conscious a nice-looking design can be made, and that's just in my blood. A lot of design ideas in the industry at the moment come from online courses or are disconnected from manufacturing. I think there's a big divide now between design that looks exciting on paper and a design service that does understand fit construction and how that garment development travels to pre-production approval.

*What would you say are the most important recent design innovations, or any other type of innovations in the fashion industry from your perspective?*

It's been a strange few years since COVID started, with many new developments halted, so the more recent would probably be in the last decade where I've seen innovation through fabrications and components relating greatly to sustainability. Innovation in our sector has also seen a big shift in lifestyle and attitude to fitness, which has moved itself from a point of sportswear seen as a commodity to now being a wardrobe staple, like a legging that's worn specifically for running or the gym has now become a high-fashion statement piece. That whole area of innovation in fabrication and fit for sportswear that is no longer just a performance garment, but now worn by the masses in everyday life, has boosted the size of this market enormously to open up design opportunity massively. To explain, NIKE not only continue to market that they are the leaders in performance, but also collaborate with luxury design and music celebrities to create a brand desired for lifestyle and fashion markets. In a similar way, there are premium designers such as Stella McCartney collaborating with Adidas and promoting the sports performance elements of the fabrics, but recognised as a fashion brand, so in many ways that's quite a change.

The other side of how the industry has seen change, particularly for sports lifestyle, is how remotely a product can now be developed. When I started designing, there was a lot of

UK manufacturing and the role was very hands-on, and big companies such as Courtaulds and Corah made the designers aware of every stage of the product development, so even if you weren't a pattern-cutter, you were aware of its importance and that the next stage goes to the sample machinist, and so on. The development stages were on-site, so you experienced the successes and mistakes and the designer had a responsibility to develop a product that could be commercially produced. Today, manufacturing is so global and, in many cases, designers work for a factory they haven't ever visited, which means that designers rely very much on the knowledge of a factory, skills and interpretation, making good communication so important. There's so much emphasis on technical packs [of details about the designs] and how much information is in there. It depends how much technicality you know as a designer as to whether you also work with a product developer. Without hands-on experience in a factory environment, I can't see how a designer is going to have that sort of manufacturing knowledge, so it's the communication and the relationship with your factory creating the garment you are envisaging. You may be a good designer, but if you're a bad communicator or your factory isn't very good at interpretation, then you're in trouble and it's going to be a long-winded process to get that garment right.

*Could you explain the process of innovation in the companies that you've worked in or the sector overall?*

In sportswear I think the process of design innovation is most commonly done overseas and is mainly driven by new fabrics, accessories and components, taking that innovation to create something new. One of the biggest processes which has obviously been missing for a few years is the trade show environment, because as a designer that's where I'd go at the start of the year hoping to find something fantastic and inspiring that I then can design into a wonderful product and present to a customer and say, "This is new innovation." Today, so much success with customers is driven by good CAD skills, but for me the real development is at sampling stage, getting that first protype in your hands and evaluating if the fabric works. Are the components sitting well, is the construction right? Holding that product is when you truly start to evolve that product to get it right.

*What would be the starting point of the creative process in your company when you're developing a collection?*

There are two sides to our business. One is the growing area of footwear, because we hold the European licence for ELLESPORT, and this development is governed by the outsole of a shoe because it's very expensive to create your own new outsole, which is for the really big brands. If we're doing large orders for customers like TK Maxx, we simply tweak and evolve the outsoles every season, so the ways that we will create a new version of a shoe would be through fabrication and colour or print. They're the things that give us a new design, with an eye on new trends. In most of our work, anything new would come from the factory, who would say, "We've got five new outsoles, give us new shoe designs for those." We will also research and send direction boards to help them. This work is branded, so we always have to consider that brand's handwriting and how to interpret that outsole for what that customer's looking for. We'll look at the market and research what's going on in Europe and beyond. In the past, we've travelled overseas to get our inspiration, and I still like to travel to see things, but a lot of the direction comes from so many influences we can find remotely online.

How we work really depends on who we're working with, we're in so many different markets. A typical case would be that that buyer would have in her mind a brief that she would give to us, and that's what kick-starts everything. For example, she might say she's looking for a fitness collection of eight pieces in a performance fabric. We'd then research and present initial concepts with mood boards, fabrications, colour palettes and maybe a bit of branding direction. From then on, we work hand-in-hand with that buyer to create and approve from the final CAD drawings. We then create technical packs for her selected styles with all finished artwork, fabrication, size specifications, construction and everything to create a prototype. We put everything in a tech-pack, which not all design businesses do because a fashion designer might have a product designer somewhere and the factory might also provide information. As we have full knowledge in our company, we can provide all information and then wait for first prototype/fit [sample from the factory] and from there follow all processes to the pre-production stage.

Our research depends on who the client is, because we have quite varied customers, we have premium-brand, and "off price" [discount] and everybody in the middle. We don't subscribe to forecasting companies because it's a massive cost to the business and sportswear is slightly less trend-driven than pure fashion, although we work in fashion sports, where you're not following specific trends necessarily, but if I go to a trade show, I'll always look at what trend books are there, and if I really like them, I'll buy them. We do more eclectic research around many different markets, along with online trend reports being readily available.

I often start designing by sketching by hand, and I love to draw. Other designers who work with me use CAD. I've kept cupboards of historical folders of colours and fabrics, which are tangible things, and I feel that is really going now. It's all very visual, with all design details written on computer. I do find a lot of students that come here with limited CAD skills, though, which shocks me that they are using easy programs like Canva, where you're mostly creating from things that already exist. To me, making a portfolio, where you draw, paint or stick in the fabrics, the colours and drawings [is] far more exciting. We use Adobe Illustrator, which creates a lot more layers with more opportunity to create your own unique work. We do print design here as well, and to be original it is important that it's not just a Photoshop® print. I must admit the majority of work experience or graduates that I get in do not work to that level of computer design, and I feel that is blocking creativity. Computer design can be so exciting, but I see that creativity is dying a little bit and can be repetitive. If I get a student in, I'll say, "Have you seen these fabrics? Have you seen these colours?" You can bring imagination to life that way, but I think we're being conditioned a little bit to follow routes that are easier, simpler, cleaner, and this definitely does reduce openness and creativity.

*Who do you consider to be the most innovative and creative fashion retailers or brands from a design perspective, and what is it you find innovative about these brands?*

There are designers that I'm always watching and I personally like. Being in a more specialised field of sportswear and streetwear, I'm looking at a crossover of sport/fashion brands like Golden Goose, and OFFWHITE, and I'll always go to people like Stella McCartney. I like to look at the mainstream trends, but I'm actually looking at more edgy brands that are using newer fabrics and crossing over products, so luggage, for instance, is more of a fashion item now, and footwear definitely. We've got a lot of trainer brands that are now evolving as high-fashion brands as well, so they're taking what they design for trainers and moving into T-shirts and all sorts of accessories. Its more exciting that they're doing head-to-toe lifestyle outfits. I'm not looking at somebody who's purely couture or somebody doing tailoring. I like to get inspiration from brands that are doing layers of styling from base to outer clothing, including accessories and all different elements of the wardrobe.

*How would you define creativity and innovation based on your own experience and knowledge?*

I think in terms of creativity, it's open wide, it's personal and anything that inspires. Over the years, looking at lots of designers, anything that sparks an idea in my head is creativity, and I can find it personally in all walks of life, so I'm looking at graphics, home wear, dance, fashion and book covers. To me, if you're a creative person, your eyes are open and one idea leads to another. Sometimes you meet people who are creative in their own way. It's taking it and putting your own spin onto something that makes you a creative person. I think there's a crossover between creativity and innovation, because if you close your mind to innovation, you're not open to creativity. I am excited if I see something new that gives you a route to create something even newer and different. I can't see that creativity and innovation can be separated, although I very much appreciate that innovation is sometimes more of a scientific skill. Maybe creative people couldn't cope with all that detail, so there are different levels of skill and focus, but do I think the two need to come together to make an innovative creation.

I think things have changed a lot now because we haven't got the big High Street stores and the traditional shopper, different sales routes are opening up the doors to many smaller start-up businesses who sometimes come to me with very set ideas. If they're the right mix with your skills, then you'll collaborate, and you can help to turn their ideas into reality. Now we certainly collaborate more with customers than we ever have. This has all evolved to the point that customers get more involved, from product ideas to marketing. In a way, this means rather than designers driving ideas to the big companies, we are interpreting their vision. Because of local industry in the UK, I still love the manufacturing side. There is still a small a pocket of suppliers here in Leicester where we'll personally go and spend the afternoon with people who sew or knit and talk about the yarns, colours and the different ways you can create.

If I was to give you my theory, I see any development as an evolution, from the start of a concept through to market, through to marketing, and selling, how an individual buys it and chooses to wear it, it will not stop evolving. When you're signing off, at that point the fabric is correct, the colour's right, it will go to production, but there is always a next stage, particularly now you see everybody recycling, revamping design, so to me, product development never stops, it always moves. I'm "old school", and have seen so many cycles of development and trends, things actually do go full circle, changing to the point where they go back to the start. I do think the issues that we've been through in the last few years

have slowed innovation, and I'm hoping we will see that circle bring back individuality, more expression and less restraints, because the confinement of being locked down, businesses lost, finance and not travelling really did stunt creative freedom.
https://www.purdy-creative.co.uk/

*Interview by Helen Goworek and Christina Goworek*

## References

CLO 3D. (2024) *3D Fashion Design Software, CLO3D*, available online at: https://www.clo3d.com/en/

Conway, S. and Steward, F. (2009) *Managing and Shaping Innovation*. Oxford: Oxford University Press.

GOV.UK. (2024) 'Patents, trade marks, copyright and designs', *GOV.UK*, available online at: https://www.gov.uk/browse/business/intellectual-property

Jobber, D. and Ellis-Chadwick, F.E. (2023) *Principles and Practice of Marketing, 10th edition*. Maidenhead: McGraw Hill.

Optitex. (2024) 'Fashion Design Software', *Optitex*, available online at: https://optitex.com/

Pedroni, M. (2019) 'From Fashion Forecasting to Coolhunting: Previsional Models in Fashion and in Cultural Production', in Vaccarella, M. and Foltyn, J. (eds.) *Fashion-Wise*. Leiden, NL: Brill, pp. 295–304.

Petter, O. (2020) 'Comme des Garcons accused of cultural appropriation after sending models down runway in cornrows', *The Independent*, 19th January 2020, available online at: https://www.independent.co.uk/life-style/fashion/comme-des-garcons-cultural-appropriation-cornrows-models-paris-fashion-week-mens-a9290576.html

Saunders, T. (2023) 'Disbelief at Reading Festival's ban on "cultural appropriation" clothes', *The Sunday Times*, 28th August 2023, available online at: https://www.thetimes.co.uk/article/disbelief-reading-festival-ban-cultural-appropriation-clothes-leeds-kq88vmg79

Sibley, G. (2014) 'A day in the life of Stephanie Kitchen', *Drapers*, 27th June 2014, available online at: https://www.drapersonline.com/insight/analysis/a-day-in-the-life-of-stephanie-kitchen

# 3

# Technical Aspects of Innovation in the Fashion Business

*Ruth Kelly and Helen Goworek*

## Introduction

This chapter explores the current major technical innovations in the fashion industry, and the potential impact and changes for the industry, garments, and consumers alike. The *Cambridge Dictionary* definition of technology as "the practical, especially industrial, use of scientific discoveries" is closely aligned with innovation. The modern world is full of technical innovations, from space exploration, healthcare and electric cars to the digital revolution. Products are made, distributed and used differently in this post-industrial age. Travel and global communications are unlike 150 years ago – gone are the horse and cart and written letter as mainstays. By contrast, clothing has not experienced the same radical disruption during this timescale. Silhouettes have changed and the fashion industry has gone through globalisation and off-shore production, with new synthetic dyes and fibres now dominating. However, since the Industrial Revolution (a large part of which was driven by textile invention and innovation), the ways in which fabrics and clothing are mass-manufactured and produced have changed very little. Vintage clothing pieces seamlessly fit into modern day life in a way that a horse and carriage or early analogue telephone would not. This chapter explores where the fashion industry is today with regard to innovative technology, and what the future has in store, focusing largely on fabric- and fashion-related innovations. We acknowledge that there are also numerous innovations in relation to other fields connected to the fashion business, such as marketing and finance, which are beyond the scope of this book.

Although the global textile apparel industry is still based on manufacturing methods conceived during and developed from the Industrial Revolution, fashion is at the brink of a seismic shift in both textiles and garment production, fuelled by advances in digitisation, robotics, science and environmental concerns. Digitisation has transformed offices, with the advent of email, mobile communications, video

DOI: 10.4324/9781003332749-3

conferencing, 3D prototyping and virtual garment simulation. One of the biggest shifts is the awakening to and new understanding of the impact on resources of the choices made in the conception, maintenance and disposal of a product. Sustainability pressure from consumers coupled with global legislation are driving technical innovation and investment. The COVID-19 pandemic has highlighted the complexity, lack of transparency and weakness in global supply chains. Another change in the fashion business is that collaboration, rather than competition, is being practised more regularly between rival companies. Furthermore, major brands have initiated corporate venture capital funding to invest in and accelerate environmentally and socially responsible start-up companies, such as Patagonia's Tin Shed Ventures™ (Tin Shed Ventures, 2024). Additionally, haute couture and ready-to-wear (prêt-à-porter) brands that are synonymous with luxury and use noble fibres such as leather, silk and cashmere are investing in innovation teams to support their designers and creative directors. Sustainability has also become more of a prevalent consideration, as designers are designing garments with the end-of-life in mind and developments have been made in zero-waste and on-demand manufacturing, repurposing and alternative consumption models. The challenge is how to develop these initiatives at a larger scale. Another key growth area of technology in fashion is virtual clothing. The fashion industry as a whole is a similar to a huge container ship, in that it can only alter its direction slowly, but it is in the process of making changes. Some of the most significant technological innovations in recent years have tended to be in the fabrics from which clothing is made, more so than technology within the content or manufacture of the garments themselves. Key facets of change and technological innovation are outlined in this chapter, in line with the chronological processes of the clothing sector, from raw materials through to garment manufacture and ultimately selected aspects of promotion and consumption. Industry specialists in the fields of product development, manufacturing, digital fashion and creative technology provide have been interviewed to provide insights into technological innovations in the context of the fashion business.

## Innovative Fibres and Materials

The textile industry constantly develops new products, but has not necessarily always innovated or invented, despite its groundbreaking inventions during the 18th and 19th centuries, which spearheaded change in other product sectors. With a globalised, fast and complex supply chain, the race has often been focused on churning out new fabrications (or versions of them) each season, to satisfy designers', brands' or manufacturers' needs to put out new ranges in ever-shortening cycles. From the 1980s through to the present day, mills (factories that manufacture textiles) have created ranges of fabrics twice per year, showcasing new yarns and constructions with finishing techniques in unique combinations. In the effort to secure future orders

**FIGURE 3.1** Paris-based textile industry trade show Première Vision in February 2024 with Spring Summer 2025 predictions. Photos by Francois Durand (top) and Alex Gallosi (bottom) with permission from Première Vision

from clients, potential future needs and trends must be anticipated. These new fabrics are displayed and presented at fashion and textiles industry trade shows around the world, such as Première Vision for fabrics (see Figure 3.1), Ispo (sportswear), KingPins (denim wear), and Outdoor Retailer. Predicting which of these fabrics will reach consumers on the streets of London, Shanghai and New York in more than two years' time is inherently challenging (see Chapter 5) and could be argued to be unsustainable in promoting over-development, as textile companies endeavour to push innovation down the supply chain. Timelines and the sheer scale of the industry make the entire process of selecting and sourcing (finding and procuring appropriate suppliers and materials) extremely complex.

According to the United Nations, in 2018 there were approximately 520,000 textile companies across the world making yarn and fabrics, and 83% of those were involved in the manufacture of fabric (Common Objective, 2018). Assuming that each of these mills offers new textile designs each season, it is likely that millions of fabrics are being developed globally per year, and there has been an abundance of invention within the fashion textiles field during the last decade (see Figure 3.2). Fibre innovation, which was once the sole preserve of large petrochemical corporations such as ICI and Dupont, is now being tackled by multiple types of companies, new and old, from the ground up. The plethora of new enterprises and new fibres being worked on is in response for the need of multiple options for sustainable solutions. This is an extremely exciting time in the world of textiles as many smart minds and novel approaches are being developed and commercialised.

The fashion industry has witnessed many innovations in fabrics since 2010, as designers and brands seek to create more sustainable and functional garments.

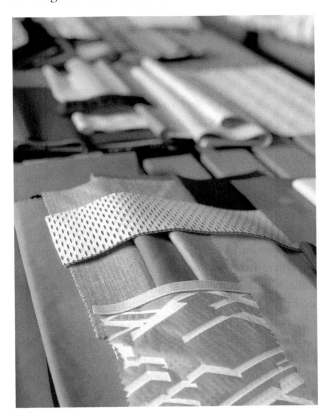

**FIGURE 3.2** A selection of swatches of new fabric designs. *Photo by Ruth Kelly*

**FIGURE 3.3** Lululemon's innovative embroidered reflective glass microbeads. Photo by Ruth Kelly

Sportswear brand Stone Island pioneered the use of reflective glass microbeads in its jackets, to produce reflective garments. Nike then adopted the technology and kitted out Team USA in the 2012 London Olympics in the Windrunner "V" jacket. In 2016, lululemon launched its Ice Queen running capsule with embroidered reflective glass microbeads (see Figure 3.3). Wood-based fibres have also been developed, such as a circular cellulosic fibre by Finnish company Spinnova, which has invented a new way of making fibres and has collaborated with designers and brands to create and launch new fabrics in their designs, including Sofia Ilmoen, Bestseller (2010) Adidas (the Terrex HS1 Hoodie), H&M and The North Face. Naia™ bio-based acetate is another new fabric innovation, used by Stella McCartney in her Autumn 2023 collection (Stella McCartney, 2023). Vegetable-based fabrics are also now available, such as Orange Fiber, which is a soft, silky biodegradable fabric made from citrus peel waste, used by Salvatore Ferragamo in 2017 (Orange Fiber, 2017). Recycled fibres are also sustainable options, such as Econyl, which is an infinitely regenerated nylon fibre made from recycled fishing nets, carpets and other waste materials. Fashion for Good, a global initiative promoting sustainable innovation in the fashion industry, is a useful source of information on innovative products (Fashion for Good, 2024). Mylo (mushroom leather), Clarus, Spiber and Keel Labs are amongst the textile brands developing innovative biomaterial technologies based on natural raw materials. In 2022, Balenciaga received widespread publicity when the company launched a coat made from Ephea, a mushroom-based leather (Cernansky, 2022).

For an industry that is synonymous with the industrial revolution, textile innovation can be surprisingly challenging, for multiple reasons. Firstly, since fabrics touch the skin, our relationship with clothing can be both emotionally and psychologically intimate. Textiles need to adapt to changing environments, to move with the wearer, not only covering and protecting the body, but also providing comfort and safety, and imparting confidence. The challenge of the fabric developer/technologist is therefore to create materials that perform, look and feel amazing, contributing to the clothing's ultimate emotional durability. Textile innovation is often therefore described as both an art and science. Another challenge facing fabric innovation is the longevity of the product, especially the need to wash and dry clothing to remove sweat, body oils, stains etc. Using hot water and detergents to clean garments can reduce their usable lifetime, as hot water causes yarns and structures to collapse and shrink. Abrasion in both wear and laundering can cause fibres to weaken and break, resulting in holes, pills and microfibre fragmentation pollution. Dyestuffs and prints can bleed and run, causing colours to fade or contaminate other garments in the wash load. Trims, such as zips, logos and buttons, can chip, peel, crack and become unsightly. Launderability has been a significant barrier in the uptake of smart textiles, as electronics and water do not readily mix. Economic factors also heavily influence decisions made during the development and innovation process. The perceived and actual value of clothing and textiles has reduced significantly in recent decades. Consumers pay less for clothing at the present time, whilst simultaneously owning many more individual items than in the 20th century, typically holding onto garments for shorter time and generating more textile waste than ever before.

Since Dupont scientist Joseph Shivers invented the stretch fibre Lycra™[1] in 1958 (after the introduction of new fibre polymers such as polyester and polyamide/nylon), there have not been any new fibre types commercially adopted in clothing. Lycra™ was invented to solve the problems of weight and degradation that using natural rubber in stretch corsetry produced, as fabrics made with rubber yarns were heavy and perished quickly on exposure to body oils, perspiration and chemicals such as chlorine. Just as Lycra™ was born out of ten years of research and the need to solve a problem, so the new materials of today are being born out of the need to solve environmental and sustainability problems.

Annual global fibre production in 2021 reached a record 113 million tonnes, almost doubling in 20 years, up from 58 million tonnes in 2000 (Textile Exchange, 2024). Extrapolating out, this figure is expected to rise to 149 million tonnes in 2030 if consumption trends continue in the same manner. However, it is important to take climate change into consideration since, according to Textile Exchange (2024),

"Without rethinking growth, the industry will not stay within the 1.5° pathway ....
To limit global warming to 1.5° Celsius, an absolute reduction of greenhouse gas
emissions by 45% by 2030 compared to the 2019 baseline is required." A combined
approach to achieve this target will necessitate a reduction in personal consumption and continued uptake of pre- and post-consumer recycled fibres, using new
sustainable feedstocks to create new materials that break the dependence on fossil
fuels. Fossil-based synthetic fibres (e.g., polyester, polyamide, elastane and acrylic)
account for 64% of all fibres produced, at 72 million tonnes of annual production
in 2021 (Textile Exchange, 2024).

Recycled polyester has been readily adopted for textiles since the fabric mill
Polartec collaborated with the clothing firm Patagonia in 1993 to launch recycled polyester fleece made from single-use plastic bottles from the drinks industry.
However, only a very small proportion of the global fibre market is currently from
pre- and post-consumer textiles, with the majority of recycled fibres globally being
derived from used plastic bottles. Moving from raw fibres to recycled to bio-based,
biodegradable and regenerative materials enables the transition from a take-make-
throwaway society to full circularity. Creating circular materials takes rethinking –
e.g., moving away from petro-chemical sources to bio-based feedstocks (the starting
material) requires much diligence with employment of evidence-based decisions as
to whether the new innovations are more environmentally responsible. Questions
need to be asked and data procured – e.g., "What exactly is the bio-based feed stock,
is it from waste, or is it being taken from land that is being used to grow food?"
Various new methods of producing bio-synthetics are coming to market, some that
generate pellets in a "plug and play" option that harnesses the existing synthetic
fibre manufacturing infrastructure. Such solutions have the advantage of being able
to scale quickly to mass industrial production. Other techniques, including fermen-
tation and DNA sequencing, are medium-term solutions requiring substantial capital investment in new hardware. Alternative feedstocks are also being explored – e.g.
aquaculture (harvesting kelp from the sea), capturing carbon from the atmosphere
and using food waste streams such as coffee grounds and fruit skins. As a response
to slogans such as "wear wool not fossil fuel", the fossil fuel industry is also now
becoming part of the solution and not just the problem. Petrochemical yarn suppliers are offering bespoke synthetic yarns, with embedded properties/colourants
added during the fibre manufacturing process (extrusion). For example, Fibrant (a
petrochemical company which supplies caprolactum, a building block of synthetic
fibres) is promoting Ecolactam as its lowest-carbon-footprint eco-friendly caprolactam (Fibrant, 2024). Additionally, materials are being grown in labs and there are
multiple novel alternatives to leather made from natural raw materials such as cactus,
mushrooms or grapes.

## New Ways of Dyeing and Finishing Textiles

Dyeing and finishing textiles and garments can be a very messy business, not only in terms of environmental impact and pollution, but also in the lack of consistency of uniformity of colour and fastness. Waterless dyeing and "dope" dyeing (adding the colorants into the fibre during the melt extrusion process) are being used to overcome these challenges. Plant-based chemicals and dyestuffs are now commercially available, and work is carrying on expanding the breadth, consistency and reliability of these products. Chemical companies such as Archroma and Beyond Surface Technologies are offering advanced green chemical solutions (Archroma, 2024; Beyond Surface Technologies, 2024). The outdoor industry is continuing to innovate in the field of waterproof breathable fabrics, transitioning out of the harmful "forever" per- and polyfluoroalkyl substances (PFAS) whilst still being able to create jackets that are waterproof and breathable for customers. Digital printing has revolutionised textile printing in the photo-realism and breadth of colours that can be achieved compared with traditional screen-printing methods. The screen-making steps have been eliminated, as the printer prints directly onto specially treated fabric, in a similar way to a home printer printing onto paper. However, colour matching can still be a cumbersome process, and improvements such as the HP Stitch with its onboard spectrophotometer (an instrument that digitally assesses colour via measuring the amount of light that a material absorbs) for colour matching, can solve this.

Haute couture designer Iris van Herpen worked with PolyJet™ technology to push digital printing further, as exhibited in Paris in January 2022. Photo-polymers with different colours and transparency were simultaneously 3D-printed directly onto fabrics. Colours of the resulting print changed depending on the viewing angle of the observer. Harnessing the laws of physics, in-yarn technologies and new processing methods are amplifying enhanced performance without the need for chemical finishes, in the field of biomimicry (mimicking characteristics of natural forms). This not only provides a more durable reliable performance, but is more sustainable in the reduced use of chemicals and water. Nextext is a company using biomimicry, utilising TurboDry®, a patent pending sweat removal technology. TurboDry® was created by Dr Jason (Jun-Yan) Hu, who was formerly a researcher at Hong Kong Polytechnic University (Textile World, 2020). Dr Hu was able to translate into knitted fabrics the ability of trees to draw up water from roots to leaves. Sweat rapidly moves through the fabric construction to enable moisture to evaporate efficiently. As the moisture processes are physical, they will not wash out, so they extend the life of the garment. Innovations are required to help with the complex chemical requirements of recycling mixed blends of fabrics. Re-polymerisation is complex, and can often result in an inferior recycled product when compared to its original counterpart. Various other recent innovations such as plasma technology and ultrasonic technology have been utilised in textile finishing. Sonovia is a company aiming to disrupt the textile industry using ultrasonic technology in its processing, developing "chemistry guns" to inject dye into yarn and break the paradigm that durability and performance mean creating pollution.

## Innovations in Clothing Design and Manufacture

Innovations in the design and manufacture of clothing in the late 20th and early 21st centuries have largely concentrated on the computerisation of existing tasks, such as drawing variations in design and colour. Moving away from the conventional steps of "cut and sew" clothing manufacturing – i.e., producing fibre, spinning yarns, knitting or weaving fabrics, dyeing and finishing fabrics, cutting fabric pieces and then sewing garments together – is a huge effort. It not only entails the employment of new machinery and practices and the reorganisation of factories, but also a re-imagining of the actual clothing by designers, technologists and product developers. Lasers, fusing and bonding technologies, ultrasonic welding and 3D printing are all being used in the production of garments to either replace stitching or as embellishment. Robotics research is also under way, which has potential to be used in garment manufacture, but which cannot yet replace the human hand in its ability and dexterity in handling and sewing pliable fabrics. Some of the key innovations in clothing design and manufacture are explored in more detail in this section.

Computer-aided design (CAD) moved into the mainstream as a fashion design tool during the early 1990s. This enabled designers to scan in hand-drawn sketches for the first time and fill them with colour or pattern digitally, more rapidly than colouring in by hand which had up until that point been done largely by designers with physical media such as flat-tipped pens such as Pantone™ or watercolour paint, then posted by mail or courier to clients. These traditional media are still in use, of course, but it has now become the norm for fashion companies in the UK to either incorporate certain aspects of CAD into their design processes or to develop ideas entirely via computer software, with drawing by hand no longer being necessary. The ease and speed with which design ideas can be sent digitally between suppliers and clients, either across the country or internationally, have been contributing factors to the widespread adoption of CAD in the contemporary fashion business, particularly in the mass market, where new designs are launched with high frequency. Despite these innovations, there is, however, still a place for hand-drawn and painted design ideas, to offer an increased sense of personal satisfaction and artistry to the designer, particularly in an era when artisan crafts, tradition and authenticity are becoming highly valued once again.

Digital creation methods are fully utilised in garment design via the use of such software as Adobe Illustrator® and Photoshop®. The product development and pattern-cutting process has been digitised with 3D design apparel software such as CLO-3D and 3D Browzwear, which can produce images with almost photographic accuracy, thus reducing the requirement to produce physical garment samples. Realistic clothing simulation and movement are still improving to deal with the challenges of accurately rendering fabrics to represent their individual stretch, drape, volume and texture characteristics. As well as digital garments reducing the burden on the prototyping process and being desirable assets in the gaming world, social media influencers and video game players can also utilise virtual outfits to maximise their creativity whilst eliminating the need for physical garments. Digital design houses like The Fabricant facilitate design, body and adaptability freedom (The Fabricant, 2024).

CAD has a further advantage, in that digitised drawings are able to connect directly to certain aspects of manufacturing systems. Pattern-cutting (making paper shapes of garment pieces prior to manufacture) has traditionally been carried out manually by technical experts in this field, as part of the process to interpret designers' 2D drawings into 3D garments. Computer-aided design/computer-aided manufacture (CAD/CAM) systems for producing garment patterns digitally as well as product life ycle management (PLM) software have been developed by companies such as Lectra. Additionally, Lectra's Gerber Accumark system (Lectra, 2024) can supply electronic equipment to produce lay plans which carefully distribute the position of pattern pieces on cloth ready for cutting in production to maximise fabric usage and to minimise waste. This is another process which had only been done manually prior to the advent of CAD/CAM systems, and whilst such equipment can be expensive, speeding up the preparation process for garment production can be a good investment.

The huge advancements and the changes to society that have been made in information technology, computing power and the the internet have made major impacts in the world of fashion. Not only have offices been transformed with the way business is conducted, enabling fast and cheap global communication throughout the global supply chain, but so havethe ways in which clothing is manufactured, ordered, distributed, marketed and even worn. The Jacquard weaving loom and attachment patented in 1804 by Joseph Marie Jacquard was revolutionary in that it used a system of punched cards to individually control warp yarns (threads which run up and down the length of a piece of fabric) in the weaving loom (a device for producing fabric), so enabling complex patterns to be manufactured. This ability to individually move yarns can now be controlled digitally, and has enabled patterning and shaping in both the weaving and knitting of fabrics and garments. The use of Jacquard's replaceable punched cards to control a sequence of operations was influential in the 19th century to the "father of computing", Charles Babbage, and his associate, mathematician Ada Lovelace, who recognised that the technology could be applied beyond just calculation, thus leading to the design of an analytical engine, which ultimately inspired the development of computers (Science and Industry Museum, 2019).

Garment machinery builders such as Santoni, Stoll, Cifra and Shima Seiki are currently pushing the boundaries of 3D knitting, taking yarns directly into seamless 3D garments. By knitting shoe uppers via its FlyKnit 3D knitting technology, Nike famously disrupted the design of running shoes. Taking yarn directly to panels or garments has the advantage of eliminating the need to produce a roll of material, therefore minimising wastage in production and speeding up prototyping turnaround times. Structures and specific yarns can be "body-mapped" (matching performance to the contours of the wearer's body) with these technologies, which is especially desirable in the sportswear and underwear industries in maximising performance and eliminating bulky and irritating seams.

3D printing is another recent development that can be applied to fashion (see Figure 3.4). Producing 3D solid printouts, usually in layers of polymer, this technology has been applied to numerous fields as diverse as art, medical items and food. Developed by companies such as Stratasys (Stratasys, 2024), 3D printers have reduced in price over the last decade, with cheaper, more compact machines becoming accessible to small organisations and even hobbyists. 3D printing has therefore become a relatively cost-effective way to produce individual items, making it potentially more sustainable than the investment involved in producing extensive samples and large production runs using traditional methods and materials. 3D printing has been used in the fashion business to make individual prototypes or small-scale production runs of solid products such as accessories and shoe soles. However, this technology has improved in its ability to produce more fluid outputs to be applied to garments, such as those used by designer Iris van Herpen in her 2016 collection (Holgate, 2016; McCormick et al., 2020). 3D printing is not yet at a scale to be used extensively in the mass market, but it has scope for future development and the potential to revolutionise clothing production.

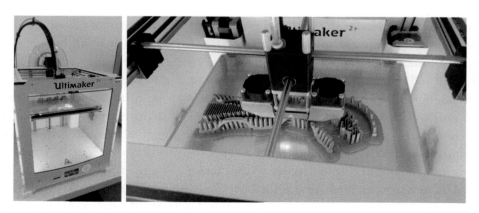

**FIGURE 3.4**  3D printer. Photos by Helen Goworek

Other contemporary aspects of innovation which impact upon the fashion business include blockchain and artificial intelligence (AI). Blockchain technology is being used to verify the chain of custody throughout the entire supply chain to certify and validate social and environmental claims relating to a specific product. Much has been written regarding the use of AI in the role of creation, specifically on the question of whether AI could replace the fashion designer. Current thinking is that AI will evolve as a tool for creatives and manufacturers alike (Textile Insight, 2023). AI could potentially be used in textile recycling centres to identify and separate different materials in physical sorting centres, or as an aid in research and development, suggesting which options might be most viable to pursue when creating new products.

## Summary

This chapter has explored technical innovations for fabric and clothing in the fashion business in recent years and their potential impact on products, business and society. Although construction techniques for fabric and clothing have seen limited change, innovations have taken place in the development of fibres, as well as dyeing, printing and finishing processes for fabrics. Innovative new fibres and materials have been developed, many with an emphasis on environmental sustainability. Contemporary innovations in clothing design and manufacture have focused largely on digitisation and sustainability, such as 3D-effect software which can replace the need for physical garment samples. In the interviews section, technical experts offer their views on how innovations are implemented in practice in manufacturing, retailing and digital aspects of the fashion business.

### Interviews with Practitioners in Innovation and Technical Roles in the Fashion Business

**Angélique Dietz is a product creation and advanced manufacturing executive in the clothing and footwear industry (VF Corporation, lululemon, Nike). Angelique studied MTS Fashion and Design in Utrecht, the Netherlands, followed by Professional Education at the Massachusetts Institute of Technology, USA. With expertise in digital transformation technologies, product creation, and advanced manufacturing, she now works as a strategic innovation consultant with tech startups and small and medium-sized enterprises in the fashion industry, bridging the worlds of digital hardware and software engineering with fashion consumer products in retail and manufacturing.**

*What do you see as the biggest innovations that are happening currently in clothing product development?*

If I think back to around 2006 when I moved for Nike to Turkey, one of the elements of the role was exploring bringing virtual (digital/3D) prototype development into the product

**FIGURE 3.5** Angélique Dietz. Photo with permission from Angélique Dietz

development process. At that time, there were three major players in that field, and they were still in the early stages. They were commercially available options, but still in early stages, with questions still to be fully answered, such as "How does the technology function?" and "What learnings are important for the software manufacturers to learn from the real-life brand and manufacturing user experiences?" Besides learning the new tools, we had to consider how virtual prototyping would impact the development and production processes and the skillsets of the people involved in that process. Almost 20 years later, there are still all too many retailers and manufacturers that are struggling to bring a 3D process to the mainstream way of working. However, many design and development experts continue to advocate and develop in the digital product creation space.

*How would you define creativity and innovation?*

Creativity and innovation for me are a natural output of behaviours and a way of being, such as being curious; being open, interested to keep learning, humility, asking questions, details matter, experience new things and try out making things. It's a way to approach life and enjoy discovery on the journey. Truth be told, my impatience sometimes gets in my own way of enjoying the journey and being too focused on the outcome. Knowing when that happens and calling myself out on it are continuous work in progress!

*To what extent does the inherent tactile nature of fabric influence the uptake of 3D prototyping?*

It's almost everything. The draping and behaviour around the soft-tissue body plays such a big role as to why technical teams still attach importance to having real-life garments produced during the product development process. The realisation of a digital true representation of a material forms a hurdle to fully removing the need for all sampling. Innovation in this space is exciting and pioneered by a few. The evolution of technology from Web 2.0 to 4.0 started with fabric layers mapped as 2D textures to now possible as a multilayer texture mapping enabling 3D visualisation and finessing the draping, stretching and also how a seam placement influences the behaviour of a fabric, pattern and thus fit of a garment. For example, let's consider one fabric behaviour: drape. It's not only how does a fabric drape, but how does that translate into the garment when on the body? How can we simulate that in an as real as possible scenario? Does the drape look right in terms of the shadows represented? This fabric component is so critical to producing the digital twin, and is one of the areas where there still lie a lot of innovation opportunities.

*Do you think that virtual prototyping has been slower in adoption because those decision-makers placing garment orders are still insisting on seeing physical samples?*

It's unsustainable, the amount of fabrics, trims and packaging in addition to global shipping and distribution required with "analogue" prototyping and additional lead time for all this, as opposed to changing a silhouette, shape etc. on a digital screen. From a sustainability perspective, it doesn't make sense to carry on producing physical samples. Sometimes I wonder if it is a symptom of habits – "We've always seen the actual products before we placed the buys" – and that people haven't been able to try the new capabilities of digital prototyping. Generation has a part to play in this. I was not raised with digital technology around me. I was raised in the business of textiles, the 100% analogue way of developing, approving etc. Younger generations are much more likely to fully digitally commit. Their education is completely digital, their shopping behaviours, experiencing, exploring, choosing and purchasing are all digital, so it gives me hope that as new generations who grew up with digital, they might be viewing digital prototypes as their normal part of the developing and decision-making process.

*Are there differences in organisational set-up that influence how extensively digital creation is utilised?*

The so-called digital native companies built their business on the basis of digital technologies. These have been able to create market share for themselves because they are able to navigate and move with the changing consumer needs so much quicker. The rise of many of these new brands certainly became an example and eye-opener to larger companies that did not have the digital infrastructure, or even a fraction of it, in place. If you have enabling software in place so that your organisation efficiently can create and sell and has real-time access to sales and manufacturing data, then you're moving into a less wasteful cycle with reduced overruns and more full-priced sales.

*If we stay on the analogue product development path, are there still innovations that can be utilised?*

I believe there are always better ways to be explored. Even if a company stays with an analogue product development process, they can utilise innovations such as utilising smaller material runs by choosing different material colouration options as part of the product development cycle and approvals, digital printing of materials or 3D printing. Lots of fabric is wasted even to make one garment sample, especially if a specific colour/print is required. When in seasonal collections you see that many of the fabrics carry over from season to season, also the basic silhouettes don't change much in fit – it's a line here and there, maybe a different trim colour, different neckline, different cuffs or smaller details that change. What is it that we need as decision-makers to enable us to move past this feeling of insecurity about deciding to buy such a similar style this year again when only seeing a digital image of it? I also think digital creation can stop us from doing the same work again and again, thinking about fabric libraries and different ways of linking previous products and materials to be able to find something really close so that you help creators using existing proven means and not by regenerating repeatedly.

*Thinking about the modern-day garment factory and how garments are made, what are you seeing there in terms of innovation?*

Manufacturers have become very skilled at driving efficiency in all aspects of their business. The need to be price-competitive is deeply ingrained. There is a cost to this, though: the dance of over-manufacturing via costing principle. To drive down the individual garment cost price, a factory requests higher volumes to be ordered to be more efficient. You can really argue, "Who wins?" It's the negotiating of pennies to get the manufacturer to agree to a lower cost price. How much of these additional bought volumes are sold at healthy margins? It's certainly not all great for the retailer, to commit to high volumes that ultimately are difficult to sell through and will be marked down or end up unsold in landfills. No one really wins in this situation. We've created this environment; how can we start to break it open to create different ways that are much healthier for everyone involved? It's great to know that many manufacturers are investing in digital technologies and quite often are more advanced in this space than their customers [retailers]. They can be good influencers for innovators and adopters of innovations and help scaling. You see that where the manufacturers have long-term relationships with their customers, there you find very optimised product creation processes and tooling in place.

*Is there anything else we should change during the creation process?*

We should start the creation with the end-of-life of the product in mind. This is such a different approach to how we've always thought about the creation process. Garment design has historically been approached through the lens of creating something unique. When we can shift to … thinking about what we want this product to be when the wearer is completely done with it, we make wiser choices at the beginning. It's maybe not as exciting to think about the end of a garment's life. My mom saved quite a lot of baby clothes from my sister and me. When I had my daughter, she gave me the well-preserved pieces. Some of them are still so beautiful, and when I put those garments on my daughter, it was a very unique experience compared to just putting on something that I bought new in a store. It was just at a different level of emotion that was in this piece, and I think if we talk about design with that end-of-life in mind, this was 40 years ago, and so how could you ever design with something in mind that maybe is or needs to be recycled 40+ years later? It's an impossible task maybe, but we continue to learn, we bring on new technologies, and when we are open to putting thought into what we expect from the product at the end of someone's use, it's a promising change.

*Are the manufacturing and design functions separated?*

Yes, the functions are separated often between brand and factory often located at the other side of the world. This also comes up for me when working with a technology company that has little understanding about the apparel industry. If you think about how many people on the creation side are making decisions, but who've never been in a factory or who've never been in a fabric mill, I mean, how can we make the right decisions if we are not fully informed or understanding the why and how?

*Is there anything else on the horizon that is out there, or you would wish would be out there, or any sort of that you're seeing?*

The topic that I am really interested in and have been blessed to be working on for the past years is automation in fashion manufacturing. It's not about fine-tuning current manufacturing machines – i.e., creating add-ons to existing machines to make them work more efficiently and therefore semi-automating – but truly rethinking the process and equipment. If we can automate and through this automation contribute to a more world-friendly method, why wouldn't we want to spend resources and capital behind this?

*Interview by Ruth Kelly*

**Helen Tarratt is Director of HT Design Consultants, a private company representing clothing and fabric companies from Bangladesh, India, dealing with UK retailers. Helen is a BA (Hons) Textiles graduate from Huddersfield University in the UK who has worked in design and sales for several manufacturers and retailers in the UK and overseas.**

*How would you summarise the creative and innovative work that you do?*

Within my job role, day-to-day I'm designing garments using Adobe Illustrator® and Photoshop®. The other big part of my role is fabric sourcing and fabric development, so that can be finding fabrics and getting inspiration from them, or further developing fabrics from the mills, looking at new yarns and trying to keep ahead of sustainable routes. That's probably as important as actually doing the sketches, design boards, presentations, and trend research. I work with the owner of the company, and all the merchandising and technical work is done in Bangladesh, where there's a manager who manages that side of it and a small portfolio of five factories that we subcontract to. I usually travel there every six months. It's all on a mutual benefit basis, but they treat me as though I work with them. The business will buy the products from the factories and sell the orders to our retail customers.

*How would you describe the creative process and innovation in the companies that you've worked in?*

In general, the process is all quite similar from the suppliers' side, so as a quick life cycle of how a supplier works, I would be looking at the season's trends, looking at past history of things that have sold, understanding the customer and what they've been selling, how we can replace those products and move them on. Then it would be a lot of trend research, fabric research going to Bangladesh, going round all the mills and seeing what fabrics they've developed, looking at new yarns, new finishes. I always ask the team in

**FIGURE 3.6** Fashion design consultant Helen Tarratt alongside one of her CAD garment drawings. Images with permission from Helen Tarratt

| REFERENCE: | SC-2378 | DATE: 15/11/23 |
|---|---|---|
| DESCRIPTION: | Waffle Granddad | SIZE: MEDIUM |
| FABRIC DETAILS: | Cotton Waffle | ETA: 30/11/23 |

## *DO NOT PRESS, LIGHT STEAM ONLY*

Herringbone BNT DTM

Rib neck trim INSET
with DTM
coverseam

Back neck buggy / DTM
single jersey

DTM Coverseam

DTM single jersey
piping on the
placket

DTM Anchor
embroidery

DTM Cover seam

Rib cuff

Follow the basic Grandad measurement chart

*Supplier & Co. Ltd.*
*International Design Corp*

**FIGURE 3.6**

| REFERENCE: | SC-2378 | DATE: 15/11/23 |
|---|---|---|
| DESCRIPTION: | Waffle Granddad | SIZE: MEDIUM |
| FABRIC DETAILS: | Cotton Waffle | ETA: 30/11/23 |

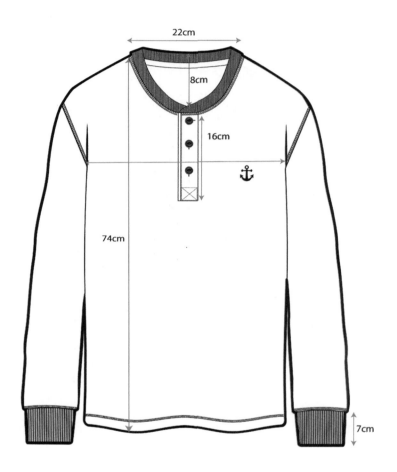

*Supplier & Co. Ltd.*
*International Design Corp*

**FIGURE 3.6**

| REFERENCE: | SC-2378 | DATE: | 15/11/23 |
|---|---|---|---|
| DESCRIPTION: | Waffle Granddad | SIZE: | MEDIUM |
| FABRIC DETAILS: | Cotton Waffle | ETA: | 30/11/23 |

Neck construction

Inspiration picture

BN print in white

## WHAT CLOTHING
— M —
### RELAXED FIT
MADE IN BANGLADESH

    Ground colour

PANTONE
19-3920 TCX
Peacoat

    Please source similar button
to this?

    DTM Anchor
embroidery

*Supplier & Co. Ltd.*
*International Design Corp*

**FIGURE 3.6**

Bangladesh to go to the laundries and the dye houses and print mills to get any new ideas and developments that they've been doing, and then generally, I'd put a small range together for the customer (usually a retailer) and then go and present it to them. Alongside that, the customer also feeds in a design brief, things that they're looking for, and then we go off and do the sampling and costing, and then I'd go back with prices and quantities. The things that change are maybe the country we're producing in or a new factory, a new fabric mill or a new yarn, but the actual process from the supplier point of view hasn't really changed at all in my entire career.

For me, the creative process is all the information that I've absorbed. If I break it down into, say, a product category such as men's jersey T-shirts and sweatshirts, I will have gathered all my information, I've maybe found some nice textured fabrics, and when I come to actually designing, I'll be thinking, "I've got these really nice fabrics, this is the shape I want to do, I want to add a print design to it or a slogan or something else." In my current company, we work with a freelance print designer, so I will brief her on the aspects that I don't do myself and I would present it using CAD as much as possible, send it to the customer to get their opinion, or I would get sample garments made by the factory. For the actual thought process, a lot of it is just filling your head with visual information. You've done your trend research, so it comes down to "I really like that neck shape, but I want to do it on this new fabric and I want to do this new rib set-out trim, I want to put a nice back-neck tape in, I want to print the back neck buggy and maybe add some contrast stitching," so I've got all the ingredients and then it's just putting it all together.

With the company I'm working for at the moment, we're still quite basic, using Illustrator® and Photoshop®, whereas the previous company that I was contracted to had a big design team and they were doing 3D designing on CLO software, so they could actually create a CAD image that looks like a garment, rather than using Photoshop® and Illustrator®, which are still quite two-dimensional. CLO is an expensive system. However, it reduced the need for physical garment samples to be made, and the previous company I worked for had the money to invest in it. They also work with American and mainland European firms who are more progressive in their way of working. For example, the design team in that company would put together a collection on 3D-effect CAD, and the buyers in Europe and the US would pick from that collection or ask us to make a garment sample, and they could also follow up with doing all the garment fittings on software as well as the grading (different sizes), whereas in the UK a lot of the buying teams want to see a sample regardless. In the UK, retailers and brands wouldn't present garments in 3D CAD with massive confidence, whereas elsewhere in Europe and some well-known retailers in the US would be willing to place orders from seeing 3D CAD images.

A lot of UK retailers still use a very traditional way of buying and selecting. There's a huge amount of waste from making samples, which could be reduced to be more sustainable. I don't know if anyone would consider investing in 3D printing instead of making samples, maybe not for garments, but certainly for more solid items like shoes. There are machines that can produce a complete knitwear garment (rather than sewing together separate pieces), but that requires investment in machinery. From a designers' point of view, you could approach Mac or Adobe to produce software to make product development more sustainable, to reduce the amount of sampling, and which would give suppliers and retailers more control over what they want and what they envisage. The whole 3D CAD system is very efficient if it's used properly. I used it in my last job for a large company with sourcing offices around the world. I did a presentation recently on mood boards with trends, fabrics and prints, and I tend to organise this by categories like polo tops with zip necks and smart T-shirts etc., rather than arranging them by trend.

I think the changes in in the fashion industry are all front-end, consumer-facing social media marketing and distribution, the whole selling side of it, data collection, that's really where all the technological investment is, but technology in product development hasn't changed as quickly as it could have changed. In the back end, you've still got mainly women on low pay in factories in developing countries making the garments, and I don't see any real evidence of automation at the moment. There are some big factories in China that are semi-automated, but even for AI or robots to do that work, you need such dexterity and agility, I can't really envisage that for a long, long time taking over any of the labour that's put into garments. There's more innovation in printing, dyeing and finishing, there's more technology for accuracy and efficiency, definitely, but the system is still people having to sew garments and packing them. I haven't seen any automated packing yet, and products are still slid under a metal detector by hand for checking their safety, so it remains a massively labour-intensive industry.

Digital printing has now become much more mainstream, used by almost all the printing mills I work with, which is more efficient and less wasteful than the roller printing or screen printing that used to be the norm. There's also been more innovation from the dyeing machine builders, so it's easier to get the colour recipes, it's quicker and more efficient, using a bit less water, and there are techniques like mineral dyeing, which is more eco-friendly. There's been a lot more sustainable innovation taken place on the dyeing and finishing side rather than it being particularly creative, but it is about being more sustainable and more efficient, causing less waste from wrongly coloured batches, for example. The data and monitoring are better than they used to be, driven by efficiency. Sustainability and new technology have come along, and the machine builders are constantly wanting to make their product better to encourage factories to buy them, so I'd say it's more of a competitive thing. Then on top of that, during the last five to ten years, there has been a sustainability drive, but prior to that sustainability was led more by reducing costs, such as using less dyestuff.

*How do you make decisions for designing with the information you've collected for inspiration?*

I don't have a lot of trend information, because to subscribe to fashion forecasting companies is just not affordable for a small supply company like the one I'm working for at the moment. A lot of my trend sourcing is looking at high-end brands and catwalks to find my inspiration. I constantly go round the shops even if I'm personally shopping. I'm always looking, especially at fabrics and trims, and for specific comparative shopping, I'll probably go to Copenhagen in March or another European city, trawling through shops, especially independents, to look for new ideas and fabrics. Then we'd buy some samples, maybe take lots of photographs so I've got a visual library. I then come back and start putting all the trends together. I specifically look after men's wear, jersey sweatshirts, shorts and trousers, so I try to visualise my designs hanging in the retail client's stores, and I will always think, "Is this suitable for the retailer? Can I really see it hanging in there?" I'm also conscious of price, so just through experience, I'll know what kind of placket opening at the front to do if I'm designing, say a Henley top, and the same with fabrics. I'll know by the fibre blend or the fabric construction, and if it's going to be really expensive and we're not going to be able to fit it into the customer's target selling price, then I wouldn't use that, even if it's the most innovative thing out there. The other important part is whether it's going to perform and pass test results, because another problem is you can find really innovative fabrics, but then sometimes they don't perform, so when I go to a fabric mill, I'll pull them out and then I'll ask whether they have any test results, and I'll ask my technical colleagues if the construction will be alright and whether it might shrink. I'll ask for a ballpark price for the fabric, and if it's US$5 a yard, it's too expensive for me to consider it.

I also have to think of the strengths of the factory and whether the designs are suitable for them to make from a technical viewpoint. The technical knowledge comes with experience, but you've definitely got to have an appreciation of it because you can't just sketch things that are not suitable for a production line, so I think it is important to learn about the technical constraints. Equally, designers have got to design and be innovative and push boundaries, otherwise you're going nowhere, and that's no good for a company either because they want innovation, so it's a balancing act. I think you can do this when you're more experienced because it's become natural to you, but I'd advise any design graduates to have an appreciation of the technology and pricing. When I first started as a designer, I didn't know all of this, so my designs were creative, but might not always have fitted into the right price. Over years of designing, it's become almost subconscious and automatic that the product's appearance in the store, who your customer is, the costs, the factory's manufacturing abilities and product performance are automatically absorbed into your design decisions.

*Do any theories about creativity or innovation influence your work?*

The one that always stays with me is the iceberg theory (i.e., that only a small amount is visible, and the problems are hidden under the water), and I still apply that. In my subconscious, I want at least half of the iceberg to be showing, I don't want to design and get an order for something that is not fit for purpose, not going to be the right price, even if it looks amazing.

*How would you define creativity and innovation based on your own experience?*

For me personally in my narrow field of what I'm doing, creativity is creating something, making something that someone buys and they're happy with, that's fit for purpose. It's bought by the customer, and that can be the buyer from a retailer. It doesn't have to be the end-consumer because I don't necessarily think in those terms. It's creating something that the company's buyer likes, and they place the order, and it's not about the money. For me, it's about the retail buyer liking and selecting my design, which gives me a real sense of achievement. I think innovation is coming up with something that is very new. I can't invent something new, but I might find something new maybe going on a trip to a laundry and finding out they want to develop – for example, waterless finishes using a powder that's eco-friendly. To me, that would be an innovation, coming up with something new that no one's really doing. If you ask me if I'm an innovator I'll say no, I'm a men's wear designer. I'm not innovating, I'm creating garments, putting lots of things together that have already been developed. If I was an innovator, I'd be working for polymer companies trying to create polymers that are not from plastic. That's how I define innovation, more invention than creative.

*Interview by Helen Goworek*

**Jade McSorley is a researcher in digital fashion and sustainability, co-founder of fashion rental app Loanhood, and a model. Jade holds an MA in Fashion Futures from the University of the Arts, London.**

*How would you define creativity and innovation within your own experience?*

I'm more of an observer of creative people, and like to understand what makes them tick and the impact that their work has. I would say creativity is taking risks and problem-solving, like being able to be creative in the face of adversity or when you feel like you can't find a solution to something, then being creative in your approach. I think innovation is part of being creative; it's essential and exciting, and can be rewarding, but I still always have this air of caution where I think we need to not just innovate for the sake of innovation. We need to innovate with an understanding of the impact it can have, and my concern is we innovate without thinking of those consequences, and I think we need to responsibly innovate. My

**FIGURE 3.7** Digitised photographic image of Jade McSorley. *Image with permission © Callum Toy*

research is looking at the fashion consumer and how digital worlds and digital fashion will change the way that they consume, or maybe they won't. I'm trying to question that, so I explore digital fashion, but also how we express ourselves and our digital identity within a digital world such as the metaverse.

*What would you say are the most important technological innovations in this field or any other kind of innovation overall?*

It is vast, and the technology depends on context and where it's being used. There's been a lot of technology that is still very innovative within 2D platforms, particularly within the circular economy, but now we are starting to look towards Web 3.0, creating new virtual environments to explore through three-dimensional virtual and digital technologies. Concepts such as the metaverse, and technologies such as AI and blockchain are exciting advancements, but we have to be careful not to give in to fear of missing out. They might be buzzwords at the minute, and particularly within the fashion context, each is fighting for their chance to shine. Yet, beyond the name, it is about understanding the benefits and value underpinning these technologies, especially for the ones who will ultimately use them – and that is us, the consumers.

The idea of blending physical and digital worlds through mixed reality is the most exciting to me. That feeling of immersion and you don't know where the physical and digital line exists. You could go into a space where elements are blended, so if you go to the Outernet in Tottenham Court Road, you could step into loads of screens that feel like you're immersed within that. The metaverse really is that blending of digital and physical worlds, but there's a lot more to be done to get to the point where you feel like they're really blended together without knowing the screen's there or a headset.

I'm focusing primarily on the fashion consumer within digital spaces in my research, trying to understand why they will consume fashion within digital worlds and if fashion has so much significance in our physical reality, will it have significance in digital reality as well? My research is split up into three themes. There's the digital fashion, digital identity, which is how we're morphing into a more digitised version of ourselves through avatars and digital humans that we can dress. Then there's how sustainability plays a role, and this refers back to the concept of responsible innovation. There's debate surrounding the potential of digital fashion because it's not quite obvious yet whether fashioning your digital self will be a more sustainable way for us to consume. There's a lot out there in "grey literature" (e.g., fashion business websites) that says that it will be more sustainable because you're buying fashion that doesn't exist, but others go against that statement. That's the gap in research that I'm trying to fill, to try to understand whether digital fashion and dressing our digital identity replace the need for us to want to buy physical fashion, or if it will just encourage more over-consumption within new environments.

Part of my research also explores the digital body we adopt within digital spaces .... What is different about [how] we dress for the metaverse, for example, compared to our physical selves, is that we need to adopt a body first to dress – that could a fantastical avatar that looks nothing like us, or a photorealistic version created through computer-generated imagery (CGI) or digital scanning. Part of my research is to understand the role of the digital body within these new digital fashion contexts. Interestingly, the scanning of humans for the fashion industry is already occurring with fashion models for ecommerce and metaverse purposes, which has become a significant case study within my research and something which I have personally explored.

*Do you think there are any particularly innovative brands or organisations involved in digital fashion?*

I would say the fashion companies that have the resources to experiment and look at research and development and innovate in that way, because it is does require a lot of resources. Balenciaga created a video game for one of their collections during the pandemic in Autumn/Winter '21 with an apocalyptic video game world where models could stand and be scanned in the Balenciaga looks, then these digital scans would be placed within this virtual world. As a customer or user, you could navigate through this world and go close to these photographic moving models in the new Balenciaga collection, demonstrating that fashion and games are colliding. Nike is also ahead in this area. They've taken over RTFKT, a digital fashion sneaker company which creates non-fungible tokens (NFTs) and different types of digital avatars that you combine and collect. For the second year running, there were lots of brands present at Metaverse Fashion Week, such as Coach, Dolce & Gabbana and Adidas, who did virtual shows where you could buy digital items from that brand or it would lead you to go and buy the physical item as well, so there was some blending. The idea of blending means that your lives in digital and physical worlds are intertwined, so the metaverse is significant to your physical life, and vice versa. If I created and dressed my avatar within the metaverse of a video game such as Roblox, it would look very different and be created very differently to another game, such as Decentraland, so the digital identity isn't directly transferable from one to the other. Industry is aiming for interoperability of avatars, so that your digital identity can exist across different portals, but the metaverse is currently fragmented, like a solar system with different worlds, rather than the single galaxy that the metaverse is supposed to be.

I'm researching into traditional fashion consumers because there's already research investigating how gamers dress their avatars and there's a lot of speculation in industry about digital fashion, being a marketing tool. It's going to be more sustainable and let you express yourselves in ways that are unbound by physical restrictions. It's unlimited creativity, but practically, we're not sure how fashion consumers are going to adopt it yet. I'm also researching into the video game industry, with gamers as an example of how things could work within the fashion world. There's a lot of research out there about how gamers use avatars and dress them as self-representation in games. There's a connection between the gamer and their digital selves, which can have a profound impact on them as a human being. It's a two-way street, but within video games, there's a boundary, a frame in which they're set, and also the intention of dressing their avatar is very different to a fashion consumer. Gamers might dress their avatar for aspects of hedonic consumption such as utility to help their gameplay because they want to win, but then sometimes they might just be buying skins because they look cool to their friends who are joining them in these metaverse gaming worlds, so there's an element of fashion within there, but also they're there to do a job. In comparison to gamers, we're not quite sure why fashion consumers will dress for these different worlds, and that is what I'm trying to explore. So how do we build that connection that we have with our physical clothes with digital ones that are immaterial? We can't wear them. We can't touch them. What do they mean to us, and will they mean as much to us as our physical clothes?

There's not currently much literature around whether the metaverse will really be in line with sustainable development and creating an industry that touches all four pillars that it should: environmental, social and economic sustainability and as Casciani et al. (2022) say, there's also cultural sustainability, how the technologies are going to change our culture and consumer mindsets etc. There are two theories that from the digital identity standpoint are really important. Belk discusses the concept of the "extended self in 1988, which he revisits in 2013 in response to a digital age within digital worlds (Belk, 2013). Others call the idea of having multiple identities within virtual worlds as fragmentation (El Kamel, 2019) and/ or "multiphrenic nature" (Kozinets and Kedzior, 2009). Are we creating multiple identities of ourselves, and how does that impact us as humans? There's also another theory called the Proteus Effect, or the Proteus paradox, formed by video game psychologists Yee, Bailenson and Ducheneaut (2009), which looks at how the behaviour of an avatar can change your perception and the way you look at other people and their actual behaviour changes in a virtual setting. They also found that being more attractive within a video game as an avatar would change their behaviour after they came out of the virtual world, which might only be fleeting, and then they would go back to being their normal selves.

*Interview by Helen Goworek*

## Note

1   Lycra™ is the trade name Dupont chose – originally it was called fibre K. The generic name for this stretch fibre is elastane, as it's known in Europe, or *spandex* (an anagram for *expands*), in North America.

## References

Belk, R.W. (1988) 'Possessions and the extended self', *Journal of Consumer Research*, 15(2), 139–168.

Belk, R.W. (2013) 'Extended self in a Digital World', *Journal of Consumer Research*, 40(3), 477–500.

Casciani, D., Chkanikova, O. and Pal, R. (2022) 'Exploring the nature of digital transformation in the fashion industry: opportunities for supply chains, business models, and sustainability-oriented innovations', *Sustainability: Science, Practice and Policy*, 18(1), 773–795.

El Kamel, L. (2019) 'For a Better Exploration of Metaverses as Consumer Experiences.' In: N. Wood and M. Solomon (eds), *Virtual Social Identity and Consumer Behavior*. New York: Routledge, Chapter 2.

Kozinets, R. and Kedzior, R. (2009) 'I, Avatar: Auto-Netnographic Research in Virtual Worlds.' in N. Wood and M. Solomon (eds.), *Virtual Social Identity and Consumer Behaviours*. NY: Routledge, Chapter 1.

Yee, N., Bailenson, J.N., and Ducheneaut, N. (2009) 'The Proteus Effect: Implications of Transformed Digital Self-Representation on Online and Offline Behavior', *Communication Research*, 36(2), 285–312.

**FIGURE 3.8** Jonathan Chippindale alongside an image of Holition's creative work. Photos with permission from Jonathan Chippindale

**Jonathan Chippindale is co-founder and CEO of creative technology and innovation studio Holition. Jonathan is a Fellow of the Royal Society of Arts in the UK and has been awarded an honorary doctorate from University of the Arts London, where he has also been a visiting professor.**

*How would you sum up the creative and innovative work that Holition does?*

We're not against technology; everything that we do is leveraging technology, but as a studio, we're profoundly pro-human, so we're very, very interested in that relationship between humans and technology. We think strategically about brands and about how they are differentiated, what is unique about that brand and the stories and the messages that are critical to that brand's DNA. Then we think creatively about how to deliver or unlock that opportunity or tell that story, and then we find the right technology, with technology last, never technology first. Some people have also called us digital anthropologists or practice-based consultants, and we often think long-term into the future, for ten or 20 years. Technology is often criticised as being a solution looking for a problem to solve. The idea of understanding human behaviour and then bespoke-crafting technology that delivers to a particular piece is very, very important to us. Part of that is looking at it through research. We were founded before the iPhone was launched, so we were right at the very beginning of all this, a brand journey of digitisation. Using foresight, we can extrapolate at learning into the future. We understand how we've got to where we are today, and therefore we've got a good sense of what the future brings, so I think that academic rigour is a very important part to our DNA, and that's where that practice-based consultancy comes from. We're computer scientists, data scientists, AI, but also artists, animators, film-makers and anthropologists and psychologists, and then there's a team of producers that keep us all on track.

*What would you say are the most important recent technological innovations that have affected the fashion sector from your perspective?*

There are giga-trends that are long-term innovation directions, and one of them is that notion of human computing. It's the idea that computing is something that we used to do using computers, but it's moving into our mobile phones, onto our wrists through wearables, into fabric of clothing through flexible computing, and into our minds with brain computing interfaces. At some point in the future there'll be very, very powerful spectacles that look cool, interesting, and look fashionable, but if we're wearing technology on our faces through spectacles, though, how will we interact with that technology in a world where we're not clicking, swiping, dragging, or typing? Then we start thinking about more human interfaces, voice recognition, emotion, recognition and predictive intelligence. That goes back to Apple in the 1970s coming up with an interface that was very human, creating files and dragging files together into folders, and then dragging folders across desktops and putting them into trash bins, so that kind of human side is interesting for us. And that's why dresses have been designed that read the mind of the wearer in real time and use that information to understand how you're feeling and change the colour according to how you feel. If we do work in-store, we try and design very intuitive, overly simplified interfaces that in some cases don't require the user to do anything. We can automatically assess skin, tone, eye, colour, hair, fashion looks, and then work out hyper-personalised recommendations. Those kinds of more intuitive things are interesting for us, too, but then everything we do is pushed into luxury, fashion and beauty, except the pieces that we do in the art and cultural space. I'm thinking more of the fashion shows that we've done for brands like Burberry. They have an artistic component, because that's another very important part of what we try to do, tell stories in beautiful ways, stories that can be told using technology rather than it being technology per se. For me, there are only really two technologies that have really revolutionised the way that retailers communicate. I think we're all at the point now where e-commerce is important. The other one is probably social media, and clearly gives you access to a hugely expanded audience, but no one's worked out fully how to commercialise it and it's a force that isn't going away, so I think those two are very, very powerful. I also think the metaverse will be there, but it's got a long way to go.

People are spending more time online, and gamers are really spending huge amounts of time in virtual worlds. We've done a lot of virtual space work for brands, and it's a very human way of engaging with a brand. During lockdown, we had a lot of clients asking us to build virtual worlds for them, because the relationship between the physical and digital for those brands was pretty weighted towards the physical brands, like Gucci or Chanel, that spent generations developing their brand as a physical entity and everything was about the store, where you could talk about architecture, design, not just products, not just logos, not just corporate colours, but aesthetic, and the way that the staff reach you as you walk in and everything is finely choreographed. Suddenly all they had was a website which told very limited stories and was all about getting people from the homepage to the basket as quickly as possible, not daring to hold you up, so there were no real stories to be told other than maybe a film or two. There's an opportunity to explore a physical space, but online you're basically breaking the sacrosanct rule of digital, by adding friction to slow people down. If you add friction, you can have more meaningful conversations, and our approach was to treat it in a different way. It isn't a lifelike representation of your store, it's a third-space kind of retail where it can be more creative. We need to put more storytelling in, that plays on that idea of walking into a space like Selfridges. You walk out with something that you didn't expect to because you stumbled across it trying to find something else, and that slightly more random way of finding product is anathema to digital, where it's "What colour do you want, what size and what product?", and so I can see the metaverse being something quite powerful in the future. We wear clothes, and they're all different, they communicate our personality, communicate our taste and our aspirations and our own individual stories. Why wouldn't you want those in a virtual world if you're spending more time there, increasingly becoming more digital? As we have expanded our digital lives, we need our own individual artefacts, and I think that is interesting for brands. I think it also plays into the tribalism of the brand and the tribalism of gaming and people that are absolutely passionate about gaming and brands, there's a slight surrealness about that which I think works quite well together, too. I think that's one for the future, about 10 to 15 years or more.

For us, the matter isn't digital space, it's a conjoined space with the physical world. We did Tommy Hilfiger's fashion show at New York Fashion Week last year, and the brief was a metaverse combined physical show. We designed this show in Brooklyn, and we also designed a simultaneous Roblox space. Web behaviour in one affected the other in real time, and the way the models moved, and what was changed in real time in the Roblox space, but also the way that these millions of gamers who are in that play changed the physical show in real time. The game can only be 50 people, but it could be several thousand of these, all playing the same game. The YouTube livestream of the show had 24,000 people watching. Tommy Hilfiger were pleased, and then we told them that 1.3 million people were playing in the fashion show. Roblox is about playing games, which may be fine if you're Vans or a skateboarding brand, but if you're Givenchy, it's not. Brands are all about the environment, the colour of the walls and the carpet and the architecture. You walk in, you look around the space. You walk into the McQueen store in Bond Street and just go "Wow! What an amazing space!", but with Roblox, they don't care so much what the space is. Brands are around the environment, and gaming is around activity. Brands aren't about activity, so it might not fit together, but brands want access to that 1.3 million people, although how many of them are their consumers? How many of them are there because they like gaming?

*How would you describe the process of innovation in your company or in the sector overall?*

I think the idea of innovation is like tumbling down a hill. Many people say "We can decode innovation," and everything is either a linear line with arrows or a circle, because then the insights go back into the process. We have a framework that's more like a series of radio waves between all the different departments. Thinking very broadly, innovation's got to start with a brief, even if it's vague, because brands have a strategic business need and we have to deliver to that brief. We will go left and right outside the brief and explore other areas completely and then bring everything back into within the brief and then have a round of feedback. In the end, we've got a proposal that has deliverables, timelines, costs, so we get to the same place, but it's very important for us to explore and not be constrained by the brief, and to see where your creativity or your technologies or your understanding goes. You need to know where the boundaries are, and you need to step past them every now and again. You don't know where the line is until you step over it. I'm not going to tell them how to design their beautiful product. We know innovation, we know what's interesting and what kind of tools to use. We did Louis Vuitton's very first retail technology project in a store, and they chose us because this was a big thing for them that they'd never done before. They realised we were good at technology and we did a lot of work with luxury, and that gave them the trust. We pushed back quite hard against the brief, and they trusted us and we delivered for them.

*How would you define creativity based on your own experience and knowledge?*

Creativity for me is searching into the unknown. Creativity is not doing what you did last week. The notion of being creative is doing something different that people notice. That just comes back to the idea of differentiation, we're all different as human beings and as we've discussed brands strive to be different. I used to look at the world in these huge homogenised groups: A, B, C1, C2, D, E, but nowadays, with digital, we can recognise individuality at a person-to-person level, so for me, creativity is about celebrating those differences and coming up with ideas that resonate to everyone that listens to them. Celebrating individuality is a very important part of what we do, and I think that's the creative bit, recognising difference and coming up with ideas that play to differences. Brands are starting to behave more like people ,because it used to be about product, corporate colour and logo and store, but now it's about "What is the brand's view on Black Lives Matter?" These kinds of things are human, and technology is a very good way of telling these stories, which means that you've got many more tools in the paintbox, and that allows you to be more creative.

I like meeting students because they're the consumer groups of tomorrow and my brands want to know what they're thinking about, so I talk to them and hear what motivates them. It means we were talking about climate change, gender and diversity several years before brands were, and it allows us to have an insight into the kind of things that we'll be talking about with brands in three or four years' time, so it's important to us, too.

# References

Archroma (2024) *Innovation*, available online at: https://www.archroma.com/innovations
Beyond Surface Technologies (2024) *Beyond Surface Technologies*, available online at: https://www.beyondst.com/
Cernansky, R. (2022) 'Balenciaga releases coat made with Ephea, a leather alternative', *Vogue Business*, available online at: https://www.voguebusiness.com/sustainability/balenciaga-releases-coat-made-with-ephea-a-leather-alternative
Common Objective (2018) 'From Fibre to Fabric – A Look At Global Mills', *Common Objective*, available online at: https://www.commonobjective.co/article/from-fibre-to-fabric-a-look-at-global-mills

Fashion for Good (2024) *Innovation Platform – Innovators*, available online at: https://fashionforgood.com/innovation-platform/innovators/

Fibrant (2024) *Sustainable Production of Caprolactam*, available online at: https://www.fibrant52.com/en/

Holgate, M. (2016) 'Meet Iris van Herpen, the Dutch designer boldly going Into the future', *Vogue*, 28th April 2016, available online at: https://www.vogue.com/article/iris-van-herpen-dutch-designer-interview-3d-printing

Lectra (2024) *Lectra Gerber AccuMark CAD Software for Fashion Design*, available online at: https://www.lectra.com/en/products/gerber-accumark-accunest-fashion

McCormick, H. et al. (2020) 3D printing in Vignali, G., Reid, L.F., Ryding, D. and Henninger, C.E. (Eds.) *Technology-Driven Sustainability Innovation in the Fashion Supply Chain*. London: Palgrave Macmillan.

Orange Fiber (2017) *Salvatore Ferragamo*, available online at: https://orangefiber.it/collaborations-ferragamo/

Science and Industry Museum (2019) *The Story of the Jacquard Loom*, available online at: https://www.scienceandindustrymuseum.org.uk/objects-and-stories/jacquard-loom

Stella McCartney (2023) *Met Gala 2023*, 3rd May 2023, available online at: https://www.stellamccartney.com/gb/en/stellas-world/met-gala-2023-behind-the-scenes-and-our-favourite-moments.html

Stratasys (2024) *Guide to 3D Printing Technologies and Materials: Polyjet Technology*, available online at: https://www.stratasys.com/uk/guide-to-3d-printing/technologies-and-materials/polyjet-technology/

Textile Exchange (2024) *Climate and Vision*, available online at: https://indd.adobe.com/view/ae34ef83-2be2-41b7-83c4-5c54f9b32aeb

Textile Insight (2023) 'Will AI revolutionize the textile industry in the years to come?', *Textile Insight Summer 2023*, available online at: https://textileexchange.org/

Textile World (2020) 'NexTex to Launch TurboDry at OutDoor Retailer', *Textile World*, available online at: https://www.textileworld.com/textile-world/2020/01/nextex-to-launch-turbodry-at-outdoor-retailer

The Fabricant (2024) *About the Fabricant*, available online at: https://www.thefabricant.com/about

Tin Shed Ventures (2024) *Investing in Returns for Nature*, available online at: https://tinshedventures.com/

# 4

# Applying Innovation Theory to the Fashion Business

*Helen Goworek*

## Introduction

This chapter will assess established theories on systems of innovation and the ways in which they can be applied to the fashion business. Key theories on innovation have been discussed and analysed in numerous textbooks and academic journals in the disciplines of business and design. However, the fashion business has specific modes of operation, such as the necessity for speed in product development and adapting products for differing cultural requirements in a global market, which make this sector differ from others, and calls for adaptation of theories to suit this area of industry. In general, innovation theories are relatively practical in focus, in comparison to those in many other business disciplines. Whilst theories may sometimes seem beneficial only in academic circles, they can often identify patterns and processes of value to industry practitioners. This chapter will explore a selection of those theories that are most applicable to the development of clothing, to assist in gaining an analytical view of fashion innovation, as well as proposing a new model to encapsulate aspects of fashion innovation, setting boundaries which can enhance commerciality.

## Innovation Theorists

Prominent authors in the field of innovation are often located in the business discipline. Steve Conway, David Smith, Joe Tidd, John Bessant and Paul Trott have published leading textbooks which offer an overview of innovation, as well as producing multiple academic journal articles and engaging in research projects. Each academic tends to specialise in a particular aspect of innovation. For example, Eric von Hippel is amongst those who have researched extensively into innovation,

DOI: 10.4324/9781003332749-4

focusing on customers' role in innovation, publishing as early as the 1970s on this topic (e.g., von Hippel, 1976; von Hippel, 1977). One of the historical figures who developed influential theories on innovation is Joseph Schumpeter, a Professor of Political Economy at Harvard University in the 1940s, who is renowned for discussing the concept of "creative destruction", in that new innovations can render their predecessors obsolete (see Schumpeter, 2010). Schumpeter's (2010) definition of innovation as "the carrying out of new combinations" is still relevant today. Gloria Barczak, Marina Candi, Roberto Verganti, Mike Saren and Michael Beverland are also amongst the foremost professors producing recent work in the field of innovation. Gohoungodji and Amara (2022) produced an extensive review of literature from 1998 to 2021 to define and assess modes of innovation in the creative industries, finding that finance, markets, technology and organisation-related factors were amongst the most significant influences.

There are various academic journals on the topic of innovation and product development, some of which have connections to academic conferences in the field of innovation, attended by delegates from both design and business schools. Before academic journal articles are published, the topics are often presented at academic conferences, such as the Innovation and Product Development Management Conference (IPDMC, 2024), thus enabling attendees at this international annual event to access cutting-edge research at an early stage. Smaller-scale academic events on creativity and innovation topics can also be of interest to academics, students and practitioners, such as regular workshops organised by the British Academy of Management's Special Interest Groups in Innovation or the Cultural and Creative Industries.

Relevant journals in which to search for articles on innovation include:

- *Journal of Product Innovation Management* (published by John Wiley & Sons)
- *Creativity and Innovation Management* (published by John Wiley & Sons)
- *European Journal of Innovation Management* (published by Emerald)
- *Innovation* (published by Taylor & Francis)

Academic journals focusing on the subject of creativity are often based in the disciplines of psychology or the cultural industries, such as:

- *Creativity Research Journal* (published by Taylor & Francis)
- *Journal of Creative Behavior* (published by John Wiley & Sons)

At the time of writing, there are no specialist journals on creativity and innovation specifically in the fashion business, but some of the business journals above feature articles on the clothing sector, and several fashion-related journals publish innovation-related articles, such as:

- *Journal of Fashion Marketing and Management* (published by Emerald)
- *Journal of Global Fashion Marketing* (published by Taylor & Francis)
- *Fashion Theory* (published by Taylor & Francis)
- *Fashion Practice* (published by Taylor & Francis)

Searching for the home page of these journals will display a list of the current and previous articles they have published, which can be accessed online by staff or students at universities or companies which have subscribed to these journals, or individual articles can be downloaded for a one-off payment. Journal articles can be used as valid sources of evidence in assignments or research projects, and assist in product innovation in industry – e.g., in support of the business case for the launch of a new product concept.

## Stage-gate New Product Development theories

Some of the best-known innovation theories in the literature are referred to as New Product Development (NPD) theories, particularly those described as "stage-gate models – i.e. those that compartmentalise elements of the NPD process into stages, each of which must be signed off (usually by senior managers or clients) before proceeding to the next stage. The standard NPD process model shown in Figure 4.1, commencing with the initiation of a new product strategy and ending in the commercialisation of products, is known as the eight-stage NPD model, as referred to in marketing textbooks by authors such as Jobber and Ellis-Chadwick (2023). The NPD model has some relevant stages for the design of specific fashion products which are replaced regularly (usually incrementally). However, this model is more applicable to the development of larger-scale innovations in the fashion business, such as the development of a new product type or concept that the company has not sold previously, rather than simply developing new individual replacement items in existing garment ranges.

This section demonstrates how the stages of the model can operate in practice for fashion. This NPD model is suited to the fashion sector, although the terminology used in industry for the stages may differ from this theory. The NPD process may pause or terminate at any of the eight stages if the new concept is found not to be financially or technically viable, in order to cut the organisation's losses, as this would be preferable for the company than an unsuccessful product launch, both for its profitability and reputation. It is also possible to insert feedback loops, so if the idea is found not to be feasible at the concept testing stage, for example, the process may revert to stage 2 to generate new ideas.

**FIGURE 4.1** The New Product Development process (adapted from Jobber and Ellis-Chadwick, 2023).

1) **New product strategy** refers to the decision to develop and implement a new strategy within the organisation. Strategic decisions, regarding the direction the company will take are generally taken by company directors or other senior managers. The new product strategies may not be completely new innovations in the market sector, but they may simply be new areas for that particular organisation. For example, many women's wear fashion retailers have increased their

market share over the years through diversification into areas such as maternity clothing, footwear or petite size ranges.

2) **Idea generation** refers to developing new product concepts which may aim to stay ahead of competitors or to maintain competitiveness in response to a competitor launching into a new product sector, usually forming part of the strategy led by the company's senior management team. For example, UK-based supermarket Tesco diversified into clothing in the 1960s, later followed into this market by competing grocery retailers Asda and Sainsbury's. Ideas for product strategies may also be conceived within other parts of the organisation – e.g., a Research and Development (R&D) or design team – or by opening up to suggestions from staff at different levels in any department. Nurturing an innovative culture within a company by providing internal communication for new product ideas, such as brainstorming sessions, can lead to enhanced profitability if these new concepts are selected and implemented successfully.

3) **Screening and evaluation** take place internally when colleagues evaluate the commercial viability of the ideas using a set of criteria to assess the potential profitability of different concepts – e.g., by reviewing the success of competitors who have launched similar new product ranges. Senior management are likely to enlist internal colleagues with specialist knowledge to support in screening new product ideas or to employ external consultants to research as effectively as possible prior to launch, to minimise the risk of product failure.

4) **Concept testing** is the stage where the company has prototype products made to reflect its new product strategy. These sample items may be made within the organisation, by its suppliers or by a specialist design agency, in the form of 3D-effect CAD designs or physical prototypes. Concept testing may also involve market research with target consumers to discuss their responses to the new product ideas.

5) **Business analysis** is often a largely finance-related stage where the company projects potential prices, sales volumes and profits. At this point, the new product idea should have become sufficiently tangible for realistic figures to be predicted.

6) **Product development** is the core stage in the NPD process, which may also be referred to as concept development. Further prototypes may be produced and refined, in either digital or physical form, using the same type of materials that will be used in production or, in some cases, 3D printing (see Chapter 3). Several samples may be produced at this stage to enhance the product's performance and its ability to meet customer needs, possibly with the inclusion of further market research input.

7) **Market testing** is the point when some level of commercial trial of the new product is implemented, where customers can buy in limited quantities. For example, a fashion retailer may initiate or adapt an individual store or some

carefully selected stores to offer a small new loungewear product range to customers before it is rolled out on a wider scale. Alternatively, samples of the new products could be photographed and sold online to a selected group of target consumers (e.g., a panel of a fashion retailer's most loyal customers) well ahead of the time when the products will be launched, to gain an idea of the products' potential popularity in advance, possibly with a discount as an incentive to buy despite the delay in delivery of the goods.

8)  **Commercialisation** is the stage when the new product idea is launched into the market. Whereas the NPD process focuses largely on the "product" aspect of the marketing mix (i.e., "the 4 Ps"), price, place (distribution) and promotion also come into play at this final stage. The final selling price will need to be set in order for sales to take place, and the method of distribution should have been planned in advance – e.g., through a website or via retail stores belonging to the company or its clients. Spending on promotion is likely to be higher than average in the launch phase in order to inform potential customers that the new range is available, and sales promotions/discounts may be offered to lower their risk in trying out a new product. Ultimately, commercialisation leads to purchase and usage of the new fashion product concept by consumers. The success, or otherwise, of the product can then be assessed and lessons learned from this prior to the recommencement of the NPD process for further new items.

## Fashion Product Development

In the fashion business, product development is a widely used term, comprising the processes prior to mass production. The prefix "new" has been removed here because the fashion market is fundamentally a constant stream of ideas to replace previous collections of garments, often with incremental amendments (such as a new colour or print) rather than radical changes or brand new product concepts. For example, mass market men's wear brands will likely continue to offer the product categories of shirts, jeans, suits and jackets each season, tweaking the shapes and colours slightly each season, rather than introducing new-to-the-world innovations every year (see Chapter 8). Fashion product development is usually led by designers, but frequently involves a wider team of specialist colleagues within the same or other organisations offering input or making decisions, such as garment technologists, textile technologists and retail buyers (see Goworek, 2007 and Boardman et al., 2020). The model shown in Figure 4.2 is a stage-gate process that has been tailor-made for the fashion business, based on empirical experience and practice from primary research with interviewees from various fashion companies. Fashion product development needs to begin well in advance of the time when the products become available to consumers, to factor in the timescale required to design and develop the products and for the fabrics and garments to be manufactured and delivered. The amount of time in each stage and in the overall process can vary,

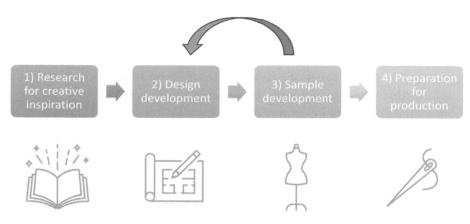

**FIGURE 4.2** The fashion product development process.

depending on the product type and company, typically lasting anywhere between one month and two years in total.

1) **Research for creative inspiration:** The fashion product development process begins when research is carried out for by designers to seek creative inspiration for new design ideas for a particular season (see Chapter 2). New fashion ranges were traditionally launched four times per year in line with the seasons, to provide clothing suitable for the climate, but it is now usual for product collections in the mass market to be launched much more frequently, depending on the company's level of fashionability. Ready-to-wear designer ranges still retain the historical approach of producing two runway shows per year, for Spring/ Summer and Autumn/Winter (see Chapter 7). Creative inspiration for fashion design is frequently derived from looking at historical, current or predicted sources of inspiration, such as viewing art exhibitions and designer collections or reading fashion forecasting publications (see Chapter 5). Maximising profitability can also play a part in the direction of creativity to be explored – e.g., adapting designs that have previously been profitable bestsellers for the company or developing product types which have been forecast to gain higher sales in future seasons.

2) **Design development** involves the generation of multiple initial design ideas, usually rendered two-dimensionally, either hand-sketched or using CAD (Computer-Aided-Design) programs. Initially, numerous provisional designs can be drawn solely for designers to assess how the garments they have created in their mind's eye may look in practice. Sketches at this stage may be generated quickly and roughly, possibly without colours being added, to save time and enable more ideas to be represented within the timescale. Designers may therefore be the only people to view the full range of garment ideas they

have generated before making a selection of those that are most viable before sharing selected images with other members of the product development team within the company. A team with various skills may be engaged in the decision-making at this point. For example, designers, garment technologists and sales staff working for a clothing manufacturer may jointly review a proposed range prior to presenting it to their clients from brands and retailers (Goworek and McGoldrick, 2015). These ideas may be presented as working drawings (from a flat perspective, rather than on a body) or represented on figures, and at each stage the numbers of designs will be filtered out both within the company and by discussing the ideas with clients, until a small number will eventually be selected to go into production. A selection of the design ideas may take the physical form of working drawings, with swatches or photos of fabrics alongside them or CAD images generated by the designer. At this stage, since there is a smaller selection of designs, these images are usually of a higher quality, including colouration, to offer more detailed information to the client to assist in their buying decision. Designers often require verbal presentation skills in addition to their technical, commercial and artistic prowess, to be able to justify the choice of garments.

3) **Sample development:** Selected designs can be made into initial physical garment samples. A specification sheet (spec) for each selected design is usually composed by a design team, featuring a working drawing (flat") with details of fabrics, componentry and costs. A "tech pack" can be compiled by the supplier to provide definitive information about the style. From this information, a manufacturer can create a sample and estimate a price for the garment. This involves interpreting a 2D drawing into 3D using pattern–cutting, using flat pieces of paper or card to define the shape and fit of clothes, then making sample garments with fabrics and components that are the same or similar to those that will be used in production. These samples can then be fitted on either mannequins or models to check how they will fit and perform (see also Chapter 8). First samples of the garments can subsequently be shown to the brands or retailers who plan to include them in their ranges. If samples are not suitable, the feedback loop on the model shows that designers can revert to stage 2 to amend the design or develop further ideas. This stage can be accelerated by using CAD technology which offers virtually 3D, almost photographic images to give a realistic view of how the garments will look after production (see Chapter 3), thus potentially replacing the need for physical samples. Although this technology can also help to save on the expense involved in producing samples, it is relatively expensive to buy, and may therefore only be invested in by larger companies. This stage is likely to be an iterative process, requiring communication internally within the organisation and externally with suppliers and/or clients to update and refine the range in response to feedback, such

as addressing technical or price-related issues. The product development phase ends when fabrics have passed quality tests and the garment shape, fit, design details, materials, colour, price and quantities have been finalised and purchase orders have been placed by retailers or brands. When senior managers formally sign off on the selection of products that have been selected for a brand or retailer's range, they are ready to go ahead with preparation for mass production.

4) **Preparation for production:** After a garment is ordered by a brand or retailer from the supplier responsible for its manufacture, preparation is required for it to be produced in practice, taking consumers' requirements and consumer usage of the product into account. Within the fashion business, this can include checking the standard of colours or prints and testing for strength and colour-fastness of the fabrics in which the products will be made, whilst pattern-cutters and machinists work in parallel to produce improved samples until the fit of the garment is approved by the client. However, some of the lower-priced mass market ranges could eliminate this stage, potentially sacrificing quality for the sake of cost savings and speed to market. Risk analysis is another potential element incorporated within this stage, when design and technical staff working on the supplier side liaise to anticipate and find ways to eliminate potential risks involved in the manufacture and wearing of the selected garments. A meeting about risk analysis may lead to an amendment of a product design – e.g., by replacing a metal fastening with a wooden one to enhance the safety and environmental sustainability of a child's jacket. A "sealing sample" is often required by client companies – i.e., a prototype product which is as close as possible to production standard, with a signature on an attached plastic seal to show that this is an approved sample, thus acting as a joint agreement of the quality that is expected in production. Fabric, trims and componentry need to be ordered by the manufacturer before production starts, therefore if the fashion brand or retailer change their minds and cancel an order at a late stage, then the factory can be left with materials it has already invested in and may not be able to use, a situation which is both financially and environmentally unsustainable.

Following these stages of product development thoroughly can lead to a more effective and efficient production process and build in sustainability, leading to improved clothing longevity (see Chapter 6). Although the manufacturing stage is not directly within the scope of a book on creativity and innovation, it is nevertheless important for designers and other colleagues involved in the fashion product development process to be aware of how this works by visiting and collaborating closely with factories. Designers would benefit from being familiar with the different types of industrial sewing machine and manufacturing processes that offer choices in the construction of garments. In summary the production process can be summarised as: bulk fabric is produced and tested; bulk fabric and trims are delivered to the manufacturer; the fabric is spread and cut in the cutting room; garment pieces are bundled and distributed to machinists before the garments are manufactured, finished and ironed, then packaged and stored before being distributed to clients who distribute the merchandise to customers.

## Boundaries for Fashion Product Development

Product development for fashion items needs to fit within four main boundaries: timing, finance, visual appeal and technical constraints (see Figure 4.3). Temporal issues cover timing, such as the season (time of year or a specific selling season, typically between three to six months for classic garments) and the weather during that phase. Financial issues can be cost-related, such as the components and manufacturing that go into a garment, or broader, such as the current state of the national or global economy. Visual appeal concerns the extent to which aesthetic aspects of fashion such as styling, colour and fabric attract customers to purchase garments. Technical aspects of producing garments to be considered by product developers

Timing                                    State of the economy

Seasonality/weather                       Costs of components and manufacturing

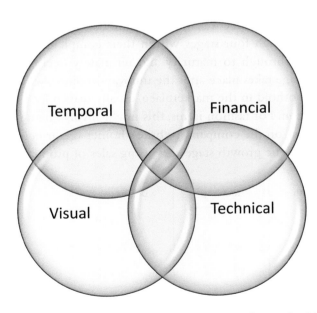

Product styling                           Durability and sustainability

Colour and materials                      Pattern-cutting and manufacturing

**FIGURE 4.3** Boundaries for fashion product development.

include their durability and sustainability, as well as pattern-cutting and clothing manufacturing techniques.

Taking the boundaries shown in Figure 4.3 into account can enable the design and production of garments to meet target customers' needs and expected quality standards affordably at a given time. For example, there could be many styles suitable for a particular season within the blue "temporal" circle, as well as having suitable visual appeal for the customer, but which don't fit within a suitable price range and are therefore unlikely to be marketable. There could also be some design ideas that fit visually into trends for the season at a suitable price (overlapping between the temporal and finance sections), but which are not technically viable to be manufactured in the factories the brand uses. The products in the central diamond-shaped section are those that are appropriate for the time, price, visual appeal to the customer and technical requirements, and are therefore those designs which are most likely to be selected to be made in production for a garment range. Although the reduction of these parameters to a diagrammatic model may make this appear to be a rational, objective decision, deciding which products fit within the boundaries of this central section is not an exact science, and may rely to a certain extent on product developers' subjective views and intuition.

## Product Life Cycle

The product life cycle (PLC) theory was introduced by Levitt (1965), who posited that products proceed through four stages within their complete life cycle, from introduction to growth, through to maturity and ultimately decline (see Figure 4.4). The introduction stage takes place after the innovation phase, with sales rising as the product takes a foothold in the marketplace, usually driven by a higher than average level of promotion. For fashion items, this might involve being featured in photos of new collections on the company website's homepage or being displayed on mannequins in stores. The growth stage sees rising sales of products, backed by

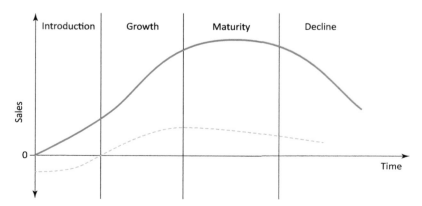

**FIGURE 4.4** The product life cycle. The solid line indicates sales volume and the dotted line indicates profits

continuing marketing communications such as featuring garments in online or printed magazines which can influence the peak sales level that the items achieve. In the maturity phase, sales can reach a plateau at this peak, appealing to the widest range of customers during the product's life cycle. In the decline stage, sales trail off, as does promotional activity, although price reduction promotions may continue, to encourage sales of remaining stock before the item goes entirely out of fashion.

The PLC is a useful model which is applicable to fashion products, yet it has various drawbacks. Primarily, the shape and timescale of the PLC cannot be predicted accurately, as it may be jagged, rather than smooth, and the extent of the timing may vary greatly in each of the four stages. Since garment styles go in and out of fashion, the PLC may become a fashion swing, with negligible sales in the decline phase, then making an upturn some time afterwards, thus repeating the cycle. For example, mini skirts and bootcut trousers, which were first introduced in the 1960s, staged a revival in the 1980s and 1990s respectively, and both items can be found in fashion ranges in the 2020s. Fashion is notorious for the development of fad items, which would follow a differently shaped PLC, with a fast upward trajectory followed by swiftly plummeting into decline, with the maturity phase being virtually absent. An updated PLC model could be developed to increase its relevance to the fashion business by inserting an NPD stage prior to introduction.

## The "Front End" of Innovation

Research into innovation tends to focus on the stages after a product has been signed off for development by the organisation, with a lack of investigation into the earlier stages prior to a team being established to develop the product ready for production. This potentially vague, embryonic phase, before the product development team meets formally, can be referred to as the "fuzzy front end" of innovation (Conway & Steward, 2009). Despite an initial lack of clarity about the idea at this stage, whilst the concept is still being specified, the front end can be viewed as particularly significant (Reid & Brentani, 2004) because it can set the direction that the innovation will ultimately take and therefore impact upon its eventual sales and profitability. The generation of initial concepts for innovation may stem from a formal process or team, such as an "ideas lab" tasked with developing innovations within a fashion organisation, or it may be serendipitous – e.g., a fashion designer may spot some inspiration at an art gallery or an innovative idea might be sparked by a passing conversation.

## Linear Models of Innovation

"Linear models" of innovation are so called because they presume a linear series of events proceeding towards an outcome. There are two types of linear model (see

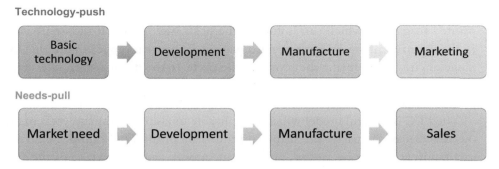

**FIGURE 4.5** Linear models of innovation (adapted from Rothwell, 1983).

Figure 4.5), as proposed by Rothwell (1983). The first model here can be referred to either as "science-push "or "technology-push", presuming that innovations usually stem from new developments in either science or technology within academia or organisations (Conway & Steward, 2009). This model would be applicable to the fashion industry when new technological innovations such as sewing machinery or technical fabrics are developed, then manufactured and marketed. However, the "needs-pull" model shown in Figure 4.5 is of most relevance to fashion, since most clothing product development begins with identifying a market need (e.g., new styles of trouser for a particular season that meet customer requirements), then developing, manufacturing and selling the resulting products. Linear models have been criticised as being too simplistic, in that innovation could more frequently be seen as a combination of both technology-push and needs-pull theories, and Rothwell (1983) therefore proposed the interactive model, which balances research and development, manufacturing, marketing, sales and innovation between both technology and the needs of markets and society (Conway & Steward, 2009).

## Diffusion of Innovations

A particularly pertinent innovation theory for the fashion business is Rogers's diffusion of innovations model (1962). This well-known model plots progression of time against sales volumes, referring to those who are the first to buy into a trend as "innovators", who then influence people known as "early adopters", with sales figures peaking as the next group, the "early majority", adopt the style. According to the model, sales plateau when reaching the "late majority group, then begin to dip when so-called "laggards" eventually start wearing these items. There is an overall presumption that consumers in the two earliest categories in this model will have higher disposable income to be able to afford more innovative products, and for the other three categories to be on lower incomes, since they are buying into a trend when it has become cheaper due to being produced in large quantities and achieving economy of scale. For example, the early majority may purchase low

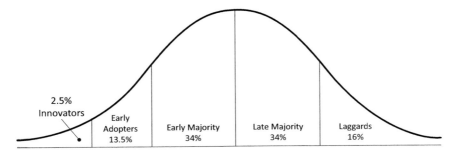

**FIGURE 4.6** Diffusion of Innovations model (adapted from Rogers, 1962).

price mass market versions of clothes that they have been influenced to buy from seeing innovators or early adopters (such as film stars and music artists) wearing them. However, those with creative fashion skills may fall into the innovator and early adopter categories without needing to be affluent, since they have the ability to create their own clothing.

Although Rogers developed this theory in the early 1960s in relation to agricultural markets, the terminology and the phases of adoption mostly relate effectively to fashion consumers (see Figure 4.6), helping product developers assess the current category for their product in relation to their target consumers and to predict which stage it will reach next. However, the model would benefit from an update in the use of the "laggard" term (as it sounds somewhat derogatory) and the percentages of people in the five categories, as there is no evidence that fashion customers would correspond to these precise proportions. The diffusion of innovations theory has also been criticised due to the likelihood that sales figures will probably not form such a smooth curve, as sales may go up and down along the way, dependent on many factors, such as the weather and other external conditions, thus forming a more irregular shape. Additionally, this theory does not specify a particular timescale when the different groups will adopt the innovation, so this has to be estimated by organisations, using data such as internal sales and market trends. Since the circular economy has become increasingly significant in recent decades, this model could now also be criticised for the term "laggard" in the final category because it implies that they are very unfashionable, whereas buying fewer clothes than average and purchasing second-hand items, which are typical behaviours in this segment, have become much fashionable, so a more positive term would be appropriate here, to acknowledge that these consumers are behaving more sustainably.

## Co-creation and Co-design

Co-creation refers to collaboration between consumers and producers in defining, producing, delivering and using products or services they buy and use (Sheth and Hellman, 2018). Increasingly, customers are enabled to collaborate with brands in the development of products to co-create value (Anshu et al., 2022; Jobber & Ellis-Chadwick, 2023). In terms of fashion, consumers may participate in the final design of merchandise by being given the opportunity to customise individual products they purchase, by requesting a personalised name or monogram embroidery. Taking this a stage further, users might be considered as "co-developers" of products, via membership of product development panels implemented by organisations (Conway & Steward, 2009). The users themselves may even be the innovators of designs, taking their own time and utilising their skills to craft their own products, which may in turn inspire fashion companies if the designs become widely visible through sharing imagery of street fashion. There is a low barrier to entry in this respect for clothing, since consumers need only relatively inexpensive sewing machines to transfer their own ideas into 3D reality, in comparison to the investment in equipment required to manufacture electronic products, for example.

Similarly, co-design is the concept that users can become involved in the design process for products or services. This field of study has expanded in recent decades, evidenced by the launch of a journal in 2005 from Taylor & Francis which focuses entirely on reporting techniques and research in collaborative design (*CoDesign*, 2024). *CoDesign* journal publishes various articles which demonstrate how co-design techniques can be applied to the context of the fashion industry, such as Jekal et al.'s (2023) research exploring developments in fashion design education for students from Generation Z (definitions vary, but Gen Z are born after 1996, according to Pew Research, 2019) and Yang et al.'s (2023) investigation into the innovative use of virtual reality environments as a collaborative design tool for fashion design. Co-design is a theme which has been discussed within both business and academic circles. At a joint industry and academia Impact+ workshop organised by Northumbria University in 2024, activist Carry Somers, founder of Fashion Revolution, proposed co-design as one of the tools that can be used to create a more sustainable fashion industry (see Figure 4.7).

## Open Innovation

Open innovation describes new ways for organisations to incorporate external sources within their innovation processes. In the more traditional closed style of innovation, products tend to be initiated and developed internally within the organisation. However, the tendency for firms to move towards open innovation enables the boundaries to be sufficiently flexible for ideas and technology from other actors to be incorporated in product development (Chesbrough, 2003). In the fashion business, it could be argued that open innovation has long been central to the way the industry operates, especially an openness with the textile manufacturers who provide the materials that are so integral to clothing. Collaboration between competing clothing companies has been somewhat limited, though, due to a high level

**FIGURE 4.7** Fashion Revolution founder Carry Somers discusses co-design at a sustainable fashion Impact+ workshop. Author's own photo

of secrecy around design ideas prior to their market launch, until the more recent trend for firms to develop "collabs" with other fashion brands evolved, which is an effective way to introduce complementary existing labels to a new set of customers. Some of the many fashion examples include streetwear brand Supreme's collabs with many brands within and outside the fashion sector, such as Louis Vuitton in 2017 and ready-to-wear label Comme des Garcons' collab with Nike trainers in 2023. Digital platforms, such as wazoku.com, act as "innovation markets" (Bessant & Moeslein, 2011), using crowdsourcing to bring organisations which have innovation issues together with firms or people who can provide potential solutions.

## Dominant Design

Dominant designs are those that are leading in their product area and set a design standard which is often followed by competitors (Abernathy & Utterback, 1978). Dominant designs flow through three stages of innovation, beginning with a fluid phase where numerous radical product innovations are launched, testing out technologies and the markets in which they are sold, to a transitional phase where designs are standardised and process innovations emerge, through to a specific phase where the number of competitors contracts and the rate of innovation reduces, becoming more incremental in nature (Utterback, 1994). Gardiner and Rothwell (1985) developed dominant design theory further, to reflect how an individual successful innovation or invention can lead to multiple divergent variations from the original firm or its competitors, before consolidating over time into a smaller selection of the most robust dominant designs. The most enduring dominant design in a product area may not always have been developed by the company that was the original innovator of the idea (the "first mover" in the market), but may instead have been created by the firm that most successfully commercialised and promoted the product.

Dominant design theory aligns well with the fashion sector, in that specific garments by particular brands often play a leading part in trend-setting, frequently referred to in the fashion media as "iconic items". Fashion styles that have dominated their markets include the Hermès Kelly bag which was popularised in the late 1950s (Hermès, 2024), Levi's 501 jeans during the mid 1980s and Roland Mouret's Galaxy dress in the 2000s (Milligan, 2009), each of which spawned in-house variants in different colours and materials and numerous imitations from other companies. Both the Kelly bag and Levi's 501s had been launched some decades prior to reaching the peak of their popularity, which was driven by celebrity connections and promotional activity, and have proven to be robust designs (literally and metaphorically) that have stood the test of time, remaining on the market at the time of writing.

## Technology S Curve

The technology S curve is a model developed by McKinsey to plot the technical performance of a technology on a vertical axis against research and development (e.g., effort/funds) on a horizontal axis (Foster, 1986), with the resulting diagram taking an elongated "S" shape. The aspect of performance needs to be measurable in some way, and the research and development could be measured in terms of financial investment or workload hours, for example (Conway & Steward, 2009). The technology S curve can consist of three stages over time: "emergent", where technical performance may be slow, the "growth phase", when knowledge about the technology accumulates, resulting in a steeper rise in the centre of the "S" shape, and the "maturity" stage where there is a shallow slope, as the technology's technical limits are reached. The model could be applied in the fashion business in various ways. New technologies are used within areas such as textile development (with a group of innovative and often synthetic performance textiles being referred to as "technical fabrics"), fabric printing and component design (see Chapter 3). Also, the fashion business is characterised by its reliance on sewing machine technology, with electronic sewing machines currently having achieved the maturity phase in terms of potential sewing speed and stitching quality after decades of development and investment.

## Networks of Innovators

Regional, national, international, social and sector-based networks are key mechanisms via which organisations can source information and technology to influence the innovation process (Conway & Steward, 2009). Additionally, Trott (2017) proposes that external networks, such as suppliers, competitors, customers and distributors, can impact significantly on product development internally in an organisation, in a more realistic sense than in a linear representation of NPD, therefore suggesting that much of the knowledge required for innovation is accumulated via external sources. Such networks can consist of a combination of individuals and groups ("actors"), with flows of information and ideas (and often friendships) being shared between the various connections in "communities of practice". Organisations within the networks may have different types of bond between them, including technical, social or legal links, and can often form mutually beneficial relationships (Conway & Steward, 2009). This network perspective is particularly applicable to the fashion sector, as individual companies would be unable to function without connections to other organisations. Regional manufacturing hubs such as Leicester Made (2024), national industry bodies such as the British Fashion Council (2024) and UK Fashion and Textiles (UKFT, 2024) and international networks such as the online platform United Nations Fashion and Lifestyle Network (United Nations, 2024) form interconnected frameworks which help to structure this global industry's innovation activities. Less formal networks are also crucial sources of creative ideas in fashion, with colleagues moving to different organisations, but maintaining friendships where information about the industry may be shared informally. Indeed, a network perspective has been responsible for the formation of the group of authors and some of the interviewees who have collaborated on this book.

## Social Innovation

A growing area of innovation which is sometimes overlooked in the literature is social innovation. Smith (2024) emphasises that innovation is not required to be exclusively technology-based (see the interview with David Smith at the end of this chapter) and that social types of innovation are also possible, which do not necessarily require commercialisation. Social innovation originally emerged in the late 18th century, and may be organised by individuals or groups without the aim of financial gain, but for the betterment of society and to affect the capacity for positive change (Smith, 2024). Based on their study of social innovation in small-to-medium-scale clothing enterprises in Vietnam, Gasparin et al. (2021:698) argue that "social, ecological and cultural values … are as inherent as economic value" in terms of managing innovation. Many not-for-profit organisations in the fashion sector, such as Fashion Revolution, Unseen, Justice in Fashion and the Ellen Macarthur Foundation (see Chapter 6), have implemented new ways of enhancing social sustainability in the workplace and other communities, often led by groundbreaking individuals or based on collaborations between interested parties with similar interests and goals. For example, the Fashion School, a community interest company featured in Chapter 2, has taken a social innovation approach by collaborating with mass market fashion retail outlets to display students' designs and to run free fashion courses on the premises, for the benefit of the community.

## Contemporary Innovation Theories

### Fiona Bailey

Some of the most popular contemporary theories of innovation are explored within the next section of this chapter. These theories originate from not only from academics, but also from entrepreneurs and business strategists. They have gained popularity through books, podcasts, social media and newsletters.

### Blue Ocean Strategy

The concept of blue ocean strategy by Kim and Mauborgne (2015) refers to the simultaneous pursuit of differentiation and low cost to open up a new market space and create new demand. The idea is to create and capture uncontested market space or untapped markets which retailers long strive to find. The blue ocean strategy is about identifying and innovating a suitable product or idea to fit these uncontested markets, making the competition irrelevant and ensuring profitability.

### Blue Oceans

The term "blue oceans" denotes unknown market space that is not in existence today, and therefore untainted by competitors. In blue oceans, the demand is created through novel innovation, rather than existing innovations being fought over by competitors. There is ample opportunity for growth within this market space that is both profitable and rapid (Kim & Mauborgne, 2015). This market space could be classed as the untapped "sweet spot", a much-coveted, lucrative and desirable space for competitors to gain access to. As competitors surge forward into this blue ocean space by releasing imitation or similar products, services or ideas, the market quickly becomes saturated with variations of the same offer. This is where, according to the blue ocean strategy (Kim & Mauborgne, 2015), the market gets "bloodied" as competitors fiercely compete for sales. The solution to continued and successful growth is to find other fresh, uncontested and untapped areas of blue ocean. This can be done by continuing to understand the needs and wants of the consumers and providing a viable, new and innovative offering.

### Red Oceans

By contrast, the term "red oceans" refers to all the industries in existence today – the known and competitive market spaces. In these spaces, companies fight fiercely to outperform their rivals to gain a greater share of the existing demand. As competition increases and the market space gets more crowded, profits and market growth are reduced. According to Kim and Mauborgne (2015), products become commodities, which leads to cutthroat or "bloody" competition, leading to the term "red ocean".

## Blue Ocean Strategy in the Fashion Industry

The fashion industry is known for trends emerging from novel and innovative ideas. As discussed in Chapter 8, mass market retailing relies on luxury and high-end brands driving trends, which are then imitated by the lower-end brands and retailers. This cycle is fundamental to the success of the mass market fashion industry. Whilst the new ideas developed by the luxury and high-end brands may start as "blue ocean" ideas, imitating competitors quickly move the market space into "red ocean" territory. This process may become quicker as competitors become more adept at moving through the research and development process and releasing new rivals at speed, soon after the original has launched. In order to maintain competitive advantage, continual original innovation is needed, making sure the research and development phases are occurring as efficiently and quickly as possible, and that any iterations are made seamlessly and with agility in order to stay ahead of the competition.

### *Doblin Ten Types of Innovation*

The Doblin Ten Types of Innovation framework (Keeley et al., 2013) provides a comprehensive approach to innovation by identifying ten distinct dimensions or "types" that any organisation can utilise to drive innovation. For a business to be successful, innovation must occur across many areas of the business. This is the concept underpinning the Doblin Ten Types of Innovation theory (Keeley et al., 2013). It is easy to assume that innovation must only occur within the product. However, the Doblin framework reiterates that the most successful brands demonstrate innovation in several areas. To achieve success, innovation must be viewed holistically, taking place across three areas of the Doblin framework – "configuration, offerings and experience" (Keeley et al., 2013). This framework can be applied to the design process of fashion brands to ensure a holistic and multifaceted approach to creating innovative products. The following sections will give examples of each of the ten types of innovation in the context of the fashion industry.

### Configuration

### *Profit Model*

Fashion brands can innovate their profit model by exploring innovative new pricing strategies, such as subscription-based models, dynamic pricing or value-added services. For example, one innovative way that Next generates additional revenue is through offering third-party brands a full-service platform which can host the brand's website, fulfil its orders through Next's warehouse, and fully manage its customer service offering.

### *Network*

Network innovations within the fashion industry often take the form of strategic partnerships or collaborations. This could involve partnering with other brands, artists or influencers to create unique and exclusive collections. Collaborations can expand the brand's reach and bring fresh perspectives to the design process, and some of the best-known network innovations involve unexpected partnerships such as Nike and Tiffany, Louis Vuitton and Supreme, and Balenciaga and the Simpsons.

## Structure

This type focuses on innovating the internal business structure of the fashion brand. It may involve reimagining team structures or deconstructing traditional hierarchies to foster a more creative, innovative and agile design process. Flexible organisational structures can facilitate better communication and collaboration among design teams, resulting in quicker decision-making and speed to market.

## Process

Innovations in design processes can lead to more efficient and creative outcomes, which is crucial in the fashion industry, especially for mass market retailers who are always seeking more efficient ways to design, create and get product to market more quickly. Fashion brands can explore new ways of working with suppliers, including adopting digital technology to speed up and enhance the overall design and garment fitting processes (see Chapter 8). The ability of fashion brands to embrace sustainable and ethical design processes is also a crucial aspect of innovation in the fashion industry.

## Offering

### Product Performance

This area of the Doblin framework is perhaps the most easily understood. Innovations in the performance of products can set brands apart from the competition, creating a source of competitive advantage. This may involve the use of cutting-edge fabrics, technologies or sustainable materials that enhance the functionality, durability or environmental impact of the products (see Chapter 3).

### Product System

Fashion brands can innovate by creating product bundles and customisable products. This encourages designers to think about how different fashion products can be mixed and matched to form multi-product sets. These sets can be sold at a discounted selling price to enhance the consumer's perception of value, believing they have got "more for their money" through product bundling.

## Experience

### Service

Service innovation within the fashion industry involves enhancing the overall customer experience. Fashion brands can explore personalised shopping experiences, innovative retail environments or technology-driven services to engage customers in new and innovative ways both offline and online. Self-service checkouts which read the garment's radio frequency identification (RFID) tag provide a quick and seamless checkout scanning experience without the need for barcodes.

## Channel

Channel innovation can include exploring new retail formats, such as pop-up shops and mobile stores, online platforms or direct-to-consumer models such as social media commerce. Fashion brands can utilise their digital channels and new, innovative technologies to create unique shopping experiences. For example, brands including Burberry, Miu Miu and Valentino are using WhatsApp to connect with high-net worth customers to alert them of new products and trigger in-store purchases (McDowell, 2020).

### Brand

Brand innovation involves reimagining the brand's identity, storytelling and values. Fashion brands can differentiate themselves through a strong and authentic mission and vision statement, leading to a brand narrative that resonates with consumers on a deeper level. An example of brand innovation is the launch of Coachtopia, the diffusion brand from the high-end accessory brand Coach. Coachtopia is centred around circularity and sustainable innovation, and helped to re-launch Coach as a relevant brand for a younger generation than its existing customers.

### Customer Engagement

Innovations in customer engagement focus on building communities around the brand. This could involve creating online or offline communities where customers can connect, share experiences and actively participate in the brand's evolution. Glossier is a direct-to- consumer beauty brand which engages its customers innovatively, through an online community of Glossier fans, posting user-generated content, including reviews, beauty hauls, tips and tutorials.

By incorporating the Doblin Ten Types of Innovation framework, fashion brands can systematically explore various strategies and methods to drive creativity, innovation and differentiation.

### Design Council's Double Diamond Framework

The Double Diamond framework, developed by the Design Council and launched in 2004, is a widely used design thinking model that helps guide designers through a structured process. It consists of four distinct phases: Discover, Define, Develop and Deliver. Whilst the framework is not specific to any particular industry, its principles can be applied to the design process for fashion brands. The following section explores each of the four areas of the Double Diamond and shows how the framework is relevant in the context of the fashion design process (see Figures 4.8 and 4.9):

### Discover

### User Research

Fashion designers can engage in thorough research to understand their target audience, market trends and cultural influences (see Chapters 2, 7 and 8). This phase involves exploring the up-and-coming trends, gaining insights into consumer preferences and identifying potential gaps or opportunities in the fashion market.

### Trend Analysis

Within this stage of the Double Diamond, fashion brands will identify emerging trends to better understand the cultural, social and economic factors that influence their customers'

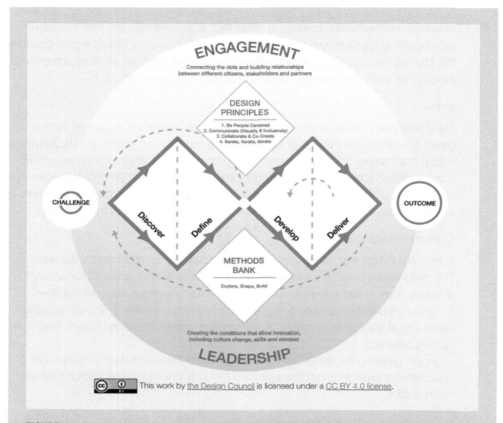

**FIGURE 4.8** The Double Diamond Framework (source: Design Council, 2005)

fashion choices. This step helps designers uncover inspiration and insights that will inform the design process and ultimately shape the product range.

## Define

### Problem Definition

In the context of fashion, this phase involves defining the specific design challenges and opportunities for innovation based on the insights gained during the Discover phase. It may include narrowing down the target audience (especially if the fashion retailer is a niche brand, like Tom's Trunks, for example – see Chapter 7), establishing brand identity and determining unique selling points to assist in creating competitive advantage.

### Brand Positioning

This stage of the Double Diamond helps to define the brand's identity and positioning within the market. This is important to fully understand the brand's direct competitors, who are most closely vying for the customer's business. This step helps in creating a clear vision

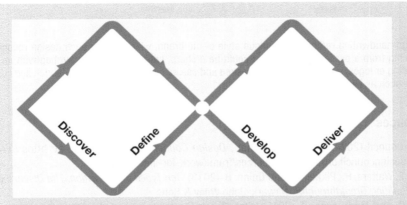

**FIGURE 4.9** The four stages of the Double Diamond Framework (source: Design Council, 2005)

for the fashion brand, setting the tone for the design direction, design handwriting[1] and necessary quality.

### Develop

*Conceptualisation*

This is the ideation phase where designers generate a wide range of ideas and concepts for the fashion collection. It involves hand sketching, using CAD design software to create initial sketches, and experimenting with various design elements, materials, and styles – often inspired by bought garment samples (see Chapters 2, 3 and 8).

*Iterative Design*

Designers can use the iterative process to refine and improve their concepts based on feedback from customers (often from website reviews or social media comments), testing the marketplace through trialling products and further research. This phase allows for creative exploration and experimentation with different design possibilities and outcomes.

### Deliver

*Implementation*

Once the final design direction is chosen, designers move towards bringing their vision to life. This involves finalising designs, selecting fabrics, trims and embellishments, and creating prototype garment samples.

*Production and Marketing*

In the context of fashion brands, the Deliver phase includes overseeing the production process, marketing the collection, and preparing to launch the product to market in a strategic and impactful way.

   By applying the Double Diamond framework, fashion designers can ensure a more systematic and user-centred approach to their creative process. It helps them balance creativity with strategic thinking, resulting in more innovative product ranges that resonate with their target audience.

## Note

1   Design handwriting refers to the unique style of the brand, which makes each design recognisable as being from a particular brand. This could be a sharp, smart, tailored handwriting with no visible branding or logos, such as Reiss, or a washed and casual handwriting, textured fabrics and laid-back style, such as FatFace.

## References

Design Council (2024) 'Design for Planet', *Design Council*, available online at: https://www.designcouncil.org.uk/our-resources/framework-for-innovation

Keeley, L, Walters, H., Pikkel, R., and Quinn, B. (2013) '*Ten Types of Innovation: The Discipline of Building Breakthroughs*', Newark: John Wiley & Sons.

Kim, W.C. and Mauborgne, R. (2015) '*Blue Ocean Strategy, Expanded Edition: How to Create Uncontested Market Space and Make the Competition Irrelevant*', Boston: Harvard Business Review Press.

McDowell, M. (2020) 'WhatsApp has big ambitions to be a shopping platform', *Vogue Business*, 15th December 2020, available online at: https://www.voguebusiness.com/technology/whatsapp-has-big-ambitions-to-be-a-shopping-platform

## Summary

This chapter has assessed theories on innovation and the ways in which they can be applied to the fashion business, as it operates differently to other sectors in certain respects. The theories which have been discussed here are of relevance to both academics and commercial organisations. Established theories such as the New Product Development process, the product life cycle, the diffusion of innovations, dominant design, networks of innovators, co–creation, co–design, open innovation and social innovation, as well as a selection of contemporary innovation theories, have been explored and applied. A model of product development has been devised to suit the fashion industry, comprising research for creative inspiration, design development, sample development and preparation for production. A new theory has also been proposed to encapsulate aspects of fashion product innovation, by setting temporal, financial, visual and technical boundaries which can meet consumer needs more effectively, thus enhancing commerciality. The interviews that follow with academics specialising in innovation explore a selection of those theories they consider to be most applicable to fashion.

### Views from Academic Researchers in Innovation

**Dr Steve Conway is Associate Professor in Innovation at the University of Leicester, UK. Steve graduated in Business Studies and Computer Science before later gaining his MBA and PhD in the Management of Innovation at Aston University,**

**FIGURE 4.10** Dr Steve Conway. Photo with permission from Steve Conway

**UK. He has also worked as a software developer at Hewlett-Packard (HP). Steve's research explores the role of social and organisational networks in innovation and entrepreneurship and their graphical representation.**

I'd define innovation as the combination of a new idea plus its commercialisation or its bringing into use. You see these two elements reflected in innovative organisations. That is, there are individuals who are good at creativity and individuals who are good at commercialisation. It is also reflected in the way that organisations organise, with some departments focused on creativity and development and others on commercialisation. In a sense, this definition of innovation highlights the two key activities that lead to successful innovation. Successful innovation teams therefore not only need to incorporate people with different skills and backgrounds, but also those from across various organisational departments – that is, they need to be cross-functional.

When I worked at HP, we had a campus that included marketers and product developers. I was in product development. What's interesting, and I suspect it's probably mimicked in fashion, is that product developers and marketers often have different personalities and aspirations, with different training, different degrees, use different "languages" and operate within different subcultures. As a result of such differences, the marketers and developers in the same building at HP hardly spoke to each other. There are two innovation concepts which are useful to consider here when reflecting on my product development experiences at HP. One is "boundary-spanning" and the other is "ambidexterity". The spanning of boundaries, whether functional, organisational, sectoral, regional or national, can be very important to the innovation process. On the one hand, innovative ideas often arise from outside the team, organisation or sector, for example, and ideas that cross over, aided by individuals whose interactions and relationships span such boundaries, can fuel the creative process. On the other hand, spanning functional boundaries, such as between marketing and product development, can be important for the successful commercialisation of an idea. However, this can be challenging given the differences that often exist between marketeers and product developers. Interestingly, boundary-spanning individuals are atypical, and thus play an especially important role in the innovation process. "Ambidexterity" in organisational terms is basically the ability to manage in two different ways at the same time. If we take the product development activities within the HP division I worked within, we had product developers working on bug fixes and incremental product refinements. This type of development required a tighter, more systematic, more bureaucratic way of working. Then there were developers in the lab working on state-of-the-art projects, which required a much more open style of management. Managing both incremental and radical innovation in the same lab, employing differing modes of management, can thus be very challenging.

When considering our definition of innovation, it is also useful to be open to the wide range of types of innovation that exist, for example from product innovation to service innovation, and from process innovation to business model innovation, as well as how organisations often bundle these together to create an offering for a customer. We should also consider what we might mean by success in relation to innovation, acknowledging that different individuals within the organisation (such as the designer, marketeer or production manager) might view success in different ways. Furthermore, we should also recognise the importance of failure and trail-and-error in stimulating learning and new knowledge that can ultimately lead to successful innovation.

**David Smith is Professor of Innovation Management at Nottingham Trent University. David graduated from BA Economics at Lancaster University, UK before becoming a researcher in various aspects of innovation, authoring over 50 journal articles and academic book chapters in this field. He is also the author of *Exploring Innovation*, now in its fourth edition (2024). David has extensive experience of corporate education, including training for the Danish footwear brand ECCO.**

In my book *Exploring Innovation* I suggest that there are broadly three ways in which innovation can arise, firstly, simply from ideas, which is the purely creative bit where people just suddenly have those Eureka moments and something occurs to them. The second source is mainly the idea of scientific discovery or the development of science, when things crop up which become innovations. The third one is technology, and the idea is that technology is something that for the most part usually already exists, but somebody applies it and uses it in some way to create an innovation. Of those three, two are very definitely to do with science and technology, and if you ask people (such as my students) to name an innovation, most of the time most people will think of something that's technology-based. However, some interesting ideas have been written about social innovation that move away from the idea of it being necessarily technological because it's about innovation in the social

**FIGURE 4.11**  Professor David Smith. Photo with permission from David Smith

relations sphere, although most people talking about innovation imply that it's technological innovation of one order or another.

My book starts with some of the conventional definitions, and I quote other people. Then in the last chapter, I try to give a slightly different perspective, to say that most people assume innovation is about technology, but it doesn't have to be, and if you look at innovations that come purely from ideas, some of those certainly are not technological. People have a Eureka moment, maybe there's a problem that they've faced for years and something suddenly clicks and they have an idea that in time probably becomes an artefact or possibly a service, and ultimately it becomes an innovation. That's how most innovation works, in my view, and it doesn't have to be technological. However, even the purely creative, ideas-based innovations have often got something to do with technology. With Facebook, for example, while there's some dispute about whether Mark Zuckerberg actually had the idea of a way of connecting with his student friends when he was at Harvard, it is creative, but there's a big technical element because in order to do it, he had to write the software and have a good knowledge of computing. If you look a lot of the more recent internet-based innovations, whilst they certainly can be very creative, there's also quite a strong technological element to it. For many of today's technology businesses, an awful lot of either their capital value or their income actually comes from the Intellectual Property that they either own or have power over.

My view of innovation in fashion would be that you rely very heavily on the creative process and it is based very much upon people's knowledge of materials, of colours and to some extent the human form and the nature of the fashion market. Some of those things are not necessarily technological, but many of them are, such as colour, material and manufacturing processes. I once worked for a company in Nottingham which became part of Courtaulds (formerly a major clothing manufacturer), and it was a really interesting experience to be there. They were a knitwear supplier to Marks & Spencer, and I was attached to the accounts department, but I managed to move around, and I met the designer, who was undoubtedly very creative. She was artistic in a whole series of different dimensions, but was also very knowledgeable about textiles, fabrics, threads, sewing mechanisms and ways of connecting pieces of fabric.

My undergraduate students tend to think that invention is creative and technical, and one of the things that I try to get across to them is the fact that invention is at best half the story, that innovation is about taking inventions, ideas, designs, all sorts of things, and one way and another, commercialising them, getting them in some way ready for the market. I occasionally teach about failed innovations, and one of the points that I usually make is you can have fantastic inventions, fantastic ideas, but it's amazing how many come to grief because they fail at the commercialisation part of the innovation process. From a business perspective, one of the things that's really important about innovation is your ability to get the product, the service or the process ready in some way to go on to the market. In the fourth edition of my book, I've got a bit more emphasis on the economist Joseph Schumpeter as one of the first people to explicate clear ideas about what innovation is, particularly some of his ideas on creative destruction, the sense that when something new comes along, in some cases it can displace existing ways of doing things.

In the chapter in my book on social innovation, I've got several case studies, such as *The Big Issue* (a newspaper that is sold on the street for sellers to earn an income). Many of the cases are not inventions, but they are definitely innovations. Social innovations often aren't sold, but they're sometimes given away or sold at a significant discount. I like to put across to students the idea that while most of the time the innovations that you come across tend to be technological, I think to some extent the media are to blame for this, in the sense that things that are bright and shiny and technical have an appeal. If you're trying to put television programmes, films or newspapers together, technical objects create quite an attractive story, and in a way this is a bit misleading because these are the things we hear about, but innovation is about much more than that. People have said to me, "We're in an amazing period of history where technology and innovation are leaping ahead faster than they've ever done before," but my argument to that is, "No, it isn't. We are not in not in such a period at all." There's a book called *The Rise of the Creative Class* by Richard Florida (2004), who says, "let's take two people, somebody who is a young man at the start of the 20th century and somebody who is a young man at the midpoint in the 20th century. Think about those two people over their lifetimes. Which one experienced the greater period of technological change?" He goes on to say that nine times out of ten, people will say it's the second half of the 20th century. His argument is that somebody who was a young person in 1900, from then up to the 1950s, experienced amazing changes in their life, in television, film, radio, transport, cars and aeroplanes, because there were none of these things in 1900. We have an obsession with technological innovation. We hear a lot about it speeding up and about transformation and that our lives are changing. I try to make the point that in fact we tend to have phases of amazing technological changes. In the last 40 or 50 years particularly, it's been changes around information and communication and things of that nature.

I'm inclined to the view that the technological aspects of innovation tend to be a bit overdone, and that innovation is about going from ideas, which requires creativity, into products, services, particularly processes. There's no doubt that one of the hardest parts of turning something from an idea into something that's marketable or usable by consumers is commercialising it. In my view, a key part of innovation is understanding consumers, understanding what they do, what they want, what they might want, understanding markets in the very broadest sense, and the processes and activities that one has to engage in to turn something from the intellectual idea into something that we can all consume. That's really what innovation is all about.

**Professor Michael Beverland is Professor of Brand Management at Sussex University, UK. Michael completed his BCom and MCom in Business and Management at University of Auckland, New Zealand before studying for his PhD at the University of South Australia. He has previously held academic posts in Universities in Australia, Denmark, the Netherlands, New Zealand and the UK. Michael's academic publications focus largely on brand management and innovation.**

**FIGURE 4.12** Professor Michael Beverland. Photo with permission from Michael Beverland

*How would you describe creativity and innovation?*

I would think of it as some type of novelty that makes an impact on a particular stakeholder audience that involves primarily a shift or a change in meaning or the communication of meaning. For more functional fashion, it could mean a more classical functional improvement or set of benefits, but when I think of the fashion industry, I think of symbolism and meaning, which means that it may not be classically new, but could just be a reimagining of something else that's relevant for the time. When I taught at a fashion school in Australia, the focus tended to be on the designer-maker, driven by the vision of one highly experimental person, the sole entrepreneur who's going to try and make their name, because it doesn't have a strong local industry there of any significant size.

We also had a lot of students who did a two-year programme in design who would often benefit from going to one of the big fashion houses that did jeans or something similar. I got the sense there that probably innovation was a bit more formal and incremental. For example, if you're just coming up with the next season where you are dealing with a look and the brand is much more established, it's therefore probably restricting your choices a lot. A lot of students found it to be quite beneficial to find their feet in the industry before they decided perhaps to go it alone. There are multiple strands, depending on where you sit in the marketplace. There's probably a group of people who are doing lots of creative things, for example with collaborations, and then there's sportswear and classical clothing, where innovation might differ in terms of the formalised stage-gate process or something like a lean process, to come up with something that's new but not too different from the design language that the brand has. I'm always intrigued about that interplay between continuing a line of things that's obviously working really well, but then knowing when it's time to do something quite radically different, that surprises people, even if you're doing quite well on the market.

*What are the most important theories in innovation or creativity in your view?*

It always depends on what they're used for. When I talked to designers in New Zealand in fashion, they used the stage-gate process. I would say you need to have a working knowledge of stage-gate theory to know why you have to step away from that or what its limits are. I've also found theories like the lean model to be quite useful and opening up different sets of practices. A lot of my work has also drawn quite heavily on design thinking. Some of the literature on design thinking is stories of methods and tools, and there's a lot of philosophical thinking around abduction and things like that which are really useful, this idea in branding of disruption and tying it back to make the brand new, but give it a broader platform and making sure that you didn't discard the brand historic image. I always think about innovation having an understanding of branding as well, particularly that interplay between consistency and relevance is really important, not being tied into a very fad-driven relevance model that isn't really saying anything about the brand. I've always found, in my experience, that fashion tends to be driven by a designer, and it's their vision. There's co-creation of meaning in a way, but not necessarily of the design per se. Those are the main theories I tend to use for research.

I've always respected Rogers's work on the diffusion of innovations. Firstly, he's aware of its limits, but I think it's always been this idea of a social influence model, which is quite powerful. I've also found Grant McCracken's Meaning Transfer Model useful, in terms of the idea of working with brands symbolically. There are subcultures working effectively now with a collaborator and being able to open up and access each other's markets, but then also changing in the process, so it's a two-way transfer, meaning that both items are changed and added to. Sense-making is another area of theory that I've used more recently, about creating customer journeys. When I used to teach luxury fashion, students really got into Holt's article on American cultural capital, and they really started to understand the sheer subtleties of cues and language and taste.

*What do you feel are most important recent creative innovations in fashion or in general?*

Sometimes I think we go for the new too often. I'm never wowed by particular social media technology or tech, I'm always a bit sceptical of that. I've just finished a piece on the analogue revival in the *Journal of Consumer Research,* and I've really been interested in things like the value that consumers find in technologies that make them work, this idea of reskilling as a form of serious leisure where people are looking for some type of meaning in their consumption rather than in their work life. Sometimes the types of technologies that have a lot of limits enable them to do that, so I became a lot more interested in terms of looking more at ideas like neo-craft, for example, this idea of a craft sector that is not hidebound to tradition, that is actually an assemblage of appreciation for a modern marketing, social media awareness and engagement, but also a passion for their particular materials and context. A paper I wrote recently was about the coffee sector as a neo-craft, that it's not a tradition of service, because, of course, most countries that have bought into this neo-wave craft thing around coffee don't grow coffee, but there's an immense craft logic around that. It's really about this idea of what Emma Bell and her colleagues have called in an *Organization Theory* paper, "Craft Imaginaries".

I'm always interested in how we talk a lot about circularity, but then, underpinning much of that is still a lot of materiality, so I think that interplay between the whole issue around sustainable fashion is very tricky because you're in a sector that's all about the new, and therefore it requires resources. In the Netherlands, almost every store is selling sustainable fashion now, and then every season they've got a new range of sustainable fashion, but it's still fashion. You're still asking me to buy a line of clothing that I probably don't need that's using up energy and materials, even if it can be recycled. I think this problem of decoupling that's inherent in those models, that we can still have it all, is highly problematic. You do see a lot of interesting things happening in that space, and I think if we could maybe marry that with a type of materialism that led people to appreciate things for longer to really engage with the stuff they have, that could be quite interesting, even if it would be not so good for the fashion industry.

I think there's an interest in eco-systems and regionality, the power of place and unpacking what is an eco-system for innovation around fashion. I tried to think about this problem when I was in Melbourne, and you realise that most of the eco-system of research and innovation tends to move its way from universities out into mainstream via start-ups and things like that. I think in fashion there's probably some element of that because obviously there's materials, there's finance, there's a greater need to connect into the finance industries and so on, but there's also a whole range of cultural capital and different pathways and connections that can be missed. Where I was in Melbourne, it was an old clothing area that most people had largely forgotten about because, of course, it moved into more of a residential space, it was really in the inner city, but there was still some of that latent trace there. There were lots of things, from little pop-up stores to clubs to cool coffee shops, which you started to trace as where people met and did events and connected and it brought people in. I think some of that research we're starting to see, and we're doing some of it at Sussex, is real interest in the creative sector and the eco-systems, but it's still very much on the surface, and no one is really getting underneath the hood of it. There are challenges from a policy point of view because things like creativity and fashion are really fragmented, and they see a handful of jobs here and there and they don't really understand it, whereas some other sectors are way bigger. For example, there's the manufacturing which we can still see in big factories, even though it's declining year-on-year, there's so much policy attention that goes into that. I think we need to understand what the community of practice are saying, what would you need to build a sustainable and resilient fashion cluster or creative cluster in a particular region that could just absorb shocks and renew?

## References

Abernathy, W. and Utterback, M. (1978) 'Patterns of Industrial Innovation', *Technology Review*, 80(7), 41–47.

Anshu, K., Gaur, L. and Singh, G. (2022) 'Impact of Customer Experience on Attitude and Repurchase Intention Inonline Grocery Retailing: A Moderation Mechanism of Value Co-Creation', *Journal of Retailing and Consumer Services*, https://doi.org/10.1016/j.jretconser.2021.102798

Be Global Fashion Network (2024) available online at: https://www.bgfashion.net/

Bessant, J. and Moeslein, K. (2011) *Open Collective Innovation*. London: Advanced Institute of Management Research, available online at: http://www.innovation-portal.info/wp-content/uploads/Open_Collective_Innovation.pdf

Boardman, R., Parker-Strak, R. and Henninger, C. (2020) *Fashion Buying and Merchandising: The Fashion Buyer in a Digital Society*. London: Routledge.

British Fashion Council (2024) *British Fashion Council's Events and Initiatives*, available online at: https://www.britishfashioncouncil.co.uk/Community/Media-Hub

Chesbrough, H.W. (2003) *Open Innovation*. Boston, MA: Harvard Business School Publishing.

CoDesign (2024) 'Aims and Scope', *CoDesign*, available online at: https://www.tandfonline.com/action/journalInformation?show=aimsScope&&journalCode=ncdn20

Conway, S. and Steward, F. (2009) *Managing and Shaping Innovation*. Oxford: Oxford University Press.

Florida, R. (2004) *The Rise of the Creative Class*. New York: Basic Books.

Foster, R. N. (1986) 'Working The S-Curve: Assessing Technological Threats', *Research Management*, 29(4), 17–20.

Gardiner, P. and Rothwell, R. (1985) 'Good Designs: Tough Customers', *Design Studies*, 6(1), 7–17.

Gasparin, M., Green, W., Lilley, S., Quinn, M., Saren, M. and Schinckus, C. (2021) 'Business as Unusual: A Business Model for Social Innovation', *Journal of Business Research*, 125, 98–709.

Gohoungodji, P. and Amara, N. (2022) 'Art of Innovating in the Arts: Definitions, Determinants, and Mode of Innovation in Creative Industries, a Systematic Review', *Review of Management Science*, 17, 2685–2725.

Goworek, H. (2007) *Fashion Buying*. Oxford: Blackwell/Wiley.

Goworek, H. and McGoldrick, P. (2015) *Retail Marketing Management: Principles and Practice*. London: Pearson.

Hermès (2024) 'Kelly', *Hermès*, available online at: https://www.hermes.com/uk/en/content/106196-kelly/

IPDMC (2024) 'Workshops and Conferences', *EIASM*, available online at: https://www.eiasm.net/workshops-conferences/introduction

Jekal, M., Brandewie, B. and Kim, I. (2023) 'Exploring the Future of Fashion Design Education for Generation Z Through Co-design as Community-Based Participatory Research', *CoDesign*, 19(4), 346–362.

Jobber, D. and Ellis-Chadwick, F.E. (2023) *Principles and Practice of Marketing, 10th edition*. Maidenhead: McGraw Hill.

Leicester Made (2024) *Directory*, available online at: https://leicestermade.co.uk/directory/

Levitt, T. (1965) 'Exploit the Product Life Cycle', *Harvard Business Review*, 43(6), 81–94.

Milligan, L. (2009) 'Being Roland Mouret', in *Vogue*, 7th August 2009, available online at: https://www.vogue.co.uk/article/roland-mouret-comes-back-as-rm

Pew Research (2019) *Where Millenials End and Generation Z Begins*, available online at: https://www.pewresearch.org/short-reads/2019/01/17/where-millennials-end-and-generation-z-begins/

Reid, S. and Brentani, U. (2004) 'The Fuzzy Front End of New Product Development for Discontinuous Innovations: A Theoretical Model', *Journal of Product Innovation Management*, 21(3), 170–84.

Rogers, E. (1962) *Diffusion of Innovations*, New York: Free Press.

Rothwell, R. (1983) *Information and Successful Innovation*, Report No. 5782. London: British Library.

Schumpeter, J.A. (2010) *Capitalism, Socialism and Democracy*. Abingdon: Routledge. (Originally published in 1942.)

Sheth, J.N. and Hellman, K. (2018) 'Unleashing the Co-Creation of Value', *Marketing Journal*, 16th August 2018, available online at: https://www.marketingjournal.org/unleashing-the-co-creation-of-value-jagdish-n-sheth-and-karl-hellman/

Smith, D. (2024) *Exploring Innovation, 4th edition*. Maidenhead: McGraw Hill.

Tidd, J. and Bessant, J. (2021) *Managing Innovation: Integrating Technological, Market and Organizational Change, 7th edition*. Chichester: Wiley.

Trott, P. (2017) *Innovation Management and New Product Development, 6th edition*. London: Pearson.

UKFT (2024) *Innovation, R&D and Sustainability for UK Fashion and Textiles*, available online at: https://www.ukft.org/innovation/

United Nations (2024) 'Fashion and Lifestyle Network', *United Nations*, available online at: https://sdgs.un.org/partnerships/action-networks/conscious-fashion-and-lifestyle-network

Utterback, J.M. (1994) *Mastering the Dynamics of Innovation: How Companies Can Seize Opportunities in the Face of Technological Change*. Boston MA: Harvard Business School Press.

von Hippel, E. (1976) 'The Dominant Role of Users in the Scientific Instrument Innovation Process', *Research Policy*, 5(3), 212–239.

von Hippel, E. (1977) 'Transferring Process Equipment Innovations From User-Innovators to Equipment Manufacturing Firms', *R&D Management*, 8(1), 13–22.

Yang, E.K., Lee, J.H. and Lee, C.H. (2023) 'Virtual Reality Environment-Based Collaborative Exploration of Fashion Design', *CoDesign* (ahead of print). https://doi.org/10.1080/15710882.2022.2162547

# 5

# Creativity and Innovation in Fashion Forecasting

*Carol Cloughton*

## Introduction

This chapter will explore the role and structure of the fashion forecasting sector and its integration within the fashion business. How fashion forecasting consultancies have evolved will be considered, alongside the development of methodologies to identify innovative opportunities for brands and retailers by recognising the importance of long-term and short-term trend analysis in predicting future fashion trends. The increasing demand for the consumer's voice to be integrated into the innovation process will also be discussed. Fashion is an important element of today's culture. The fashion industry is challenged by rapid and constant change, and the sector needs to be fully informed of the contemporary social and cultural dynamics that will influence consumers and the products they create for them. It is also important to be clear about what fashion means in the context of fashion forecasting. "Fashion" is either a consumer product or a behaviour that is adopted by several individuals in their social group because either the behaviour or the product is perceived to be socially relevant at that moment (Sproles and Burns, 1994). "Fashion" is not, of course, just about clothing, but is applied to other categories such as hairstyles or make-up. It also includes the adoption of behaviours and ideas that influence our lifestyles, such as social networking services like Instagram, TikTok, X or Facebook, sustainable fashion, or a brand of smartphone as the social pressure to conform and be accepted by peers influences a consumer's choice and behaviours. We need to feel that we belong to our social group, so we will modify our behaviours to fit in (Kim, Fiore, Payne & Kim, 2021). It is not just about the material culture, the objects that are fashionable; it is also important to look at the ideas that are connected to them. What unifies both the objects that are created and the ideas that have inspired them is that they constantly change, and this is the essence of fashion.

DOI: 10.4324/9781003332749-5

## How Fashion Forecasting Has Evolved

Pre-1960s, the fashion system was largely influenced and centralised in Paris through haute couture. Haute couture originated in Paris in the late 19th century, and it represents the highest level of fashion. Designer companies such as Karl Lagerfeld, Chanel and Christian Dior use skilled ateliers (workshops) which have a unique specialism, such as tailoring or dresses, and produce handmade, bespoke pieces for clients seeking the highest standard of quality, service and privacy (Renfrew & Lynn, 2022). The classical model as identified by Simmel (1957) was driven by the so-called "upper classes" who dressed to reflect their social position, their wealth and status, and these styles were emulated by "lower classes". Although social classes are difficult to define in contemporary society, upper, middle and lower classes were more clearly delineated and significant in society prior to the 1970s. This top-down, or "trickle-down", model was prevalent in Western societies, but the dramatic shifts in the social and cultural landscape from post-World War II up until the late 1960s disrupted this top-down approach to fashion influence as new social groups emerged. Aspiring to imitate the upper classes was no longer the primary motivation as fashion became a means to express a sense of individuality and distinctions through age, race, ethnicity, sexual orientation and gender (Crane, 1999; Garcia, 2021).

Fashion influence was emerging from the working classes, and there was a shift from conformity through imitation of the higher social classes to individuality as new, younger consumer groups were creating their own style tribes. Adolescents and young adults were becoming increasingly interested in fashion and were seeking "to differentiate themselves from the middle-aged and the elderly" (Crane, 1999:13). This reversal of influence disrupted the fashion system, as the dominant inspiration was coming from the lower classes and creating bottom-up, or trickle-up, opportunities (Field, 1970). Developments in ready-to-wear and retail were producing shorter and faster fashion cycles. The need to anticipate and translate these new fashion innovations with minimal business risk led to the creation of fashion forecasting agencies (Crane, 1999; Garcia, 2021). The first launched in Paris in 1966, when Promostyl was founded, followed by Peclers in 1970 (Divita, 2019). This new fashion system was no longer driven just by the designers, the top-down approach, but by emerging influences from popular culture, that were being embraced by new consumer groups in the UK and the USA, including young adults and adolescents who were developing their own identities. Urban subcultures were starting to emerge that were inspired by music, and these subcultures were creating their own, innovative street style clothing. A very good example of this was the creation of punk in the 1970s, a powerful British street fashion that evolved from the streets of London that would influence designers for years to come (Crane, 1999). The growing influence of streetwear continued into the 1990s with the development of other street-inspired subcultures such as hip-hop in the USA, and led to multiple sources of influence as fashion was being developed by experimental consumers rather than designers (Garcia, 2021). The industry wanted to create innovative fashion for this more accessible fashion consumer and fashion forecasting agencies offered them the resources to do this. The agencies would anticipate the future by linking commerce, manufacturing and culture to the aspirations and lifestyles of new, predominantly younger consumer groups who were seeking the styles that would reflect their need to develop their own identities (Crane, 1999).

As the fashion industry became more global, so the need for more resources to anticipate the needs of those markets increased and new forecasting agencies were formed. In 1980, Trend Union in Paris was founded by Lidewij Edelkoort, followed by NellyRodi in 1985 (Divita, 2019). Street style and fast fashion started to dominate the retail landscape in the 1990s, and the High Street and key global players such as H&M and Zara had developed business models that could rapidly translate catwalk trends into stores at low costs. To succeed in what was becoming a very competitive marketplace, the speed at which the right trends could be transformed into innovative ranges for very fashion-driven consumers would be an advantage. In 1998, Marc Worth launched WGSN, the first agency to offer fashion trend forecasting online. Although the likes of Promostyl, Peclers and NellyRodi had expanded their reach by opening offices in key fashion centres such as New York, London and Tokyo, they still relied on producing trend books with the latest trends and swatches for their clients. This presented problems when challenged with faster trend cycles, as inevitably many of the forecasts would be out of date by the time they were published, and this came at a high cost for a lot of their clients. WGSN, on the other hand, created more value for brands and retailers in cost and time savings by offering its trend information on a platform that could be updated continuously via its global network of trend researchers. The success of online fashion forecasting services has now been adopted by trend agencies globally, as the format has offered more opportunities for their clients to develop more accurate product, marketing campaigns and understanding of their consumers, as well as growing as a valuable outsourced specialism within the sector. As an example, WGSN was sold by Worth to Emap in 2007 for £142 million (Hesse, 2014), and its value at the time of writing is estimated at £800 million (Crowley and Farr, 2023).

Technology hasn't just disrupted the way that trends are communicated to clients. In the 2000s, the acceptance of social media along with the global reach of popular culture via the internet and its influence on diverse consumer groups has created multiple challenges for trend agencies. Hyper-connected consumers are constantly changing key elements in the fashion industry such as retail business models, but more specifically the speed of the fashion cycle. Social media influencers, livestreaming of fashion events, social media platforms, live shopping events and peer-to-peer networking are examples of developments that have made the identification of the key cultural drivers chaotic and complex. The consumer has developed a digital voice, and the narrative it produces is now an essential element in the creation of trends. Definition of the word "trend" is now more flexible. Rather than just predicting trends, it is the role of agencies and trend spotters to track the trends that are developing on social media in varied global markets created by the consumers themselves, the subcultures that are emerging, the music styles and the influence they are having on their fashion choices, and select the ones that will be relevant for their brand or chosen market. Social media is the new street.

## Fashion Forecasting and the Fashion Business

In contemporary markets, the role of fashion forecasting is to align the opportunities for creativity and innovation to the future vision of a brand or retailer, in line with their values, resources, and crucially, the aspirations and lifestyles of their customers. Executive teams use trends to develop innovative ranges, develop marketing strategies to drive retail sales and reduce the possibility of excess inventory, and even to re-evaluate business models. As there is not one single, centralised source that predicts and starts a trend, it is imperative for brands to look to fashion forecasters to filter through this pool of opportunities and uncover the ones that will work for their markets and their consumers in the short term and the long term.

## Long-term Trends

The world's population has grown exponentially in the last few years. There has been a significant increase in the population in Asia, Africa and Latin America. This has had an impact on the fashion industry as it has created not only opportunities for growth, but challenges in understanding these new markets. To uncover long-term market opportunities to innovate for the future needs of their consumers, brands and retailers need to look at long-term forecasts – i.e., macrotrends – in their development cycles. Macrotrends impact on all industries, and are identified by mapping large-scale changes in society, such as the uncertainty or stability of politics, the state of the economy, developments in technology or science, environmental concerns and changes in legislation, and anticipate how these will impact on the future values, behaviours and lifestyles of consumers in national and global markets (see Figure 5.1). The long-term view must be considered in contemporary fashion markets, as we now recognise that fashion is a vehicle that has evolved to represent the personal views and values of consumers' perceptions of themselves and how they express their personal identities (Crane & Bovone, 2006). The consumer's values may well change, triggered by major shifts in society, and the long-term view is important in anticipating and planning for these.

**FIGURE 5.1** Brainstorming a trend at TrendBible. © TrendBible

Consider the impact of climate change on the industry, and the very pressing need to create more sustainable processes and products. Fashion is an element of material culture when it becomes a product, such as clothing, footwear, accessories or beauty products. Future trends in sustainability may create a more mainstream trend in the desire for pre-owned products as there is a major shift from new product to resale, vintage and charity shop finds. Pre-owned fashion therefore holds more value to consumers as they have been influenced to control their buying behaviour because they're also worried about the planet and have chosen to express this to their surrounding social world by wearing pre-owned. The symbolic value of what we wear cannot be underestimated. However, as a brand or retailer, if your business model relies on developing new product for your consumer, how will this trend impact on your profitability and future growth? Long-term forecasts give businesses the opportunity to create a strategic direction that sits with their resources and market reach (see Figure 5.2). It is important to stress that the opportunity to develop creative and innovative business opportunities through marketing campaigns, range developments or business models stems from a customer-driven approach. How consumers think, feel and act changes rapidly as the impact of world events becomes more complex and the business environment becomes more competitive, so a long-term forecast of two to five years ahead can improve a company's future prospects.

**FIGURE 5.2** TrendBible digital forecasting services include macro reports, predicting the future of life and home. © TrendBible

## Short-term Trends

Short-term forecasts, or microtrends, are when the fashion forecaster translates cultural cues into future fashion trends that will work for brands and retailers, their values and identities, and will appeal to specific consumer demographics up to two years ahead of the market (see Figure 5.3). The speed of fashion cycles and the demands of the globally connected consumer mean that fashion forecasters need to be listening, observing and responding quickly to the multiple sources of inspiration to satisfy the needs of their global clients. A fashion trend transforms the macrotrends into inspirational, creative, new product that meets the aspirations and lifestyles of consumers. By comparison to macrotrends that evolve over time, microtrends, or style/fashion trends, move much more quickly, and fashion trend forecasters need to constantly look at changes in ideas and cultural outputs in areas such as music, film, art exhibitions, travel, lifestyles and experiences. On their own, these signals are quite weak; however, when they are observed in differing consumer groups and industries, these weak signals collectively create a strong story that a trend is evolving or that a major trend is about to emerge that will affect mainstream, global markets. Forecasters can produce trend reports that have translated these cues into actionable ranges or marketing strategies for their client base. In the late 20th century, trend agencies would deliver a broad theme for a specific

**FIGURE 5.3** Illustrations of lingerie design predictions for Autumn/Winter 2025/26 by Concepts Paris. Photo with permission from Jos Berry

season, and it would be the role of the designer and the marketing team to translate these ethereal visions for their consumers and business goals. Now fashion trend forecasters need to realise trends for specific business objectives due to the volume and speed of available trend information. They must offer the right trend into the right market at the right time.

The size and scope of the global market and the diverse consumer demographics that can offer so many opportunities for fashion businesses have led to the creation of four areas of specialism in the industry that provide long-term and short-term forecasts. As with so many roles in fashion, they have become intertwined as one feeds into the other. It also worth noting that these areas offer new career opportunities in addition to the more traditional role as fashion forecaster. The four areas are Futurists, Foresights, Trend Forecasters and Consumer Insights. Futurists and Foresights specialists deal with long-term trends, and Trend Forecasters and Consumer Insights deal with more short-term opportunities.

**Futurists:** Their role is to look at the future in a very broad sense. Futurists often utilise scenario planning, trend analysis and speculative thinking to develop their insights. They might draw on a combination of quantitative data, qualitative research and expert opinions to construct plausible narratives about the future. The goal is not necessarily to predict a single, definitive outcome, but rather to offer a range of possibilities through scenarios to help individuals and organisations shape the future into what they would like it to be. An example of a leading Futurist is Andy Hines and his consultancy, Hinesight.

**Foresights:** Their role is similar to Futurists, as they too want to create an understanding about the future; however, they are often working within specific industries, and work closely with stakeholders to identify key drivers of change, assess potential future scenarios and develop strategies that enhance an organisation's future opportunities within the scope of their abilities and consumer base.

Foresights specialists might employ methodologies such as trend analysis, scenario planning and horizon scanning. Examples of agencies that offer foresights are TrendBible, WGSN and The Future Laboratory.

**Trend Forecasters:** Their role is to predict and analyse emerging trends in the fashion industry. Fashion is deeply intertwined with culture, and Trend Forecasters need a keen understanding of societal changes. This involves staying abreast of cultural, political and economic developments worldwide, taken from the long-term macrotrends. By recognising shifts in values and attitudes, Trend Forecasters can predict how these changes will manifest in fashion preferences. A strong skill employed by Trend Forecasters is creativity, to anticipate the direction that fashion, and style will take in the future. Trend Forecasters play a crucial role in helping fashion designers, retailers and brands make informed decisions about their collections, ensuring they stay relevant and appealing to consumers. Examples of agencies that offer trend forecasting services are WGSN, Fashion Snoops, Trendstop, Stylus and EDITED.

**Consumer Insights:** Consumer Insights involve the interpretation of data collected from various sources, such as market research, surveys, social media and other analytics tools. Think of Consumer Insights as the "why" behind consumer choices. It's not just about what people buy, but understanding the reasons driving those choices. Imagine it as unlocking the secret code to consumer behaviour, helping businesses tailor their products and strategies to better match what people truly want and need. It is generally accepted that businesses which invest in understanding their consumers are more likely to succeed. In the realm of fashion trends, Consumer Insights are crucial – e.g., understanding the growing preference for sustainable and ethically produced fashion helps brands align with consumer values. Brands and retailers continuously collect quantitative and qualitative data about their own consumers, and these insights help fashion forecasters identify the right trend for their consumer base.

## The Role of a Fashion Forecaster

Many trends can now co-exist within a season. The role of the forecaster is to ensure that the cultural and social sources they look to for inspiration are signalling a trend that will fulfil the emotional and aspirational needs of a consumer or group of consumers. Therefore, the process starts by evaluating the changes that have already started to happen in the many diverse global cultural fields such as music, art, catwalks, streetwear and cultural spaces such as social media, blogs and online communities. This process is often referred to as "cultural brailling" by trend practitioners in the industry. The fashion forecaster takes these sources of research and transforms them into narratives that will inform future trends.

Fashion forecasting has traditionally been used predominantly by the fashion industry; however, fashion trends have cross-disciplinary benefits. In 2016, the client list for WGSN was broken down as follows: 60% were retailers and fashion brands, 20% were manufacturers, and 20% were from industries outside the fashion sphere, including advertising, interiors, cosmetics, technology and the car industry (Lantz, 2016). Much of the future growth for subscriptions and consultancy work for leading trend agencies is predicted to be in areas such as beauty, consumer tech, and consumer insight (Taylor, 2023). This illustrates the broad influence of fashion on lifestyles and product, as colour direction and fabrics from future trends can be absorbed into car interiors, or the patterns from another trend can be used on phone covers in the next two years. Cross-cultural analysis also comes into play when the fashion forecaster is looking at the connections of influence in other industries to the trends they are developing.

The formats and presentation of trend research can take many forms. All trend teams, either in-house within a design department or from an agency, produce mood boards that offer direction for future product trends with colour, fabric, print or graphics and silhouette direction (see Figure 5.4). These will be created for specific categories such as apparel, accessories, intimate apparel, sportswear or footwear. Trend teams will also produce forecasts on categories such as men's knit

**FIGURE 5.4** Mood board for Autumn/Winter 2024/25 by Concepts Paris. Photo with permission from Jos Berry

and jersey, footwear and accessory materials, and in specialist areas such as denim fabrics and their wash and finish. Alongside the directional images, the trend teams will present sketches, termed as black and white "flats", that summarise the key shapes that represent the direction the product will take. More details of the process are outlined in the next section. Marketing, buying and merchandising departments look for reports that track trends that have been delivered into the market that are generating data on sales and competitor activity and their range or line plan strategies. These are often referred to as buyers' briefings.

Trend agencies tend to develop the long-term forecasts, the macrotrends, with details of the shifts in the global market that are driving the trends, the innovations that the trends have already triggered in the fashion industry as well as other industries outside of the fashion sector, and suggestions of how to realise the trends in future products, marketing or business models. Agencies also compile reports from all the major fashion shows, textile or yarn shows and fashion trade exhibitions. These are invaluable for fashion companies which do not have the budget in their development cycles to attend them. Some agencies also produce cultural guides from their observations from intelligence they compile from global cities that are developing their own contributions to the arts through the creation of elements of culture such as unique exhibitions, retail experiences, streetwear or music festivals.

Both agencies and in-house design teams will monitor the lifestyles and expectations of their consumers. Trend agencies will develop consumer trend reports, such as the digital expectations of Generation Z in two to five years' time in China, for example. The in-house design team will produce consumer insight reports on the current behaviours and lifestyles of their consumer base, and use these as a starting point to anticipate their future needs. Large retailers and brands buy into the longer-term consumer trend forecasts offered by leading trend agencies to confirm their own insights or use them to identify new consumer groups that are emerging that align with their values and product offers. An agency's consumer trend reports are also an invaluable asset if a company is planning to launch in a new country where the company has limited experience or access to intelligence on the expectations of country's consumer groups. This helps brands or retailers to adjust their product offers, marketing approaches and/or manufacturing bases to minimise the risks associated with international expansion.

## Identifying Creative Opportunities: The In-house Design and Trend Agencies Approach

As stated previously, trend teams can be found in-house within many brands and fashion retailers. The design department which creates the trend intelligence for their markets and consumers works in tandem with the buying department and manufacturing bases at the company's head office. This approach allows the design team to incorporate consumer insights into its interpretation of the trends that will fit with the customer's values and lifestyles. Creating the trends alongside the buying and product development teams also ensures that the product can be realised within the timescales and resources of the company. A fast fashion company can react to trends quickly because it has a responsive manufacturing system in place and can realise product in-store within six to eight weeks in some cases, whereas other retailers focus on a "speed to market" principle and can respond within four to six months. Brands which do not have a distribution system, such as their own retail stores or transactional websites, need retail partners to sell their products on their behalf. Therefore, they must plan ranges one to two years ahead of delivery as they use the predictions of the number of sales per collection that are calculated by heads of marketing, buying or sales in their key markets using the consumer insights they have generated from their past and current sales data. Many in-house design departments from fashion, lifestyle and textile companies also subscribe to trend information from trend agencies as this allows them to review the agency's trend predictions against their own to support their interpretation of future colour, fabric, and design direction. In some cases, the trend agency is employed on a consultancy basis to decode the major trends for the market in the short term, or to give additional direction for product and marketing when the company is looking to extend its offer into new categories or new markets globally in the long term (see Figure 5.5).

**FIGURE 5.5** TrendBible includes consultancy services for leading global brands. © TrendBible

Within a trend agency, the timing and format of trend intelligence to develop fashion product are varied to accommodate the needs of its client base, such as timescales and diverse consumer bases, as outlined previously. Trend agencies offer a variety of services, such as general trend direction for delivery to consumers in one to two years' time for colour, fibre and fabric, and print and graphic direction, followed by trends for specific segments of the market, such as street style or sportswear, and for the larger retailers or brands which have teams that deal with specific categories, the trends are applied to silhouettes such as dresses or knitwear in specific markets such as men's wear or women's wear. As the fashion market has evolved and become more competitive, the need to track trends mid-season has become important for many mainstream retailers. The development of algorithms and the generation of big data by some agencies (e.g., EDITED and Trendalytics) have given companies the option to review the success of drops and sell-outs of not just their own ranges or categories, but those of their competitors, in real time. This is starting to replace the traditional, human-generated comparative shop report (comp shop) with accurate and instantly accessible data (see Chapter 2).

For both approaches to trend development, either in-house or trend agency, many work to similar timelines. Colour palette confirmation is needed by the manufacturers, retailers and brands 12–24 months prior to the selling season as the need to develop colour batches and dyes in time is crucial. Brands and retailers can confirm the colour palettes internally for their own markets. Textile mills also buy into the trend reports to be more proactive in the development process, to ensure they are creating their own innovative product in time for the season/s ahead. The next stage is confirming the fibres that will be used to develop the key fabrics for future seasons. Yarn shows are often 10–14 months ahead of the selling season, and textile fairs around 12 months. Both trend forecasters and in house designers visit yarn fairs, such as *Pitti Immagine Filati* in Florence, as well as fabric and knitwear fairs such as *Texworld* or *Première Vision* in Paris to confirm any new directions or innovations available for sampling (see Figure 5.6). With an indication of colour palettes already in place, it's also an opportunity for the teams to look at print and graphic directions that have been created for that season by leading mills or textile designers.

Important elements of research for trends are catwalks and garment fairs. Analysis of the fashion weeks in New York, London, Milan and Paris gives silhouette and design direction for many trends, but other trade fairs such as *Pitti Uomo, Copenhagen Fashion Week, MAGIC Las Vegas* or specialist trade fairs such as *ISPO* (sportswear), and *Interfilière* in Paris (lingerie and swimwear) are also key sources of trend direction and vital in confirming elements of colour, print and shape for future ranges (see Figure 5.7). Budget and time constraints with many in-house design and buying teams have given trend agencies the opportunity to attend and produce reports from trade fairs and offer these to their clients.

**FIGURE 5.6** Yarn and fabric exhibition stands. Photos by Francois Durand, with permission from Première Vision

## Trend Agencies as an Asset to Creativity and Innovation

An advantage to outsourcing trend direction to agencies is the scope of research into cultural change that they can make available to their clients. The agencies employ multiple trend spotters, often referred to as "cool hunters", in most global markets, who map changes in culture and feed these back. They look for signals that there are innovations or new ideas developing within their markets, predominantly in urban areas that are breaking away from current cultural norms such as new art forms or employment of technology or even luxury dining experiences that are emerging from diverse global markets. Trend agencies pool these cultural clues and use these

**FIGURE 5.7** Jos Berry and colleagues forecast colour and fabric trends. Photos with permission from Jos Berry

to map new trends, either short-term or long-term, that have the potential to transform the lifestyles or product needs of mainstream markets.

Smaller brands and designers often do not have the funds to access the trend information that larger brands and retailers include in their market development strategy, or simply choose not to. This may seem contradictory to the trend identification system that many fashion companies have adopted. Entrepreneurial brands and designers that sit on the outside of the mainstream system are often motivated to push against the current trends that are flowing through mainstream markets or simply rely on their intuition and what they feel would appeal to a smaller, more innovative consumer group. The role that these "outsiders" play is important, as this is where new ideas and new fashion directions emerge from, and the fashion cycle is triggered again. This is a key point to make, as there has been criticism that an over-reliance on trend forecasting services has resulted in a "copycat" approach to the trends themselves, rather than a starting point of inspiration for creating innovative product that meets the consumer's future aspirations (Hesse, 2014). There need to be those who want to challenge the cultural norms from the bottom up and develop a counter-offer. Although the entrepreneurial designers and brands may not have looked to a trend agency for inspiration, these small-scale designers are an important source of research for trend agencies, as observing these innovators on the edge of the system are the ones that drive new trends that the trend agency will monitor for future trends.

In some instances, a trend agency as an external resource, employed on a consultancy basis can help overcome the barriers to developing innovative new product or communication approaches within a brand or retailer. In more mainstream markets, trend agencies can translate the potential of trends across multiple departments to limit the tension between design and marketing. The goal for both functions is to realise the potential of the trends within the company's market to increase profits, avoid stock-outs, and offer ranges and an approach that sit with the consumer's future needs, lifestyle and buying behaviour.

Marketing and design are motivated by differing goals. The first is the concept of time. Designers want to shape the future, forget the past and imagine the potential of future scenarios through the designs they want to create, whereas marketing tends to think in terms of shorter timescales, and what customers have said in the past and what they are saying now will dictate what they need in the future (Beverland et al., 2016). Design wants to create demand; marketing is motivated to meet demand. In addition, the language that differing specialisms use can exclude their colleagues from other departments from their thought worlds and create confusion in understanding the motivation for their approach to an opportunity (Beverland et al., 2016). As an external resource, a trend agency acts as a mediator between the two thought worlds by translating the trend into the appropriate language using quantitative (statistics) and qualitative data (text-based research). In addition, trend agencies have the reassurance of an extensive global research base, a global client base, often including the client's competitors, and multiple data-driven assets, including in-season trend tracking to evaluate the impact of the trend adopted against the client's competitors.

## The Future of Forecasting: A New Era of Consumer-driven Innovation

Definition of the word "trend" is becoming more flexible. "Big data", a term used to describe very large data sets, is creating more opportunities for fashion, and the industry is moving more towards data-driven insights to predict trends in certain scenarios. Advanced algorithms can collect and process data from multiple sources at great speed, and present data sets in varied formats, such as financial transactions or online consumer behaviour.

Rather than solely predicting trends based on the intuition of the trend forecaster, it is going to be the role of more trend agencies and creatives to monitor and report on the trends that are developing on, say, social media in varied markets, select the ones that will be relevant for their brand or chosen market and include these in their trend predictions. Looking at innovators in the creative industries and cultural developments in the arts for inspiration is now no longer enough, as trends are also being created by the consumers themselves. Trend agencies have already started to adapt their methodologies to generate insights about the digitally savvy e-commerce consumer (Bendoni, 2017). WGSN now offers an INstock service, and EDITED has created a trend service based on new AI technology that is quite unique in the sector. Heuritech offers big data and AI by analysing millions of social media images daily, using tailored consumer panels, and using its algorithm to generate the key fashion colours, prints and fabrics (Heuritech, 2023).

Although there are opportunities to utilise multiple data sets in fashion forecasting, the industry sectors that need to be able to predict demand with such accuracy to maximise profits are those with short product life cycles due to very fashion-aware consumers and responsive supply and manufacturing systems. Fast-fashion retailers benefit from the real-time data created from user-generated content on social media and their consumers' product reviews, in addition to the sales, stock outs, promotional activity and reductions that their buying behaviour creates. This data can be invaluable in building a current and future strategy. This is achieved by analysing the views, shares, discussions and images that have been generated by their core consumer base (Rudniy et al., 2023). There does, of course, need to be a balance maintained between a data-driven and creative approach to trend development. Generalisations generated by big data have their place, but the thoughts and feelings of consumers are fragile by comparison, and generalisations cannot be made from emotions and opinions. DuBreuil and Lu (2020) recognised the limitations of big data in trend predictions, as a consumer's need for innovative and inspiring design is complex and unpredictable. Using a more intuitive approach in fashion forecasting allows for more creative interpretation, and crucially for a lot of brands, will offer more opportunity to maintain a brand's image and integrity when using the trend as their source of inspiration (DuBreuil & Lu, 2020).

## Summary

Fashion forecasting has evolved from predicting trends based on a centralised source of creativity and innovation to multiple sources of inspiration. In addition, fashion forecasters must look at long-term trends, or macrotrends, to uncover long-term market opportunities to innovate for the future needs of their diverse, global consumers. Short-term trends take the signals from the macrotrends and translate them into inspirational, creative trends that meet the aspirations and lifestyles of consumers. Fashion forecasting roles can be in-house in the design department or be created by external trend agencies. The future of forecasting is becoming more challenging with the advent of AI-generated big data and the active role consumers play in creating trends. Future fashion forecasting will need a balance of quantitative research extracted from big data and consumer insights, as well as the qualitative approach taken by Futurists and Foresights specialists. Trend forecasters can translate these rich sources of market and consumer intelligence into the right fashion trends for an increasingly complex, diverse global marketplace

**FIGURE 5.8**  Fran Sheldon, left, and a student presentation, right. Photos with permission from Fran Sheldon

## Interviews with Fashion Forecasters

**Fran Sheldon is currently a Lecturer in Responsible Fashion Management at the London College of Fashion, developing teaching and research around Fashion Futures, Sustainability, and Market Analysis. Fran gained an MA in Fashion Promotion and Imaging from the University of the Creative Arts, UK. Before working in higher education, Fran was Head of Education at EDITED (Retail Data Analytics), and designed and launched the online education platform and accreditation for fashion retail professionals. Fran is part of the Education Committee for Fashion Roundtable.**

*In what ways have you been involved with fashion trend forecasting and big data?*

I started working at EDITED in 2016, and the area of retail data analytics was still new to the fashion industry, so it was an exciting time demonstrating the opportunity for using data in fashion retail. My role as Head of Education meant I was able to work directly with students at fashion schools to adopt data analysis in their research, as well as working with departments within retailers to better understand how to use data alongside traditional concepting techniques. My time at EDITED resulted in the formation of a certification programme which was specifically developed to help clients utilise data-driven insights from trading decisions to concept development. My education work was also centred around "data sympathy", which is about understanding how information is collected, classified and presented. AI learning models are different from the human brain, so it is important for users to know how to navigate that difference and how to combine intuition, experience and data together. Even in the short time I was working at EDITED, I witnessed the app learning and improving, partly in machine learning capability, but also with the creation of new features, specifically designed in collaboration with clients. When I changed career and entered academia, I continued to bring my knowledge and enthusiasm for data tools into the curriculum because I felt this was still lacking in many fashion management programmes. My goal was, and still is, to empower the fashion experts of the future to feel confident using data alongside their intuition.

*How does big data feed into trend forecasting? Is it used more to develop future trends or for tracking delivered trends?*

I think the two approaches work well together, and probably at an entry-level exposure to a data tool, the first experience might be in tracking the trend. Product performance data is key to understanding how the trend is emerging, evolving, developing and diminishing. That kind of insight is an asset to brands and retailers, to gauge when and how to engage with a trend. From this you get a robust trend life cycle viewpoint. Simple indicators like sell-outs, new-in products, and discount depth and breadth, when viewed in aggregate over time and via an easy-to-navigate interface, is highly valuable. I think a more advanced use of data comes from being familiar with the life cycle data over a long period of time. Super-users at EDITED gain so much from long-term exposure and familiarity with the tool, so that they start to recognise patterns in the data and have become attuned to the way products are moving to assess emerging behaviours and detect early change. So, combined with the more traditional methods of forecasting in recognising and sensing change, users benefit from the ability to look backwards and forwards all at once.

*What are the advantages for your clients in the trend process to look at big data to create innovative product?*

I think, interestingly, when you're using retail data in an immediate way, perhaps in the trading phase, you are primarily focusing on accuracy; minimising risk and maximising opportunity, and again I think this is a great use of data as a starting point. To create innovative product, you can also introduce data insights into the creative process by including the perspective of the consumer into the concepting phase. The data is an advocate for the consumer within the creative process, and I think that changes the development of product. In a way, it becomes more of a conversation, or a moderation between consumer and designer, and we can consider what is the consumer interested in? What are the trends that are emerging that we may have missed? I think using consumer-generated data from an inspirational point of view like that, to combine two inspiration sources, then that's where innovation can come from.

*How and where is the data sourced that is used to develop fashion trends?*

This is one of the main interesting aspects about working with big data that I really enjoyed from my days at EDITED, and even now when teaching about big data systems. The data for most retail data analytics platforms will come primarily from product data that comes directly from retailers' sites into EDITED, and that's what creates big data. Crucially, it's coming in at real time in the case of EDITED. You're able to get a day-by-day view of what's changing, which completely transforms the traditional idea of processes like the comparative shop, for example. Big data is impressive, but the real innovation comes from what you can do with the data through classifying it and presenting it through interactive and easy-to-use data visualisations. The EDITED product team work closely with the in-house fashion experts and client intelligence to classify the data into different product categories, as it can recognise, for example, a trainer versus an espadrille. So there's a lot of work that goes on behind the scenes with the data and developer expertise. This SAAS [software as a service] model means that although insight reports are a key part of the service, the main purpose of the tool is to provide real-time, easily accessible data for retail experts to navigate and personalise for their specific operational needs. The Customer Success team at EDITED ensures that the customer understands how to use the data and best ways to achieve what they want from the tool. It's a completely revolutionary service model for insights for the fashion industry, and quite different from report repository and consultancy models.

*Which brands or retailers do you think are drawn to trends that include big data? Is it at all industry levels?*

Naturally, mass market retailers tend to be more drawn to big data because of the pressure on speed-to-market in a super-competitive and crowded market, and the loaded risk that inaccuracy has on smaller margins. So whilst mass market retailers have tended to be the early adopters of data, most brands now depend on improving their accuracy and pace, from luxury all the way down to budget. In the past decade, we've witnessed the decline of a seasonal model toward a "drop" model inspired by streetwear hype-brands; now couple this with a general decline in customer loyalty, and the interest in big data insights has really taken off. The past decade has also been defined by a global supply chain crisis, so it's really no surprise that accuracy has become a recurrent strategic concern to minimise the issues like "bullwhip" (BoF McKinsey & Co., 2023) that have been problematic for so many companies across the sector.

Employees at all head office levels have a use case for big data. The great thing about most big data-based retail analytics companies like EDITED is it's not just the data that's provided. There's also reports with data presented in an easy to digest way. These are often a staple of weekly trading (sales figures) meetings, and useful for department leaders to gain an overall perspective on their category. Those that tend to work directly in the analytics screens are the trading teams and planners, so often buyers and merchandisers, but also visual merchandisers and marketing teams, so they can understand performance from a communications perspective as well. Trend reports are created continuously. There will be trend reports created around runway analysis as well as retail reports, and many will combine multiple insight leads. Retail reports can happen multiple times within a week because the data is real-time, so there's always something quite interesting to observe. So one day you might have a buyer's guide for children's footwear, and then a day later it might be men's wear trousers. The analysts are working on a cycle of these reports, keeping on top of the analysis for each category on a timely basis. The fashion industry works to an operational model which combines creativity with commerciality, so there is a distinct need to balance foresight and insight, especially between buyers and merchandisers; adding data into the creative vision can help mediate these discussions.

*How do you feel tracking social media as a source of big data will work in the future?*

I think it's probably going to be similar to when product data came in and disrupted the traditional forecasting and insights method, so it may further amplify the ability to detect

change. Social listening has always been a part of the research, of course but the ability to aggregate this in with product performance data has been an exciting development. I am particularly interested in the evolution of social media and influencer culture towards micro communities. A lot of forecasters and consumer analysts have done a lot of great work in understanding communities, so being able to track these behaviours and quantify them at a more nuanced and micro level is important, especially details like how products are being defined and styled. A universally accepted truth by futurists is that the future is plural. When you talk to most trend forecasters and futurists and scenario planners, they talk about this idea of the scope of change in that sense. Big data is really a helpful tool for understanding that plurality and understanding from the consumer perspective that lots of multiple things can be happening all at once, all at the same time, all in the same demographic and region. The ability to track that all at once can be difficult from a sensing, intuiting perspective, so if we add the two together, data and intuitive forecasting, I think that's where we can uncover some fantastic social driven insights.
https://edited.com/

*Interview by Carol Cloughton*

## Reference

Business of Fashion, McKinsey and Company (2023) "The year ahead: Mapping the next wave of supply chain pressures", *Business of Fashion*, 12 December 2023, available online at: The Year Ahead: Mapping the Next Wave of Supply Chain Pressures | BoF (businessoffashion.com)

**Jos Berry is the CEO of Concepts Paris, a company producing body fashion design intelligence for industry professionals, which she established in 1990. After an art-focused education, whilst working as a textile trade journalist Jos researched the lingerie-buying attitudes of women, and later became a consultant for lingerie firms and the *Salon de la Lingerie* and *Interfilière* trade shows in Paris.**

*How would you summarise the creative and innovative work that you do?*

It's a combination of knowledge and inspiration. I need to inspire people, and within that inspiration, where you are coming from becomes more and more important. Inspiration and knowledge are what I would say they expect from me. A big part of my work is based on what I would do if I was in the shoes of a client, and you have to realise what inspires them. We have seen over the years that the majority of our client base are fabric manufacturers.

*How do you find creative inspiration for trends?*

What has inspired me the most was when I was a journalist for a professional trade paper, and they asked me to research women and lingerie in the early 1970s, when there was also

**FIGURE 5.9**  Jos Berry in her Paris studio and with colleagues at a trade show. *Photos with permission from Jos Berry*

the schism related to changed attitude and changed mentality of women, in such a way that they had difficulties with the rather arrogant attitude of salespeople in lingerie shops. In a time of emancipation, that group of women, the baby boomers, came of age, they wanted their own lives, and they had really had enough of being told, "That's how we do it." That's when I realised that women in general, when it comes to their bodies, are insecure, and it has nothing to do with taste. It has something to do with their emotions and with the urge to feel at ease with themselves. I found this social-psychological link with fashion very interesting, because I was related in fashion to Trend Agency, which looked only at street fashion and what designers did, and then linked their predictions to that. In lingerie, that was not at all the case. You had to really cleverly understand how women were thinking, and that made it very interesting and a rich area of research and trending. It was not surprising that when COVID started and women were again focused on their own strength basically to survive, that the whole discussion started again, so it's funny that in very specific times in history like, for instance, the 20s and the 30s where women suddenly discovered a new way of being and then in the 60s and 70s when they again talked about a new being, with an enormous crisis in the economy and very often they go together. It's shaking women up to their core, because women, in my opinion, remain insecure, they are still not, in a society which is masculine, helped to know who they are, and perhaps that insecurity makes them so fantastically resilient.

A lot of what we are doing is based on a sort of memory of style, of beauty, of things that happened already, and then the next step, of course, is technology, which at this moment is overriding in a big way on all kinds of levels. For example, in our current work in-house, we just had a discussion and we feel that there is an enormous longing for the comeback of the real French lingerie style that I'm calling "beauty", and then we say, "Why is that and how can we do that?", which is a very important discussion about how that look would be able to be sold online where everything is based on visuals. If the delicateness is not communicated, you can't do it at the moment, so there are different elements playing roles, so now we are looking at French style in a completely different way. We are looking at graphical, strong statements in materials or in shape.

*What is the creative process in your company when compiling trend packages?*

There is a creative process, and since we are specialised in thinking about this constantly, we know our biggest clients' needs and that they have dates when they need to have the next spark. Timing is an important part, but in general we constantly think about it, and being involved on so many levels as a specialist with our clients makes it easier if you have a lot of experience in saying what will and won't work. The next phase is a gathering of a group of people who work in luxury fashion. It used to be in Paris, in a place where we all came together with little pieces of fabric and ideas to start the season, and it is now online. This is a blessing in disguise, because it has become international, whereas in the past it was organised twice a year by the team that owns the lingerie trade fair in Paris or the famous Fédération de la Lingerie, the big brands who have their own federation. This is what we call the "consultation de la couleur". It used to be only very colour-based, but now, of course, colours without materials, without communication, don't work. It has become much more broad in its observation, and we talk with specialists there, which used to be a majority French affair, but now it's very international. We invite people who are really important in their work. Of course, fashion trends and creativity have become a very multinational affair. That is the beginning where we come together, basically saying what everybody thinks is happening with trends. We gather all that together and say, "Okay, this is the logic of the world around us plus what everybody wants. These are the logical and inspired directions." We wait until that presentation to decide our trends for our own companies, then that information is given to my team, who then start to look, to think and to sketch.

There is an enormous influence at the moment of artificial intelligence. AI is in the line of 3D design, which is starting an enormous discussion, because according to some people, it's killing creativity. I see it as a problem-solver, because in our international world it's a new way to process the data and the whole communication internationally. Everybody talks about it, but I don't see it replacing the designer or things like fitting or grading, and I certainly think that the way the data is processed and implemented, AI will have an enormous effect and is very interesting. Body size and the fact that stretch fabrics react are particularly important in design in our industry, and there are academics who are busy with data based on how the body moves which you can feed into a computer.

*How would you define creativity and innovation based on your own experience and knowledge in your sector?*

Creativity is a sum of deep knowledge, because it's a very technical area, and that spark of something which is unquantifiable, very emotional and instinctive also, and I believe that the more you know, the more that instinctive part of your brain is a very important thing to develop. Creativity is always based on being aware of what is happening and all that information and data processing plus emotion. In fashion at this moment, creativity is very much driven by money and needs. Designers are creating things that can be part of their promotional or their entertaining communication, because fashion is currently very much part of entertainment.

https://saloninternationaldelalingerie.com/evolutions-2025/

*Interview by Helen Goworek*

**Jo Feeley is the founder and Chief Executive of TrendBible, a trend consultancy which is a leading authority on the future of life at home, established in 2006. Jo studied BA (Hons) Fashion Design at Kingston University, UK, and subsequently pursued a career in fashion, where she was engaged as a trend consultant for multiple global clients, as well as working directly with leading brands such as American Eagle and the Arcadia Group.**

*How does TrendBible work in practice?*

We forecast the future of life at home, mainly for brands, retailers, but also for investors and charities, and even more recently, for the National Crime Agency! Any company that wants to know about how householders will live in the future at home. We have a blended business model, so it's part agency, part publisher and part subscription. We have three verticals: consultancy, subscription and standalone individual forecasts. We have global corporate clients that include brands, retailers, charities and organisations. We have a global network of trend scouts who ping us intel every day to our Slack[1] app, and we host eight expert

**FIGURE 5.10**  Jo Feeley. Photo with permission from Jo Feeley

panels a year to speak with researchers, academics and foresight specialists; from these we craft seasonal forecasts for some of the world's best-known brands.

*What inspired you to start TrendBible?*

I decided I wanted to leave the fashion industry when I was consulting for Tesco. It was at the time when something like 50 pence in every pound was being spent in Tesco in the UK. It was a massive company. Consumers were motivated to buy ten T-shirts for, say, £2 each, as it was all about "buy as much as you can" rather than buy one T-shirt for £10 at a better quality. It was all about having more. It didn't sit well with me, and it was one of the reasons why I wanted to start thinking about moving to something a little bit more sustainable. So that was the point when I started to think, if I want to work as a trend forecaster, how else might I use my skills? And I started to look at the market where I might apply trend forecasting to, and there was an opportunity in the home and interiors sector. Over time, it became more about the future of home rather than furniture and the interior, to the point where we weren't being asked about the next cushion colour or what would be the next motif that might go on some bedding. It was more about "Can you help us figure out what fence paint should we be producing given that more women than ever are getting involved in DIY and what kind of colour palette should we develop to offer her?" As lifestyles have become more diverse, so have the opportunities to predict them. There's even a travel trend forecasting agency now.

*How would you define consumer insights and foresights, based on your experience and knowledge of trend forecasting in the lifestyle and fashion markets?*

There are people who work in futures, people who work in foresight, people who work in insight, and then there are trend forecasters. We are in the business of foresight and forecasting, really. Insights, on the other hand, is more qualitative and quantitative customer research. We have a lot of clients who work in consumer insight, and they gather customer data to inform their view of what their customer thinks. For example, one global toy company we work with have an internal consumer insight team that spend their year traveling around the world speaking to children about how they play, and see what their family life looks like. They develop a set of data from their research and use this to really understand who their consumer is for future developments. When you are trend forecasting, you plot in a line of something that's happened already, and then you project what might happen next. At TrendBible, we do some trend forecasting, but we use foresight as well. With trend forecasting, we see something is happening, and we see it building statistically – as an example, we see more people have bought camper vans since 2019, and the number is increasing. The Google search for "van life" is going up year on year, so we can trend forecast against that and say when we think it's going to hit the curve and become relevant in key markets.

We use foresight as well, which is developing a hypothesis about where the trend will go. It's not just using the data to project forward. I think that's probably quite an important distinction to make. Having a blueprint for the future is super-helpful for any company that has a two-year or more development cycle. For example, we work with kitchen appliance manufacturers and companies like laundry detergent manufacturers who have complex chemistry and rigorous testing to do to a launch a new product safely, and baby car seat, stroller and mattress manufacturers who have lots of safety and environmental testing to fit in their process, so it takes years to get to market. They really need to know what will be shaping their customers' tastes, values and behaviours in two to five years' time, so foresight is an essential tool to help them get that future blueprint.

*How important do you think trends are to developing creative and innovative solutions for your clients?*

Our job is to paint a picture of the future and work with companies to find out what a preferable future looks like for them as a business. Trend forecasting as a discipline leans much more towards foresight these days, as companies want to use trends to set themselves apart rather than all look the same. Originality matters more after decades of copying. The pace of change now has had an impact on large corporations who can't get behind copying another company quickly enough to be relevant. So it's better to do something original instead, and trend forecasting helps you understand the context of the future you'll be trading in in two years' time.

*Where and how do you and the team find sources of inspiration for your trend development?*

We have developed our own RISE™ model that is our research framework and ensures we're collecting data points and "weak signals" across four key pillars that influence life at home: Relationships, Identity, Society and Environment. There are category breakdowns underneath all of these, and we have trend scouts all over the world collecting "weak signals" of any changes in these areas and filtering them in through Slack, the app. Weak signals are examples of a new attitude or value system or value starting to emerge. They are indications that change is happening, but we would never develop a trend based on one weak signal. We would always cluster together weak signals from lots of different areas to give the trend a stable base. That reassures us that the trend is broadly referenced across a number of different industries, not just one, so we are constantly looking for something interesting that might be happening in global markets that signifies that people's values or the way they want to shop has changed. It can start with a change in a consumer's attitude that is driven by a shift in their thoughts and feelings. We start to recognise those indicators, and that would be the beginning of our process. It's our job to make sure we pay attention to the right weak signals and put these together. We are 24/7 brailling society and culture for these changes, and my team's job is to cluster them and find the meaning. There may be thousands of these "weak signals" popping up at any moment, and the team need to make sense of this for our clients, track the pace of forthcoming change, and look at which markets and audiences have appetite for a new trend first.

*In what ways do your clients use your trend services in their product development and overall business models?*

We have some clients who use trend forecasts at a strategic level among senior execs, and some who are more vice president or design director level who want to feel informed about the change that's coming and how it will impact their business and customer. Also marketing teams use trends really well to read the social mood and craft good marketing messages – but often they can afford to work to a closer deadline than two years. As a general rule, our long-term trend forecasts are within about five years and the shorter term is two years. However, we have already been asked twice in the last year to do a ten-year forecast. Sometimes there are certain teams inside certain companies that will have an appetite for a ten-year forecast, and when we do create one, we use a completely different set of methodologies to produce it because the trend forecasting method isn't useful at that point. You need to be in that foresight and futures approach, like developing scenario plans. You might develop between ten and 12 different scenarios, and the motivation for this long-term projection is what would a preferred future look like for that brand: what would we like to choose for ourselves, and how could we make that happen? So yes, we do get asked for ten-year forecasts, but it's usually a really particular kind of projection. Not all companies have the stomach for it, as they don't all have the ability to act on what you predict so far ahead.

Our customers that want a five-year forecast are companies like kitchen manufacturers, appliance manufacturers, vacuum cleaners or microwave ovens, carpets: companies that have products with a slower shelf life, as you expect the home sector to have products that sit with the customer for a much longer period than fashion. With fashion, you only ever need that product to physically last for six months to a year, to a couple of years maximum for some people, and for some customers that might only be six weeks, it might be something that they only want to wear and be seen in once. That's not the case with home interiors, where you're dealing with an audience that wants something to still look contemporary and relevant in about ten years' time. With a kitchen, consumers used to expect a kitchen to last 20 to 25 years. Now consumers expect their kitchen to last about ten years from an aesthetic perspective as they realise that after ten years the aesthetic they desire will alter, and they'll want something different. So they will want to be able to change it in some way: maybe they take the doors off, but leave the cabinets in place. So they want to have the option be able to amend and update it, the aesthetics in line with their lifestyles, their changes.

We ask ourselves where is somebody in their householder journey? Are they off to university for the first time and they're taking their first set of cutlery? Are they first-time homeowners, where they want something affordable, but that does the job well? Are they second- or third-time homeowners, where they're making an investment for their lifetime home? Are they retiring and they're down-sizing and they want things to be practical and compact, but maybe want the quality to be better? So there are different considerations versus fashion, as it drives a completely different set of behaviours.

*Is there anything else you'd like to add in relation to foresights, forecasting and consumer insights and the industry generally?*

Insights give you a good picture of what's happening *now* with your customer, but it isn't foresight, which helps you explore what might happen *next*, because allegedly, as the great Henry Ford once said, if you asked customers what they wanted, they'd have said faster horses. Insight isn't a good place to exclusively forecast from; you need to use foresight and future methodologies like scenario planning to unlock opportunity.

*Interview by Carol Cloughton*

## Note

1 The Slack app is a communication tool used by companies to give real-time access to co-workers to the right information to collaborate, to share messages and media, or to live chat.

## References

Bendoni, W.K. (2017) *Social Media For Fashion Marketing: Storytelling in a Digital World*, London: Bloomsbury Visual Arts. http://dx.doi.org/10.5040/9781474233347.ch-003

Beverland, M.B., Micheli, P. and Farrelly, F.J. (2016) 'Resourceful sensemaking: Overcoming barriers between marketing and design in NPD', *Journal of Product Innovation Management*, 33(5), 628–648. https://doi.org/10.1111/jpim.12313

BOF Team, McKinsey & Company (2023) The Year Ahead: Mapping the Next Wave of Supply Chain Pressures, *Business of Fashion*, 12 December, available online at: https://www.businessoffashion.com/articles/retail/the-state-of-fashion-2024-report-bullwhip-effect-supply-chain-volatility-manufacturing-consumer-demand/#:~:text=This%20turmoil%20is%20known%20as,yarn%20and%20raw%20material%20suppliers

Crane, D. (1999) 'Diffusion Models and Fashion: A Reassessment', *The Annals of the American Academy of Political and Social Science*, 566, pp. 13–24, available online at: https://search.ebscohost.com/login.aspx?direct=true&AuthType=ip,shib&db=edsjsr&AN=edsjsr.1048839&site=eds-live&scope=site

Crane, D. and Bovone, L. (2006) 'Approaches to material culture: The sociology of fashion and clothing', *Poetics*, 34, 319–333.

Crowley, A. and Farr, E.V. (2023) 'Ascential unit attracts at least two bids as other buyers drop out', *Reuters*, 28th June 2023, available online at: https://www.reuters.com/markets/deals/ascential-unit-attracts-least-two-bids-other-buyers-drop-out-sources-2023-06-28/

Divita, L.R. (2019) *Fashion Forecasting*, New York: Bloomsbury Academic.

DuBreuil, M. and Lu, S. (2020) 'Traditional vs. big-data fashion trend forecasting: An examination using WGSN and EDITED', *International Journal of Fashion Design, Technology and Education*, 13(1), 68–77, available online at: https://search.ebscohost.com/login.aspx?direct=true&AuthType=ip,shib&db=edsbl&AN=vdc.100102644983.0x000001&site=eds-live&scope=site

Field, G.A. (1970) 'The status float phenomenon', *Business Horizons*, 13(4), 45. https://doi.org/10.1016/0007-6813(70)90157-6

Gaimster, J. (2012) 'The changing landscape of fashion forecasting', *International Journal of Fashion Design, Technology and Education*, 5(3), 169–178. https://doi.org/10.1080/17543266.2012.689014

Garcia, C.C. (2021) 'Fashion forecasting: An overview from material culture to industry', *Journal of Fashion Marketing and Management: An International Journal*, 26(3), 436–451. https://doi.org/10.1108/JFMM-11-2020-0241

Heuritech. (2023) 'Quantify and predict what people wear with the power of AI', *Heuritech*, available online at: https://www.heuritech.com

Hesse, J. (2014) 'Top fashion entrepreneur slam 'Lazy, Copycat' fashion designers', *Forbes Magazine*, 29th August 2014, available online at: https://www.forbes.com/sites/jasonhesse/2014/08/29/top-fashion-entrepreneur-slams-lazy-copycat-fashion-designers/?sh=631582b11611

Kim, E., Fiore, A.M., Payne, A. and Kim, H. (2021) *Fashion Trends: Analysis and Forecasting*. London: Bloomsbury Visual Arts.

Lantz, J. (2016) *The Trendmakers: Behind the Scenes of the Global Fashion Industry*. London: Bloomsbury Academic. https://doi.org/10.1177/0094306117734868w

Renfrew, E. and Lynn, T. (2022) *Developing a Fashion Collection*. London: Bloomsbury Visual Arts.

Rudniy, A., Rudna, O. and Park, A. (2023) 'Trend tracking tools for the fashion industry: The impact of social media', *Journal of Fashion Marketing and Management*, ahead of print. https://doi.org/10.1108/JFMM-08-2023-0215

Simmel, G. (1957) 'Fashion', *American Journal of Sociology*, 62(6), 541–558. http://www.jstor.org/stable/2773129

Sproles, G. B. and Burns, L.D. (1994) *Changing Appearances: Understanding Dress in Contemporary Society*. New York: Fairchild Publications.

Taylor, N. (2023) 'WGSN owner says revenue rises, but non-fashion is growth driver', *Fashion Network*, 30th March 2023, available online at: https://ww.fashionnetwork.com/news/Wgsn-owner-says-revenue-rises-but-non-fashion-is-growth-driver,1501957.html

# 6

# Sustainability and Innovation in the Fashion Business

*Helen Goworek*

## Introduction

Creativity and innovation are central to sustainability in product development, manufacturing, retail, usage and disposal of clothing, since developing sustainable concepts can be considered a creative process. In order to create innovative, sustainable ideas, it is essential for designers and other employees in creative roles to understand sustainability, via their education or through experience in the workplace or leisure interests. Forward-thinking companies provide training and information about sustainability for their workers, offering agency to act sustainably to those involved in product development processes (Goworek et al., 2020). This chapter will assess the significance of innovation in environmental and social sustainability in the fashion sector, covering the topics of sustainability and innovation in product development, sustainability in clothing manufacture, sustainable innovations in clothing retailing, hire and exchange, and innovations in garment disposal and recycling. The chapter also features interviews with specialists in sustainability in the fashion business, offering their views on innovation.

## Overview of Sustainable Fashion Innovation and the Circular Economy

The clothing life cycle usually flows from selecting raw materials through to yarn production, fabric manufacture, product manufacture, consumption and eventual disposal of garments, with the stages mapped out in Figure 6.1. Many products may also go through additional phases such as printing. In each of these stages, which are likely to take place in different companies and possibly different countries, opportunities arise for innovation which can have positive or negative sustainability impacts on the environment or society. This life cycle is often represented as a linear process, but this model has been made circular to depict that many products

DOI: 10.4324/9781003332749-6

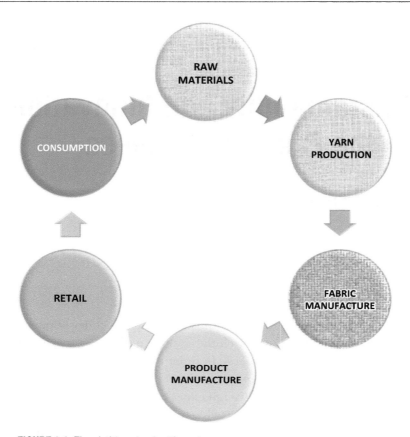

**FIGURE 6.1** The clothing circular life cycle

can be reused or recycled after use to form raw materials used in new products. Consumption – i.e., wearing and maintenance – is usually the lengthiest part of the fashion life cycle, but the degree of products' sustainability and lifespan and consumers' ability to care for their garments are greatly affected by decisions in the early stages of product development, particularly choices made by designers such as colours, fabrics, components and styling.

Sustainable garments fall into two main categories, environmentally or socially sustainable, and a limited range of products can be categorised as both. For example, garments containing recycled or organic fibres can be considered to be more environmentally sustainable as they have a reduced impact on the environment, and Fairtrade items are socially sustainable because they pay the raw materials suppliers fairly and contribute to improvements in society. Sustainable fashion plays a major part in the circular economy, which has been defined by the European Parliament (2023) as "a model of production and consumption, which involves sharing, leasing, reusing, repairing, refurbishing and recycling existing materials and products as long as possible". Reflecting the structure in Figure 6.1, the circular economy benefits from reduction of waste, and the productive reuse of products which can continue to create value in preference to being discarded. Both commercial and not-for-profit organisations, including the Ellen Macarthur Foundation (2024), promote the shift towards a more circular economy, supporting sustainability and aiming to eliminate waste and pollution. The fashion trade publication *Drapers* helps to drive sustainability in the sector by hosting an annual *Sustainable Fashion Conference* and conferring several awards to businesses, including "Sustainable Textile Innovation" and "Best Circularity Initiative" (*Drapers*, 2024). Fashion brands which can provide extensive evidence of a sustainable approach throughout their organisations and suppliers can apply for "B Corporation" (B Corp) status to demonstrate their sustainability credentials (see Head, 2023). UK-based brands Finisterre and Joanie are amongst the fashion companies which have achieved this, having undergone detailed assessments of both their environmental and social responsibility standards (see Joanie, 2024).

## Sustainability, Creativity and Innovation in Product Development

In the clothing industry, product development describes the design and preparation of goods for manufacture by selecting appropriate materials, components and design details prior to retailing these items to consumers. Gwilt and Rissanen (2011:13), who have written extensively on the topic of sustainable fashion, stress the importance of the designer's role in sustainable innovation:

> Fashion is often perceived negatively in terms of sustainability and yet one of its inherent qualities is innovation and the search for new solutions… it could be argued that the fashion design process, as it is commonly understood, should be challenged… If fashion designers do not understand what sustainable design strategies are, how to engage with them and the possibilities that they offer then they are unlikely to alter their fashion design process. It is imperative that the contemporary fashion designer sees sustainable strategies in terms of the opportunities for innovation.

## Sustainable Innovation in the Selection and Usage of Materials and Components

The materials and components used in the manufacturing of garments impact upon the environment, since resources are used and carbon emissions are created during their production. Decisions made by fashion designers, buyers and pattern-cutters are responsible for determining the amount of fabric used, which can affect the level of wastage of materials. In general, garments with lower fabric usage are likely to be more sustainable due to lower consumption of raw materials. Minimising fabric wastage is not a new concept, since this has historically been done to save money, such as the UK government's "Utility Clothing" during the 1940s. However, it is a recent innovation to minimise wastage for sustainability purposes, and the software which can be used to achieve this is innovative – e.g. digital lay-planning systems can be used to lay out garment pattern pieces as efficiently as possible (see Chapter 3). The term "frugal innovation" has been used in various other sectors, largely for technological products, and particularly for low-cost items in emerging economies, based on simplifying key functions and focusing on value (Tidd & Bessant, 2021). A frugal innovation approach can also be taken in relation to clothing in more affluent markets, with the intention of waste minimisation, rather than being driven by cost reduction, which would be very apt for a revival of the 1990s trend for minimalism.

The selection of a sustainable fabric is usually the most significant factor in defining a garment as sustainable, since it forms the majority of the product. However, fabrics are rarely produced within the same organisation as the garments, therefore clothing manufacturers or brands are dependent upon receiving reliable sources of fabric and information about its sustainability characteristics. The notion of sustainable fabrics is a relative concept, with no definitive way in which they can be categorised. The general consensus currently seems to be that a fabric which has an increased level of sustainability compared to the standard version, may be described as "sustainable", "green" or "eco" – e.g., fabrics may be made from recycled fibres or knitted from yarns created from renewable fibres. A growing area of innovation in fabrics in recent years has been in those with sustainable features. Innovative new fabrics have been developed, such as those made from pineapple fibres – e.g., Piñatex® (Ananas-anam, 2024) or mushrooms (Mylo™, 2024, as used by designer Stella McCartney) (see also Chapter 3). Such fibres are initially innovations in the textile industry which can then proceed to be considered as innovations in clothing when they are used to make garments.

Probably the best-known environmentally sustainable fabric is organic cotton, which can be cultivated without herbicides or pesticides. To be classified as organic, the cotton must contain a minimum of 70% organic fibres, as verified by Global Organic Textile Standard (GOTS), which can offer independent certification of suppliers' textile processing in both social and ecological terms (GOTS, 2024). Although producing cotton organically seemed novel and therefore innovative when it began to be popularised in the 1990s and 2000s, in a world where use of pesticides had become standard practice in agriculture, it was about returning to traditional, historical methods of plant cultivation by removing or reducing the intervention of chemicals. Another organisation which can approve the sustainability of fibres with regard to both biodiversity and employment conditions, is the Better Cotton Initiative (BCI, 2024). Certification of sustainability is important evidence for an organisation's customers, but it must be paid for and also requires time from the company's employees to arrange it, hence why sustainable garments may understandably cost more than standard clothing. However, fashion companies need to research the level of sustainability of fabrics, with fibres such as bamboo appearing to be environmentally friendly due to the plant's rapid growth, but this can depend upon the ways in which the plants are grown and the fibres are produced (Sanders, 2020).

Another traditional aspect of clothing which has gained renewed interest is durability, which can also be designed into garments in the product development phase (Goworek et al., 2020). Problems such as seam slippage, where seams can easily be pulled apart, and pilling of fibres on a fabric's surface (also called "bobbling") can be addressed when products are designed, through making choices of materials and using technical tests that can extend garments' usable lifetimes (Claxton et al., 2017). Since extending a product's life cycle is a more sustainable approach, consumers can be encouraged to buy clothing which is of good quality. However, this may not be an affordable option for many people, particularly during a cost-of-living crisis, and buying less clothing overall or purchasing second-hand garments can be the most effective ways to be sustainable. Whilst buying pre-worn clothing is not novel in itself, innovations in technology have enabled this option to become more widely available to consumers, with increased choice due to the widespread use of eBay and newer garment-focused apps such as Vinted, depop and Loanhood. These platforms help to facilitate the longevity of clothing, in that it may have an increased chance of passing through the hands of various users within its extended lifetime.

Choice of colour is usually a central decision in the design of garments. The fabric for mass market clothing is usually made to order after the garment is selected by a brand or retailer, therefore the designers have a chance to select more sustainable colours with different methods of dyeing. Textile dyeing can result in many impacts on the environment, from water pollution to chemical usage and possible health risks for textile workers (Saha, 2023). Fabric's original colour before being dyed is usually described as "greige", but the importance of having the "right" colour for a specific season or appealing to customers' tastes means that it would be unusual for fashion items to retain their natural shade. Printing is another aspect of colouration of fabrics, which involves the application of printing inks to the surface of fabric, and the chemicals used within the inks can also have sustainability impacts. Designers can request information from textile companies to help them make more sustainable choices in dyeing and printing – e.g., synthetic dyes may be more toxic than dyes from natural raw materials. Choice of colour is creative, but not innovative as such, although it can give an element of newness to clothing at a certain time. However, there have been recent technical innovations in the equipment used for dyeing, particularly in terms of improving sustainability (see Chapter 3).

Fastenings such as buttons and zips are garment components that are visible to customers, with other inner components, including interfacing and shoulder pads, being concealed within tailored clothing to enhance its structure. Designers are responsible for selecting the components which can affect garments' environmental sustainability by using renewable or non-renewable sources. Component manufacturers can respond to demand from fashion designers and technologists working for fashion brands or retailers to innovate in terms of developing new items or adapting existing items that can take sustainability into account – e.g., by using renewable or recycled materials. It is important for designers and technologists employed by fashion companies to gain understanding of sustainable innovations in fabrics and components to influence their decision-making, and for senior managers in their organisations to gain awareness of sustainability and support their colleagues in this respect (Goworek et al., 2020). The selection of materials and components can clearly have a significant impact upon the maintenance, durability and lifespan of garments.

## Sustainable Design Features

There are many opportunities to incorporate sustainable innovations into garment designs, including the minimisation of fabric wastage, as mentioned above. Modular styling is another potentially sustainable feature of garment design, where parts can be removed or adapted, to offer different looks from the same garment (Gwilt & Rissanen, 2011). Modular garments have more recently been defined in research by Zhang et al. (2024) as "a clothing assemblage":

> Structurally, a modular garment is not a piece of a complete garment, but a clothing combination assembled with detachable garment modules through standard closure interfaces… to function as a wearable garment, different garment modules need to be assembled and serve different functions.

The life cycle of clothes can be extended when retailers or brands do not solely follow mass market fashion trends, an approach termed as "slow fashion" by various authors (see, e.g., Gwilt & Rissanen, 2011; Minney, 2013). Slow fashion's meaning can go beyond references to speed of product development, relating also to small-scale garment production and craft skills (Fletcher & Grose, 2012). Additionally, Cataldi et al. (2013:22–23) considered slow fashion to be an innovative direction:

> Slow fashion represents a new future vision for the fashion and textile industry, one where natural resources and labour are highly valued and respected. It aims to slow down the rate at which we withdraw materials from nature… In this movement, the people who design, produce and consume garments are reconsidering the impacts of choosing quantity over quality and redesigning ways to create, consume and relate to fashion.

To test how clothing will look before it is manufactured, suppliers often make individual physical samples for clients to check that they fit effectively. Sample garments may be posted internationally, creating carbon emissions via transportation, and it is therefore preferable to produce a minimal number of garment samples. Alternatively, companies can use software which gives high-resolution images of garments, some with a 3D effect (such as CLO-3D), from which product selections can be made, and the use of this innovative software can therefore be more sustainable (see Chapter 3). Designers and garment technologists are usually responsible for selecting the thread, style of stitching and types of sewing machine that will be used in the garment manufacturing process, which can also have a significant impact on the quality and durability of garments.

After finalising the fit of a garment in a standard size (usually a 12 for women's wear in the UK), the pattern pieces need to be graded – i.e., adapted for smaller and larger sizes that will be sold to consumers. Innovations in software can be used to accelerate the grading process and increase accuracy. Employing designers and pattern-cutters with strong technical skills and grading as accurately as possible should result in fewer prototype garments having to be made and a lower level of returns from customers, therefore improving sustainability by reducing wastage. There is scope for the product development stage itself to be more sustainable, as outlined here, but academic discussion on this is scarce. All of the product decisions mentioned above are taken prior to production, and can impact significantly upon the sustainability of garments when they are manufactured in the next stage.

**FIGURE 6.2** Dr Jo Gooding. Photo with permission from Jo Gooding

## Innovation in Adaptive Fashion and Disability-related Design

**Dr Jo Gooding is co-founder of StyleAbility, which aims to help people find fashion to accommodate their dressing needs. Jo studied Design History at the Royal College of Art (RCA) and the Victoria & Albert (V&A) Museum, and she holds a PhD in design from Northumbria University, UK. Jo has taught design students at various institutions, and she is an expert on research in adaptive fashion and disability-related design. Jo has been invited to be an expert contributor for both the Science Museum and the BBC.**

Like most children, I was very creative and I found comfort in libraries and museums, excited to uncover stories in objects. I was born in Staffordshire, near to the Wedgwood pottery factory, and I recall frequent trips to museums where I became curious about the connection of arts, sciences and innovation and their part in the Industrial Revolution. During and following my degree, I worked in art colleges teaching contextual studies for creative students from all types of creative subjects, ranging from fashion to graphics, and supervising students undertaking their final year projects or dissertations. For our major degree project, we were encouraged to choose one category of object and examine its design change as technologies of production and social context altered. I looked at eyewear, and I focused on National Health Service glasses. This was particularly interesting as the frame styles were limited to a standardised range, so the medical and professional committee explicitly rejected any fashion element and their style did not change for nearly 40 years. The frame design became a recognisable symbol of state-supplied help, and a huge number of people were affected by the stigma of wearing a "badge of poverty". It was only from the mid-1980s, when regulations and provision changed, that more fashionable styles became available and opticians could advertise and act as retailers on the High Street. Fashion, style and innovation were now permitted for this scientific appliance. Eyewear has since become an exemplar of the importance of fashion and choice in medical and disability-related objects. This shaped my interest in disability-related fashion.

Those two years based within the incredible V&A Museum and connecting with creatives nearby at the RCA shaped my connection to creativity and innovation. I was entranced by Sir Ken Robinson's talk, discussing the importance of creative education, and recognised the privileged experience I had training at the RCA. My doctoral thesis looked at the emergence of design history as a subject and discipline, which included an understanding of the history of arts education in Britain. I became immersed in theories of how to teach critical thinking in a creative way, mainly because there was often a little bit of resistance from creative students when challenged to reflect on their work in context or to write about that work. I revisited this knowledge when I was connected with the Durham Commission on Creative Education in 2019.

I became a research fellow on creative economy engagement at the London Doctoral Design Centre, and in this study I explored the barriers that prevent creative projects having real-world impact. Here I revisited my connection with disability-related design and eyewear and working with Professor Graham Pullin's team in Dundee on the collaborative design project "Hands of X", exploring the importance of choice in prosthetic limbs. I also contributed to the V&A Dundee's exhibition *Design Meets Disability*. Since then, I have been exploring entrepreneurial routes, using creative approaches, to support inclusive design. I started by focusing on fashion and clothing, primarily due to realising the importance of fashion style and choice for psychological well-being, via the NHS glasses example and "Hands of X" project. Yet when I was a lecturer on a fashion marketing course, I experienced a chronic illness and struggled to get dressed. I recognised that the design of clothes had a huge physical and psycholocial impact, and we should all have access to clothing that works for us. This has informed my current mission, StyleAbility, a purpose-led business with an innovative digital fashion solution to help everyone find clothing that works for them, to solve many of the problems in online retail.

*StyleAbility: Helping everyone find fashion (https://www.styleability.co.uk/)*

## Innovations in Sustainable Clothing Manufacture

Clothing is usually produced by specialist garment manufacturers which operate independently of retailers and brands and are considered to be part of the supply chain. A few brands and retailers are exceptional in owning their own factories to produce a proportion of their merchandise, such as Zara, which originated as a manufacturer and still owns production facilities in Spain, as well as ordering many of its products from overseas. In addition to taking into account the sustainability of fabrics, components and manufacturing techniques to produce clothing, companies have to consider the factory environment — e.g., lighting, heating, air conditioning and operation of machinery. Innovations in these areas may be adopted to reduce energy usage whilst making sure working conditions are also acceptable for employees.

Social sustainability is also a key aspect for consideration when making selections of textiles or clothing manufacturers for garments. The best-known label for social sustainability is probably the Fairtrade Foundation, which offers the Fairtrade mark to certify that products have reached certain social, environmental and economic standards for producers in the supply chain, ensuring that workers receive fair pay (Fairtrade, 2024). Other socially sustainable accreditation options for clothing include Fair Wear, used by Danish sustainable fashion brand Filippa K (Fair Wear, 2024). Problems with social sustainability in the clothing industry have been discussed extensively in the mass media, such as the tragic collapse of the Rana Plaza factory building in Bangladesh in 2015 and the disclosure that certain factories in the UK paid employees well below the minimum wage (Hammer et al., 2015). Another major global social sustainability issue is "modern slavery, defined by Anti-Slavery International (2024) as: "when an individual is exploited by others, for personal or commercial gain. Whether tricked, coerced, or forced, they lose their freedom. This includes but is not limited to human trafficking, forced labour and debt bondage."

Modern slavery has often been linked to clothing manufacture as well as child labour, which has led to the development of relevant legislation in various countries. The Modern Slavery Act (2015) in the UK requires businesses which supply goods or services and have an annual financial turnover in excess of £36 million to make modern slavery statements publicly accessible – e.g., through their websites (UK Government, 2015). Smaller companies may also choose to offer modern slavery statements online voluntarily. Modern slavery is a major social sustainability issue which has been addressed for some years by non-governmental organisations and activists who work to support employees, such as Labour Behind the Label and Unseen. Whilst activism and support for workers are long-established ideas, rather than being novel, setting up a non-profit organisation that supports workers which is not a union could be considered to be engaging in social innovation (see Chapter 4). Justice in Fashion (JiF) was initiated as a community interest company in 2020 to build relationships with communities of workers in the clothing industry during the pandemic and some of its events and services are open to designers and employees in other roles in the fashion business (JiF, 2024). For example, fashion designers may wish to attend JiF events to learn more about how modern slavery can be addressed within their work. However, JiF Managing Director Jennifer Wascak suggests that as modern slavery relates mainly to labour exploitation, "forced labour" is a more appropriate term to use.

## Sustainable Innovations in Clothing Retailing, Hire and Exchange

Clothing is delivered from manufacturers to retailers in the final phase of its journey to consumers. During the last decade, it has become the norm to feature a selection of sustainable products within brands' or retailers' ranges – e.g. Emporio Armani's Sustainable Collection. However, certain brands approach sustainability in a different way by producing high- quality clothing in classic styles, which can assist in extending the lifetimes of their garments. COS (part of the H&M group) offers a variety of aspects of sustainability, from using sustainable fabrics in its products to taking back used garments in its "Full Circle" strategy, which can then be retailed in its "Resell" section online (COS, 2024). Although selling second-hand merchandise is not novel in itself, offering pre-worn clothing alongside new garments is a more recent innovation which is now becoming a more mainstream retail concept. Similarly, department store Liberty of London contains a vintage clothing area and its competitor Selfridges offers a "reselfridges" option for customers to resell used items from brands that have been sold in the store (Selfridges, 2024). As a precursor to this, in the early 2000s Selfridges sold garments via a concession for the renowned vintage designer clothing company Steinberg & Tolkien, and the former Topshop flagship store at Oxford Circus in London also offered a selection of pre-worn merchandise. Stores such as Circle Vintage in Durham (see Figure 6.3), Flip in Newcastle and The Wardrobe in Leicester are amongst the many established independent retailers of vintage clothing throughout the UK. Additionally, vintage fashion fairs run by small-scale stall-holders are held regularly in local areas, such as *Frock Me!* in Kensington and Chelsea in London, and others operate nationally, moving from city to city, such as Lou Lou's *Vintage Fair*.

A novel sustainable retailing concept is the ReTuna Återbruksgalleria in Eskilstuna, Sweden (see Figure 6.4), a modern shopping mall where every item sold is reused, recycled or produced sustainably (Retuna, 2024). Retailers which sell products under their own labels will probably also have been involved in the product development stage, via their designers, buyers and technologists. The transportation of garments from suppliers to retailers (or directly from online retailers to consumers), usually referred to as logistics, can potentially have a negative effect on the environment, especially due to the use of fossil fuels and the resulting carbon emissions. In a similar way to factories, bricks-and-mortar retailers with their own stores and distribution centres (warehouses) also impact upon the environment by using energy for lighting, heating and transportation, as well as resources such as retail fittings and carrier bags within retail stores. Fashion retailers as well as brands and manufacturers can use the Higg Index, a framework developed by the Sustainable Apparel Coalition (SAC, 2024) to assist in the assessment and measurement of sustainability strategies – e.g., to calculate water use and carbon emissions or to review labour conditions. Systems to manage data are recent innovations which can be used to support fashion companies in achieving social and environmental sustainability goals within supply chains, using companies such as Sedex (www.sedex.com) to collate relevant data.

**FIGURE 6.3** Vintage clothing for sale in a department store concession, a vintage clothing fair, Circle Vintage store and a charity shop vintage section. Top: Author's own photos. Bottom: Photos with permission from Christina Goworek

Fashion consumers can also assume some of the responsibility for sustainability during the retail phase by assessing whether or not to travel to retail outlets to make a purchase. Buying online and using "click and collect" were retailing innovations popularised during the early 2000s. Other innovative business models have also emerged or been revived to sell fashion products – e.g., clothing libraries which are available in the Netherlands, where customers pay a monthly subscription to hire clothes (Boztas, 2018). Garment rental has long been a tradition for weddings, and has been relaunched as a method of retaining clothing in the circular economy by companies such as My Wardrobe and Hirestreet (see Figure 6.5) for consumers to hire garments for a short time at a more economical cost than purchasing.

**FIGURE 6.4** Sustainable retailing at ReTuna Återbruksgalleria in Eskilstuna, Sweden. Photos with permission from retuna.se © Lina Östling

Whilst retailing primarily caters for business-to-consumer organisations, there has been increasing engagement in selling garments via consumer-to-consumer channels, particularly since the launch of eBay in 1995 in the US, Vinted in 2008 in Lithuania and depop in 2011 in the UK, reviving the second-hand clothes market, which had previously mainly focused on garments donated to charity shops or jumble sales. Another innovative method for consumers to acquire garments is to attend a clothes exchange, which may be arranged on a not-for-profit or charitable basis to allow attendees to swap clothing with each other after paying a small admission fee (see Figure 6.6). Loanhood is a community interest company launched in

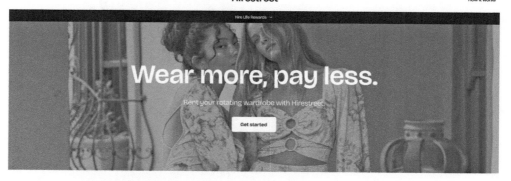

**There are two ways of renting with us**

Choose a hire box size, add items and checkout with a one-off payment. Simple.

**FIGURE 6.5** Hirestreet fashion rental website. Photos with permission from Hirestreet, image credits: Winona and Runaway The Label

**FIGURE 6.6** A charity clothes swap in Leicester UK and a Loanhood clothes exchange event in London. Author's own photos

the UK in 2018, initially running clothes exchanges, then later using crowdfunding to develop an innovative app that consumers use for peer-to-peer clothing rental. "Loaners" who have signed up to the Loanhood app can either send or drop off their own garments to renters (Loanhood, 2024).

## Innovations in Wearing and Maintaining Clothing

The stage between purchase and disposal is usually the longest part of the garment life cycle, and can have the most significant impact on the environment (Allwood et al., 2006). As discussed earlier in this chapter, consumers' potential to care for clothing effectively is dependent to a large extent on decisions concerning materials and construction that were made at the product development phase and quality standards in manufacturing. Washing and drying can have a significant impact on the environment in terms of energy consumption, as well as adding costs to clothing care. Many fashion firms have therefore adopted the practice of using their wash-care labels to encourage customers to launder at lower temperatures (e.g., "if it's not dirty, wash at 30"). Brands and retailers may also liaise with manufacturers of washing machines or detergents and stain removers to develop the most effective washing instructions for clothing, to reduce energy usage, with the additional benefit of reducing the cost of laundering for consumers. Fashion brands that wish to have a positive impact on the environment beyond the point of purchase can supply information to their customers about how to care for clothing more responsibly – e.g. on garment labels or on their websites and apps, thereby assisting in the reduction of carbon emissions.

Whilst research has shown that consumers often profess to intend to behave sustainably in the purchase of clothing and other goods, there is also evidence to show that they frequently do not follow up on that intention, a situation referred to as the "attitude–behaviour gap" or "value–action gap'" (Blake, 1999; Carrington et al., 2010). Fashion brands and retailers can seek to bridge that gap by supporting consumers in behaving more sustainably. Increasing numbers of fashion companies are now prolonging their responsibilities after consumers have purchased their products, offering repairs and advice on maintaining the products they have sold – e.g., outdoor clothing brand Regatta's website includes advice about cleaning and reproofing its waterproof clothing (Regatta, 2024). Swedish company Nudie Jeans takes this approach further by offering free repairs on its products within its stores (see Figure 6.7) or via mobile mending (Nudie, 2024). Similarly, Blackhorse Lane Ateliers, a craft jeans company, manufactures and offers repairs in its London-based premises (2024). These examples are indicative of growing appreciation by fashion consumers of the traditional craft skills that had become distanced from the market due to the rise of global manufacturing. The revival of such traditions may be perceived as innovations by customers who are not so familiar with repair services,

**FIGURE 6.7** Nudie Jeans store and repair shop in London. Author's own photos

which used to be widely available in the UK, but began to diminish in the 1990s. US outdoor wear brand Patagonia, which has one of the strongest reputations for sustainability in the clothing sector, offers mending guidance online and in-store repairs for its products, as well as repairs by post (Patagonia, 2024). These policies form part of the company's innovative business model, with an emphasis on social and environmental responsibility, which are not profit-orientated, yet enhance the brand's values. The prolonged customer service offered by these organisations demonstrates a practice that has become known as "extended producer responsibility".

Consumers are also becoming more interested in aspects of clothing repair, such as visible mending of knitwear, where the repair becomes a way to enhance the decoration of a "garment (Noguchi, 2022). A frequent problem with knitwear, as well as some woven garments, is that they are prone to pilling ("bobbling"), which can be addressed by using either "sweater stones" made from volcanic rock or battery-powered pill-removers, to remove the surface build-up of fibres. There has generally been reduced emphasis on sewing in the UK school curriculum since the 1980s, but there is now renewed interest in repair skills in the media, with video tutorials being shared more easily online. Repair cafes have also become popular events, where people meet at an existing venue to help each other mend clothing and other items in a sociable environment. Overall, most of the innovative or revived methods discussed in this section can help to extend the lifetime of clothing before it is discarded and therefore limit the need to buy new products, lowering the impact of clothing on the environment (WRAP, 2012).

## Innovations in Garment Disposal and Recycling

Disposal of clothing can create a vast negative impact on the environment, as it has been estimated that 336,000 tonnes of clothing are thrown away each year in the

UK (WRAP, 2012). Discarding garments in landfill sites can also affect the environment by increasing greenhouse gas emissions. Research shows that consumers have a hierarchy of disposal methods for clothing, giving their most valued items to family and friends or selling them online, donating items to charity, repurposing or recycling (Birtwistle & Moore, 2007; Recycle Now, 2024). According to a study by Zhang et al. (2020), consumers in Nanjing, China retain clothing for an average of 3.75 years and mostly retain it until it is worn out. Whereas in the past fashion retailers and brands usually relinquished responsibility for clothing post-purchase, apart from legal obligations for faulty goods, certain companies offer the opportunity for consumers to take back products after use, as described above, in preference to discarding them. Retailers such as H&M and Marks & Spencer have encouraged their customers to be more sustainable by allowing them to dispose of used clothing in their stores (see Figure 6.8). Although collecting used clothing is not innovative in itself, it is a novel idea to operate this system within a mass market retail context.

US brand Eileen Fisher takes back used garments bought by customers from its range for its "Renew" collection, then uses visible mending before reselling them, a form of upcycling (Eileen Fisher, 2024). Upcycling is the reuse of items that appear to

**FIGURE 6.8**  Used clothes donation container in a fashion store. Author's own photo

have reached the end of their useful life – e.g., through combining them with other products in new ways, such as patchwork. Repurposing is also possible for used clothing – e.g., when it can be used for a different function such as a tote bag. Circularity platform Recomme offers various retailers and brands different ways of reselling, repurposing or recycling used clothing (see the interview with their CEO Simon Platts at the end of this chapter). Conversely, several fashion brands have become infamous for unnecessarily destroying their unsold products – e.g., by incineration or landfill, or cutting garments to make them unwearable. Ironically, although their aim is likely to be to avoid the brand image being diluted through the companies' unsold goods being retailed at low prices, disposing of products using such unsustainable methods would be more likely to negatively affect their brand image.

## Summary

This chapter has discussed how creativity and innovations in product development, manufacturing and retailing of garments can affect consumers' sustainability behaviours when wearing, maintaining and disposing of clothes. Sustainability in the fashion sector addresses both environmental and social responsibility, and the move towards a more circular economy is being driven by not-for-profit organisations and businesses which prioritise sustainability. Sustainable innovations are taking place at the start of the clothing life cycle in fabric and garment design and development, with a requirement for enhanced education in this area to promote continued progress. Sustainable innovations in clothing manufacture and innovative business models in retailing, hire, exchange and garment disposal have been discussed, which can lead to reductions in the fashion sector's environmental impact. Change is imperative, and all areas of society, including businesses, consumers and policy-makers, have a part to play in leading the fashion sector towards a sustainable future. Interviews with specialists in sustainability in the fashion business are featured below, expressing their views on sustainable creativity and innovation in practice.

### Views on Creativity and Innovation from Sustainable Fashion Specialists

**Alison Gwilt is Professor of Design at the University of New South Wales (UNSW), Sydney, Australia, and is the lead author of four books on sustainable fashion. Alison graduated with a BA (Hons) Fashion and Textiles at Central Saint Martins, London, and she holds a PhD in sustainable fashion design from RMIT University, Melbourne, Australia. Alison formerly worked in the fashion business and academia in the UK.**

*In what ways can brands and retailers in the fashion sector be innovative when they're embedding social or environmental sustainability into design?*

My priority would be to determine the sustainability mission for the brand or retailer, as this should underpin everything that you do and then seek innovative ways to embed

**FIGURE 6.9** Professor Alison Gwilt. Photo with permission from Alison Gwilt

sustainability into the product design. These are some of the significant points where change can be made. As you begin to plan your product range, it is paramount to change your thinking on product lifetimes, and to consider the end-of-life of your product before you have even begun the design process. If you can think of an endpoint first, it will completely change the way that you design, construct and retail clothing. Another really important point to consider is understanding what consumers do with your clothing. If you knew how people interacted with your products at home, this [could]can influence the way that you design and manufacture your products – for example, you might discover that the fabrics you routinely use are not very durable during repeated laundering. There are many variables around how clothing users maintain and discard clothing items, no two people have the same clothing care routines. But with an understanding of what goes on in the product life cycle phases, you can change the way that you design and make clothes for the better. I would say that in the clothing sector we don't always listen to consumers, which is a big issue because they are the gatekeepers between purchasing a product and where it goes next. Clothing users play a critical role in whether or not products remain in use for as long as possible. Retailers are also in a prime position to educate and encourage consumers to adopt best practices whilst also gathering insights that can be fed back into the industry. While brands can employ their own loyalty schemes to best understand some of their consumers, retailers are in a fantastic position to gather information from casual consumers. This helps brands overcome the issue of reaching unidentified consumers who purchase their products and provides data that can be fed back into the design process, which can make a big difference to how products are designed and manufactured.

In terms of what the sector is doing in relation to sustainability, currently there is a real drive to develop textile recycling technology to solve the problem of textile waste. There is a race to develop new tools and systems that will help us break down clothing products at scale and reuse their materials to create new fibres or materials. While it may seem ambitious to think we can recycle all of our clothes, money from various sources, including large brands, is being pumped into start-ups and small companies to develop technology that can recycle large quantities of clothing. However, the underlying problem is that our current fashion system perpetuates a model of consuming more stuff, and recycling technology will not slow this down. In fact, it may even encourage brands to create more clothes and allow consumers to buy more garments. I prefer to advocate that we should keep our clothing in use for as long as possible. Brands could be doing so much more around this point during design and manufacture, while retailers could be supporting customer on methods for maintaining and circulating clothes. When I look across brands, particularly where I am here in Australia, there's a big emphasis on encouraging people to repair their clothes, but there is so much more that needs to be considered when we want long-lasting and actively worn clothes – for example, improving their durability. This goes right back to the design stage and creating products that are not just physically durable, but also aesthetically durable and functional. If we consider these factors in design, then we encourage consumers to keep clothes for as long as possible by nudging their behaviour. Our UNSW Art and Design collective, Design ForCE, works with local textile, jewellery and object designers in Sydney to transform waste into products that fit within the circular economy's biological or technical cycle (see Figure 6.10).

Currently, it seems there are two strong tracks of thoughts on what fashion can be. While the race is on to recycle textiles as quickly as possible that enables our industry to produce

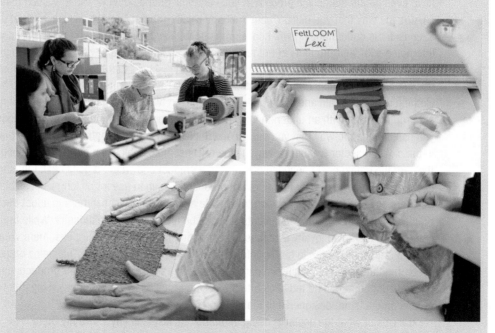

FIGURE 6.10 A group of designers at Design ForCE explore industrial felting methods that reuse the smallest of fabric scraps to create new cloth. Photo by Jennifer Chua with permission from Alison Gwilt

more clothing, there is also recognition for a slower fashion system that at times relies on predictable approaches to designing long-lasting clothes, such as using fabrics that are more durable, but designers can explore more innovative approaches. For example, we seem to be ignoring the conversation around how people wash clothing, which greatly affects the lifespan of a garment. Some years ago, Marks & Spencer led the 30° wash campaign, but there are now fewer campaigns encouraging people to wash clothing less or wash differently. Meanwhile, for a long time there was a discussion around designing modular clothes, but no real innovation in this space has appeared in the High Streets yet. There are, then, many approaches to innovation still yet to be uncovered in design and construction that could enable a whole variety of opportunities to keep materials in use or to more cleanly situate them in the technical or biological cycles. In Australia, some brands are assessing the opportunity to work with natural materials, which in the right conditions can be compostable. Creating innovative clothing for the biological cycle would really open up the brand's opportunities for the circular economy. For some unexplained reason, we seem to be stuck with the notion that fashion only fits in the technical cycle, and yet with more innovation we could design and construct clothing that fits into the biological cycle where it is compostable at the end-of-life. Currently, I sit on a Standards Australia committee to develop a textile standard for composting textiles, which the *Guardian* newspaper states may be a world first. Although there is a lot of complexity in composting textiles, we are hopeful that it will get off the ground.

*What sort of solutions do you think there might be in in the overarching environment? What might educators do to help this to change?*

I'd like to see a more coordinated response in education to the problem of sustainability in fashion. I still think there's a very ad hoc approach in institutes about how they introduce or explore sustainability in design and construction programmes. I suspect that's still going on, and I think the real problem there is that it can still be treated a little bit as an add-on – where we continue to teach the same design process which does not truly integrate sustainability. I feel quite strongly that there needs to be a co-ordinated approach in the very first year of programmes so that students understand a new way to design and produce clothes. Sustainability education should be scaffolded so that skills and knowledge are built – we don't want students uncovering fundamental knowledge later in their programmes. It's also important to acknowledge that design is only one part of the whole system of clothing design and use, consumption and production, so there are many factors that need to be considered in depth.

Some of the most exciting brands to me have been those who are very flexible in their business model. They don't just produce the clothing, but they may also offer a service, or provide a community service, or they might diversify and develop different types of products. I think I've always found those to be the most interesting businesses, because they've appear to survive one storm or another. When we look back at the impact of COVID-19 on the fast fashion industry, the whole supply chain was disrupted, and more so here in Australia due to our remote location. We import huge amounts of raw materials and finished products from countries such as China, and the pandemic showed how fragile our supply chain is. Particularly for small clothing brands in Australia, those that survived the impacts of the pandemic did so because they diversified by, for example, producing new product lines such as scrubs for the healthcare sector. I feel that business leaders and educators need to observe the practices in brands and retailers to explore and encourage the diversification of the traditional business model, especially if we encounter another pandemic in the future. The pandemic has been a big lesson for all of us. There are also brands that probably still aren't making great use of social media channels and all those other fields that are clearly important to consumers, so there's a lot that could be done to support business practices within the sector. It's interesting that small brands are usually agile and flexible, and I can see that doesn't quite happen in large-scale brands, so I do think there's a place for business leaders to go into both types of organisations or any small to medium enterprise to encourage diversification of business models.

*Is there anything that you would say that could encourage or facilitate designers or businesses to be innovative in terms of sustainability? How would you recommend that they go about that?*

We have still not discovered the motivating reason for why some firms are engaging sustainable, ethical or responsible approaches towards design and manufacture when others aren't, and I really would like to know more about that. I'd like to know why we just can't motivate some people to take this more seriously, and I think there's still a lot of work that needs to be done into that area, because there are still brands in the industry today that are obviously making very little contribution in terms of improving practices, or they're very focused on only specific practices; meanwhile, some brands are doing terrible things, so it's no wonder it's confusing for consumers. I believe there's greater opportunity for designers in the industry to be more innovative, and to question how their brands can engage more with sustainability. I find it amazing that people think it's not important, when it clearly is to consumers. I'd love to see some great innovation from designers and product development teams, and brands and manufacturers, to come up with solutions that we know can help address some of the environmental problems, but aren't being explored – e.g., preparing garments for reduced washing or encouraging people to wash their clothes less. There's so little work that's been done in that space, and there's so much that could be done with manufacturers of washing machines and detergents.

Another aspect for designers and businesses to explore is the clothing rental model, as there are still many brands that only produce clothing to sell, but never think about manufacturing garments for the rental market, so there's certainly space for innovation there. I wonder how differently designers need to think if they're developing products for a rental market and not for a singular sale, and whether there need to be some differences in terms of design practice, so there's still more to uncover. There is so much momentum in the sector currently to be more responsible that it's quite surprising that some brands do not engage. Data from consumers is so important, because if your customers are telling you that sustainability matters, surely that is how you do something innovative as a designer. For designers and businesses, this means speaking to your consumers in a way that moves beyond understanding what colours or styles they like, and instead gather real information that could drive innovation within the sector so much more.

# Further Reading

Gwilt, A. (2015) Fashion Design for Living, London: Routledge.

Gwilt, A. (2020) A Practical Guide to Sustainable Fashion, London: Bloomsbury Visual Arts. A Practical Guide to Sustainable Fashion: Basics Fashion Design Alison Gwilt Bloomsbury Visual Arts.

Gwilt, A., Payne, A. and Ruthschilling, E.A. (Eds.) (2019) *Global Perspectives on Sustainable Fashion*, London: Bloomsbury.

Gwilt, A. and Rissanen, T. (2011) *Shaping Sustainable Fashion: Changing the Way we Make and Use Clothes*, London: Routledge.

Tonti, L. and Gorman, A. (2023) 'Bras fit for burying: Australia to set a world-first standard for composting textiles', *The Guardian*, 21st March 2023, available online at: https://www.theguardian.com/fashion/2023/mar/22/compostable-textiles-australia-world-first-standard-for-composting-biodegradable-fabric-material

**Simon Platts is CEO and Co-Founder of Recomme, a circular fashion service provider. Simon was formerly Responsible Sourcing and Environmental, Social and Governance Director of ASOS, and his experience includes visual merchandising, buying and product development in the fashion business.**

*How would you sum up the sustainability work that you're involved in relating to fashion and innovation?*

The current work I'm most closely involved in within environmental sustainability looks at different opportunities to support various parts in the circular economy. During my time at ASOS, I was working on how we embedded that into the heart of everything we were doing when we're designing products and materials we were using: where we were getting them from, how the customers were getting that product, how they cared about it, what packaging was used, how they not only cared for the product, but how they could then possibly have alternatives once they're finished with it. Then we looked at recovery of products that can

**FIGURE 6.11** Simon Platts. Photo with permission from Simon Platts

then be made, if possible, into new materials to be used in new products that could be put back into the circular economy. Now, in my current role with Recomme, this is a platform solution service provider that enables brands and retailers to engage with their clients or their customers directly on those aspects. This could be anything to do with potentially offering a repair or recovery for resale, rental, repurposing or recycling. One of our clients, Oliver Spencer, has called its platform "repurpose", which I think is a great word to use, because recycling is a bit like the word "sustainability", it's very broad, and it's got a lot of nuance, a lot of edges to it, that are a bit blurred.

The key areas that Recomme is working in are recycling, resale, reuse, facilitating a white label platform solution that enables brands and retailers to talk to their customers. "White label" means that the brand would embed this platform into their systems to be able to then customise and start encouraging recovery of goods back from customers through the various different ecosystems behind it to get the best from that product. They can use it internally within the company as well, for example with stock that has been returned that they can't resell or that are faulty or damaged, but they want to get into the recycling route, so it can work business-to-business (B2B) as well as business-to-consumer (B2C). We recover product and we capture data on what products are being returned, what value they may have had when they were bought, what they're made of and their weight.

I have had a background in visual merchandising, buying, product development and sourcing in the fashion business over the years, and I've seen how important data is to making sure you are acting in the smartest way. Data now, more than ever, is a vital tool for brands to ensure the actions taken are the most effective and efficient. This use of data will also help them develop their circularity models and to work on their own science-based targets around how they're capturing and reducing carbon and how they manage their water consumption and biodiversity impacts. Visual merchandising, buying and product development in the fashion business help to give valuable data to the brands as well, so that they can then use that data to work on their own science-based targets around how they're capturing and reducing carbon and water consumption. It also gives them a good message that has cadence to it to be able to talk to their customers about what they're doing, because consumers are becoming more aware of the issues on the planet, whether it be for people or the environment. I think they want to know when they're shopping that they can trust the brand through various pieces of education, so we can tell them a little bit more and we can verify that information, so they can rest assured the brand is giving them a product that's been designed in a circular manner. The brand has designed that way, and we've looked at materials that we're using that can be used over and over again. We put that into a great, fashionable product, and we've not compromised the quality. What we should still be doing is designing for durability and longevity. That could be through the diversity of the product in terms of wearing it or accessorising it in different ways so they keep that customer wanting to use that product for as long as possible.

By its very definition, fashion means it moves and not everybody wants everything forever, so that's why a circular economy and being more responsible is important, giving customers the option to sell that product, through take-back and recovery, making it easier for them, or directing them to existing propositions like eBay, depop and Vinted. We are realising that the commodity that we've got, which is a sweatshirt today, for example, when it's finished with, shouldn't just be discarded to the point where it goes in the ground. It could be used in many ways. We can use new technologies and innovation to get the product right for the customer when they want it. Let's not try and second-guess what a trend is going to be, because data, AI and technology can give us that ability to do things differently at the front end now and be smarter and more efficient. Let's then design and make that product so that it can stay around a long time, but if it is going to be deconstructed, it can be used again, so even if there is a lot of consumption, we're not constantly just taking and taking from the planet and causing issues.

The circular economy is the ecosystem of fashion, and I think a lot of the brands now that are really understanding what this looks like are looking into their biodiversity, water and alternative materials. Circularity at its purest would be circulating good things. Ideally, we move to a point where actually what we're bringing in at the front end is good feedstock that allows it to stay in the ecosystem a lot longer, rather than just bad feedstock. Designers today, with a cradle-to-cradle mentality, really need to think about every aspect of what they're about to design and produce. There's so much more to consider. Who is it for? Where? What is it? What is its facility? Where would it be made? What would the cost be of that? Which country? Historically, that was done through a team consisting of buyer, designer, merchandiser, product development people, which is still there, but I think the onus on the designer now is phenomenal, to know what the latest trends are and to know what people want. That designer needs to understand what impact that product that they're designing is going to have and how they can design something that can tick all those boxes of circularity, from reduced impact at the beginning to longevity, reuse and ultimately to recovery, to be recycled into something that can then ideally go back into a new product.

When I worked in garment sourcing, I got even closer to the supply base. I was always on the lookout for innovation in fabrics, and I remember introducing recycled polyester into swim shorts because I surfed and I saw that one of the big brands was doing swim shorts made from recycled plastic bottles. This was always what I wanted to do in, in terms of striving for better all the time and respect for people, so that gets you into the human rights element and modern slavery. Sourcing needs to be done in a considered way, and I think with a company like ASOS, it needs to be done for speed and agility. It needs to be efficient, avoiding overproduction, it needs to be on time and on demand, which means we need to look at different regions and different materials that come from there. We can put it together and ensure that we're doing things right both for people and planet, and also for profit. Towards the latter years, sustainability and ethics have become a massive part of the fashion industry. My interest in it started by having an affinity with not wanting to destroy everything, and it's something that I've always had a passion for. I guess the majority of my work is about creativity and innovation at the moment, because we need new solutions to the issues that we've wandered into by using a model to buy fashion fast for stores.

*What do you think are the most important recent sustainability innovations in fashion from your perspective?*

There are recent initiatives and innovations like Kornit Digital's and Aeoon's technologies for printing materials. We're at the point now where you could design, sell and make a product individually, which is usually called made-to-measure or haute couture. You're going to get a different price, but you're also going to get a different level of sell-through (selling at full retail price) and a different markdown (selling at a reduced price), and therefore a different level of profit, which is potentially higher by being smarter and using innovation, technology and circularity.

I think we need more work on innovations in material. We need scale recycling and mechanical and chemical recycling to break down because there's a legacy of products that are out there that need to be recovered and have something done with them. We've got to deal with the short- to mid-term issues, and as we then feed in better stock, it should get easier, and we start to get a clean circular economy. I think innovation and scaling of that innovation in recovery and recycling and materials needs accelerating. For example, it could be that brands don't just get taxed for not selling recycled materials, but they might get a tax break on a more sustainable material that they sourced, so there could be a carrot-and-stick approach, instead of the stick all the time. I know that's something that people are talking about. I think there's a lot of innovation going on in materials like hemp and nettle, Piñatex® (pineapple fabric), lots of lab-grown leathers and mycelium. Lots of things seem to be trapped in the lab or through lack of investment, that can't get up to scale, and therefore we'll just carry on using the old stuff. It's important that people in the industry decant this learning, whether it's good or bad, and pass it on to the next generation so they do everything they can to embrace the technologies and new ways of doing things and don't go making the same mistakes again.

*How would you define creativity based on your own experience and knowledge? How does that creative process work for you?*

I'm constantly looking for things that are going to make things better, different and smarter. By definition, creativity creates innovation. The guy who came up with the idea for Recomme is not from the fashion industry, he's a tech guy, and he used this tech logic in an industry that was struggling with the problem. I think people are looking outside of our industry for creativity, but we should be talking as a fashion industry. I call it co-opetition rather than collaborating with people. We shouldn't be trying to compete with each other. We should be working together, and then, when you've got it, it's free to air. For me, creativity is having that ability to look at something, and not looking at it with a muddled-up brain that knows it and therefore can't fix it.

*Who do you consider to be the most innovative and creative fashion retailers or brands from a sustainability perspective?*

I know there are brands working really hard on different things. If you look at Patagonia as a brand, obviously Yvon Chouinard set that up, starting with metalwork that he used for climbing, and he did what he did because of the outdoors and caring about the environment. He's passed the business now to the people, and it's an open-book business. I think in the outdoor world there's a lot happening in innovation in materials that could filter down into the mainstream. I think any brand that is using new technologies to reduce their overall production, designing, selling then making it by using technology and innovation, talking and planning where their factories are and ensuring that their workers are being paid a living wage etc., could open the door to customers understanding more about the value of what they're buying. It worked for Toms, and in a slightly different way, Gandys, Alpkit and Finisterre. I love what Finisterre stands for, so it's my go-to brand in the UK. Patrick Grant is another sustainable brand, and Cookson & Clegg, who make great stuff that you'll have forever. I'd like to see more of the innovation from that level being used lower down [pricewise], where we let people buy a lot of clothing, but let them know how to look after it and what to do when they don't want it any more.

**Elizabeth Stiles is the owner of a UK-based consultancy for fashion retailers and brands, offering online courses, coaching and mentoring, as well as podcasting (*The Fashion Brand Clinic*). After graduating with a BA (Hons) Fashion Buying at De Montfort University, UK, Elizabeth worked in the fashion business for ten years in buying, design and supply for companies including Next and Miss Selfridge before launching her company in 2018.**

*How does your company work in practice?*

I'm a fashion brand consultant, and I worked in fashion, buying and also in the fashion supply chain. I now work mainly with independent businesses on their manufacturing, marketing and a bit of their mindset as well. I run online courses, I do one-to-one coaching ,and I run a "mastermind" group where brands can all talk to each other, like group coaching. My podcast, *The Fashion Brand Clinic*, has been going for a few years now, and there don't seem to be many fashion business podcasts, so it covers a niche.

**FIGURE 6.12**  Elizabeth Stiles. Photo with permission from Elizabeth Stiles

*What's been your involvement with environmental and social sustainability in the fashion business?*

It only really started after I left my career in the High Street. I would say it was next to nothing when I was actually working in fashion, buying and being a supplier to the High Street. We suggested using recycled polyester to one brand in 2017, and they just completely said they weren't interested, it was pointless, their customers wouldn't be interested, and there was nothing more I could do with that because it was a flat-out "no". Working with independent brands has been much more interesting. Working with a brand called Lucy and Yak has been probably the one that has had the biggest impact, just because of the scale of the business. Very early on, they were using recycled polyester for fleece jackets, recycled wool for their coats, and all the cotton they use is organic. They don't use dead-stock fabrics (unused surplus fabric left over from garment production) any more due to the scale of the business, as it just wasn't feasible any longer, but lots of other brands I work with who are on a smaller scale find dead-stock fabrics to be really useful because they don't have to meet minimum order quantities for fabric to be produced to order. When you're starting out, being able to use stock fabrics, obviously they don't have a minimum quantity, you can just buy however much you need, whether it's as little as 1 metre or 10 metres ,it works for them, but they can also say it has a sustainability benefit. A brand might have bought too much stock and just cut the garment order in half and said, well, so 500 metres of fabric is left over as dead-stock. It's beneficial because you're using something that's already in existence, rather than creating a brand new resource, so good on the environmental side. For some brands, it's their life's work to be more sustainable. I would say some of them are all about sustainability and it's their passion, but then with others, I think, it's more accidental than purpose-driven.

*How do you incorporate sustainability into your training courses?*

I have a course called "How to Grow a Fashion Brand" online, and everything that I talk about in there is about sustainable practices. I give people two options from the outset about how to set your business up, whether it's made-to-order or it is made like a production run, and so obviously the majority of the High Street use a production run format where the product is made before it's sold to consumers. I'll list out the pros and cons of each so, for example, it's much more scaleable to have production runs, the delivery time is much quicker to the customer, you get better prices because you're ordering more stock at once, but the cons are that you know there does tend to be wastage. Some of that stock will inevitably end up in a sale, so it won't all be sold at full price. When you pre-order, there is zero waste, because you only make what people have ordered, so the factory makes the production after you've sold it to your customers. It's much better for cashflow as well when you're starting out, because you get the money upfront, and you can use that to create the product. Not all manufacturers will do this, because it's risky as to how much product you'll actually sell, depending on how much web traffic you have, and it's less scaleable in a way, but as time has gone on, I would say more brands are doing it, because people are more receptive to understanding why they would have to wait maybe two to three weeks for their product to arrive if it does have the benefit of much lower waste. This is generically across the board in the business, and there is a new brand called Odd Muse, and I've noticed that she's managed to scale her business through pre-order, which is quite unusual. There's also another company that I work with called Humphries and Begg that uses pre-order from a sustainability perspective, such as on Black Friday they've made it "pre-order Friday", launching their Spring collection in the previous November.

*In what ways do your clients incorporate sustainability into their products and overall business models?*

I tell my clients to be really careful about using the word "sustainable" in their marketing, because the meaning of the word is very subjective. It's such a controversial topic because there's no real definition as to what sustainability means. I advise customers to get more niche: "So what are you? Are you a zero waste company, or are you a company that reduces the amount of water that you use? Are you a zero plastic brand? Are you a Vegan brand? Are you an organic brand? Are you a brand that pays fair wages? Do you only use recycled materials? Do you only upcycle garments?" All of those things are sustainable, and they're easier to define to a customer than sustainability.

*How would you define sustainability in in the scope of the work that you've done?*

I think it's about longevity personally, so when you look up the word "sustainable", it's something that can sustain. I remember going to the trade show *Make It British*, and everything there was made in the UK, which could be viewed as sustainable because everything's made in small batches, locally produced and has a low carbon footprint. A client who was with me was asking about bamboo socks, which seemed more sustainable than cotton socks, because bamboo grows at a faster rate, so it's easier to produce. However, we were told at the trade fair that bamboo socks are so thin that the heels wear away, and the lifespan of a bamboo sock is much shorter than the lifespan of a cotton sock, so the growth of the raw material is more sustainable, but the longevity of the product is less. It's not necessarily useful to tell people not to buy anything from the High Street, although I think some High Street brands are better than others. In a cost-of-living crisis, the majority of people are on a tight budget, and we have to consider what's more sustainable. Is it something from Zara that you wear 500 times for the rest of your life, or something that you spend £300 on and is made from dead-stock fabric, but you only wear it once? I think also what people say and what people do are very different things. Nowadays, people are saying they want to be sustainable, but they don't want it to be more effort, and they don't want to pay more for it, so that's why habits are going to take a lot longer to change than the thought process. I think the thought process has changed and almost everyone wants to do better now, so you'd probably struggle to find somebody who says they really don't care. They recycle and give clothes to the charity shop etc. Even buying items from the charity shop isn't embarrassing any more, it seems to be cool, but actually doing it when it's a little bit more difficult than ordering next day from H&M is where it's going to take a bit of time to change.

*Which brands, if any, do you think are most innovative in terms of sustainability?*

I think Vinted has used technology to make sustainable shopping no more hassle and no more expensive than the High Street, and I think that's why it's become such a popular way of shopping for people of all ages. They've made it as easy as shopping on ASOS, but cheaper. I think the entry point to people's shopping habits changing is going to be buying second-hand online, just the way that the shipping labels are printed and the buyer protection fee. Everything is so slick that it's become very popular. Vinted is a much smoother process from a tech point of view in comparison to competitors, like the way it uploads something and it already knows what colour it is and the suggested postage weight just from the description. I think it's amazing what they've done.

*What do you think about the fashion business overall? Do you think it's making progress towards being more sustainable or not?*

I want to think so, but it's a tale of two halves. I've read that Shein's market share has grown exponentially, but so have the likes of slow fashion brands, so both streams have grown, but what has dipped is the gap in the middle, so High Street names that are neither cheap nor sustainable. Yes, we are moving in the right direction, but there is a massive community of people who still want to buy cheap products, and the good news is that there are people who want to buy more slow fashion as well.

*Which brands or retailers do you think are most innovative in terms of their sustainability strategies?*

Where people are collaborating together, I think that's where more sustainable strategies are going to happen, such as Lidl's Christmas jumper rentals in collaboration with a sustainable designer. Also, rental platforms By Rotation and My Wardrobe are great examples of companies who are using tech to improve the sustainability experience.

*Where and how do you find sources of creative inspiration in your own work?*

There are lots of places. I love still receiving physical copies of magazines because I think it would be sad if they disappeared, which might happen if we don't buy them. Even though I don't read them every month, I still like to get them through the post and I like that there's no algorithm in a magazine. If you like one picture of an item on Instagram, your feed is then filled with it, so you think it's on trend when actually it's not. I think you get a more balanced view of what's happening in the world when you're flicking through a magazine, and you might see something that you wouldn't necessarily search for online, so yes, I still love reading magazines and being around creative people. For my work, though, my inspiration is predominantly online.

*How would you define creativity?*

With maths and science, there's a right answer and a wrong answer, whereas with creativity, I think just anything goes. It's a creative outlet for a messy mind, maybe, of things that don't always make sense. It's a task to make sense of what's going on inside your mind, like putting colours together.
https://www.elizabethstiles.co.uk/ and @elizabethstilesuk

## References

Allwood, J.M., Laursen, S.E., de Rodriguez, C.M., and Bocken, N.M.P. (2006) *Well Dressed? The present and future sustainability of clothing and textiles in the United Kingdom.* Cambridge: Institute for Manufacturing, University of Cambridge, available online at: https://www.ifm.eng.cam.ac.uk/insights/sustainability/well-dressed/

Ananas-anam (2024) *Pinayarn,* available online at: https://www.ananas-anam.com/pinayarn/

Anti-Slavery International (2024) *How we work to end slavery,* available online at: https://www.antislavery.org/what-we-do/how-we-work/

Better Cotton Initiative (2024) *Introducing better cotton traceability,* available online at: https://bettercotton.org/

Birtwistle, G. and Moore, C.M. (2007) 'Fashion clothing – where does it all end up?', *International Journal of Retail and Distribution Management,* 35 (3): 210–216.

Blackhorse Lane (2024) *Made to Measure,* available online at: https://blackhorselane.com/pages/made-to-measure

Blake, J. (1999) 'Overcoming the value-action gap in environmental policy: Tensions between national policy and local experience', *Local Environment,* 4 (3): 257–278.

Boztas, S. (2018) 'Check me out: The library where you can borrow clothes instead of books', *The Guardian,* 18th January 2018, ;available online at: https://www.theguardian.com/business-to-business/2018/jan/18/check-me-out-the-library-where-you-can-borrow-clothes-instead-of-books

Carrington, M.J., Neville, B.A. and Whitwell, G.J. (2010) 'Why ethical consumers don't walk their talk: Towards a framework for understanding the gap between the ethical purchase intentions and actual buying behaviour of ethically minded consumers', *Journal of Business Ethics,* 97: 139–158.

Cataldi, C., Dickson, M. and Grover, C. (2013) 'Slow fashion: Tailoring a strategic approach for sustainability', in Gardetti, M.A. and Torres, A.L. (eds) *Sustainability in Fashion and Textiles.* Sheffield: Greenleaf Publishing, pp. 22–46.

Claxton, S., Cooper, T., Goworek, H., Hill, H., Mclaren, A. and Oxborrow, L. (2017) 'Pilling in knitwear – a clothing longevity problem beyond design', in Bakker, C. and Mugge, R. eds., *PLATE: Product Lifetimes And The Environment: Conference Proceedings of PLATE 2017, Delft, the Netherlands, 8th–10th November 2017.* Research in design series, 9. Amsterdam: IOS Press, pp. 89–93.

Clean Clothes Campaign (2024) *Rana Plaza,* available online at: https://cleanclothes.org/campaigns/past/rana-plaza

COS (2024) *Sustainability at COS,* available online at: https://www.cos.com/en_gbp/sustainability.html

Drapers (2024) *About the Conference,* available online at: https://sustainablefashion.drapersonline.com/dsf2024/en/page/home

Eileen Fisher (2024) 'Renew – Lightly Used Clothing', *Eileen Fisher*, available online at: https://www.eileenfisherrenew.com/

Ellen Macarthur Foundation (2024) 'What We Do', *Ellen Macarthur Foundation*, available online at: https://www.ellenmacarthurfoundation.org/about-us/what-we-do

European Parliament (2023) *Circular Economy*, available online at: https://www.europarl.europa.eu/topics/en/article/20151201STO05603/circular-economy-definition-importance-and-benefits

Fairtrade (2024) What is Fairtrade?, *Fairtrade Foundation*, available online at: https://www.fairtrade.org.uk/what-is-fairtrade/

Fair Wear (2024) Member Brands, *Fair Wear Foundation*, available online at: https://www.fairwear.org/brands/

Fletcher, K. and Grose, L. (2012) *Fashion and Sustainability: Design for Change*, London: Laurence King.

GOTS (2023) *Global Organic Textile Standard and Certification*, GOTS, available online at: https://global-standard.org/

Goworek, H., Oxborrow, L., Claxton, S., McLaren, A., Cooper, T. and Hill, H. (2020) 'Managing sustainability in the fashion business: Challenges in product development for clothing longevity in the UK', *Journal of Business Research*, 117 (9): 629–641.

Gwilt, A. and Rissanen, T. (2011) *Shaping Sustainable Fashion: Changing the Way We Make and Use Clothes*. London: Routledge.

Hammer, N., Plugor, R. Nolan, P. and Clark, I. (2015) *A New Industry on a Skewed Playing Field: Supply Chain Relations and Working Conditions in UK Garment Manufacturing*. Leicester/London: University of Leicester/CSWEF, Ethical Trading Initiative.

Head, A. (2023) 'B Corp brands', *Marie Claire April 2023*, available online at: https://www.marieclaire.co.uk/life/sustainability/b-corp-brands-738665

Joanie (2024) 'Joanie B Corp Certification', *Joanie Clothing*, available online at: https://joanieclothing.com/b-corp

Justice in Fashion (2024) *JiF method*, available online at: https://www.justiceinfashion.org/how-we-do-it

Lectra (2024) *Gerber AccuMark CAD software for fashion design*, available online at: https://www.lectra.com/en/library/gerber-accumark-3d

Loanhood (2024) *How it works*, available online at: https://www.loanhood.com/how-it-works

Minney, S. (2013) *Naked Fashion*. Oxford, UK: New Internationalist Publications.

Mylo (2024) *Mylo Unleather*, available online at: https://mylo-unleather.com/

Noguchi, H. (2022) *Creative Mending: Beautiful Darning, Patching and Stitching Techniques*. North Clarendon: Tuttle Publishing.

Nudie (2024) 'Where can I get my jeans repaired?', *Nudie Jeans*, available online at: https://www.nudiejeans.com/help-center/where-can-i-get-my-jeans-repaired

Patagonia (2024) *Repairs*, available online at: https://eu.patagonia.com/gb/en/repairs/

Recomme (2024) 'How Recomme Works', *Recomme*, available online at: https://www.recomme.co/

Recycle Now (2024) 'How to Recycle', *Recycle Now*, available online at: https://www.recyclenow.com/how-to-recycle

Regatta (2024) *Garment Care*, available online at: https://www.regatta.com/garment-care/

Retuna (2024) 'The stores at ReTuna: Clothing and home textiles', *ReTuna Återbruksgalleria*, available online at: https://www.retuna.se/butiker-och-verksamheter

SAC (2024) *Our Impact*, Sustainable Apparel Coalition, available online at: https://cascale.org/about-us/our-impact/

Saha, S. (2023) 'The toxicity of textile dyes: Unveiling the hidden colours', *Fibre2Fashion*, available online at: https://www.fibre2fashion.com/industry-article/9722/the-toxicity-of-textile -dyes-unveiling-the-hidden-colours

Sanders, L. (2020) 'Bamboo: Eco-friendly fabric or environmental disaster?', *Euronews*, available online at: https://www.euronews.com/green/2020/11/30/bamboo-eco-friendly-fabric -or-environmental-disaster

Selfridges (2024) *Reselfridges*, available online at: https://www.selfridges.com/GB/en/features/ project-earth/resell/

Tidd, J. and Bessant, J. (2021) *Managing Innovation: Integrating Technological, Market and Organizational Change*. Chichester: Wiley.

UK Government (2015) *Publish an Annual Modern Slavery Statement*, UK Government, available online at: https://www.gov.uk/guidance/publish-an-annual-modern-slavery-statement

WRAP (2012) 'Valuing Our Clothes: The cost of UK Fashion', *Waste Resources Action Programme*, available online at: https://www.wrap.ngo/

Zhang, L., Wu, T., Liu, S., Jiang, S., Wu, H. and Yang, J. (2020) 'Consumers' clothing disposal behaviors in Nanjing, China', *Journal of Cleaner Production*, 276. https://doi.org/10.1016 /j.jclepro.2020.123184

Zhang, X., Le Normand, A., Yan, S., Wood, J. and Henninger, C.E. (2024) 'What is modular fashion: Towards a common definition', *Resources, Conservation and Recycling*, May 2024, 204: 107495. https://doi.org/10.1016/j.resconrec.2024.107495

# Creativity and Innovation for Branded and Ready-to-wear Fashion

*Erica Charles*

## Introduction

This chapter examines innovation sources and processes used in the development of branded clothing and "designer" ready-to-wear collections (a translation of the French term *prêt-à-porter*, describing garments from the runway that are not hand-crafted or individually fitted haute couture). The differences between these collections will be explored, alongside discussion of how leadership and organisational structure of these differing market levels affects innovative processes. The fashion industry has seen significant changes since the COVID-19 pandemic began in terms of practices and processes, and that too applies to the design and manufacturing of branded and designer fashion. This chapter examines some of the key changes in this sector, by highlighting innovation sources and processes used in the development of branded and designer ready-to-wear collections. Key drivers of innovation within the creative process will also be discussed.

The terms "branded fashion" and "designer brands" are often used interchangeably, and although they do share similarities, they differ in terms of production scale, price points, target audience, and the degree of emphasis on innovation and artistic expression in the design process. Branded fashion often involves mass production and typically involves creating styles for a wider audience. However, it differs from "own-label" fashion, which is developed for specific retailers, as brands focus largely on designing and promoting clothing and accessories. As branded fashion companies are rarely retailers (although they may have a limited number of their own outlets), they usually act as intermediaries (similar to wholesalers), selling most of their products via other companies, mainly small independents or large department stores that specialise in retailing and offer a range of brands (see Figure 7.1). Given the need to appeal to many, branded fashion typically aims to have more accessible price points than designer clothing and is more responsive to emerging fashion trends. In this

DOI: 10.4324/9781003332749-7

**FIGURE 7.1** An independent fashion store selling a range of different brands. Photo by Helen Goworek

space, brands have relied on a strong retail presence and wide distribution networks to maximise reach, be it through bricks-and-mortar stores or online. In order to meet high demand, a highly efficient production process, the use of cost-effective materials and standardisation in design are typical in branded fashion.

Typically, designer ready-to-wear brands focus on creating a sense of uniqueness and exclusivity, and as a result create limited production runs. Also known for their higher price points, designer brands look to reflect craftmanship and quality whilst appealing to a target audience that is willing to invest in these core values. Designers working for these brands, are often given more freedom to explore and experiment, be it with unconventional materials or innovative designs, thus keeping innovation and creativity at the forefront. Often reflecting the creative vision of an individual or a small design team, the artistic expression and storytelling of the brand extend to its luxury retail spaces. These spaces often offer a more elevated and immersive shopping experience that aligns with the designer brand's image. It is worthy of note that clothing in all price ranges will require fashion designers, but the inference at designer level is that the name of a designer will feature on the label, whereas mass market designers remain anonymous to the consumers who wear their designs.

## The Design Process for Branded and Ready-to-wear Fashion

The design process for branded and ready-to-wear fashion is a dynamic and collaborative journey that encompasses trend analysis, conceptualisation, sketching, prototyping, fittings, fabric and trim selections, and production. Balancing creative innovation with commercial viability is key, and as a result, designers in the branded and ready-to-wear sectors must navigate a complex landscape to deliver cohesive, accessible and trend-right collections that resonate with the target consumer whilst still maintaining the unique brand DNA. Typically rooted in market research, designers immerse themselves in the ever-evolving fashion landscape, analysing current market trends, consumer preferences, cultural influences and even societal shifts to inform their creative decisions (see Figure 7.2). Scrutinising everything from designer runway shows and street style to social media influencers and developments in the art and music scene, these observations inform the creative direction for the collection (see Chapter 2).

The design process is intricately linked to a brand's identity and ethos, so designers have to operate within a framework which is defined by the brand's overarching mission and values. Brand guidelines serve as a compass, dictating colour palettes, silhouettes and overall design "handwriting" (see Figure 7.3 and the interview with Gemma Shiel at the end of this chapter). This structured approach ensures a cohesive narrative and recognisable brand image, allowing consumers to identify and emotionally connect with the brand across various platforms. This is even more important in the contemporary e-commerce landscape, given the sheer amount of products displayed. A robust brand aesthetic and style play a crucial role in ensuring easy identification amidst the vast array of choice available to customers online. For

**FIGURE 7.2** A co-ordinated collection of branded products. Image with permission from Karen Purdy

**FIGURE 7.3** Products from Lazy Oaf indicate the brand's identifiable design handwriting. Photos with permission from Gemma Shiel

designer collections, although they too are informed by consumer insights and key market dynamics, the design process is characterised by a more exclusive and artisanal approach that involves a more intricate and time-intensive journey. Creative freedom, craftmanship, attention to detail, the importance of the brand and managing the brand image at all levels provide the foundation for its creative process. Given that designer brands are unrestrained by the need for mass market appeal, the design process is initiated by an in-depth exploration of conceptual themes, artistic inspirations and innovative ideas, with an emphasis on pushing the boundaries of fashion (see Chapter 4). Designer brands probably consider themselves as innovators, rather than imitators (see "Diffusion of Innovations" in Chapter 4). The Creative Director of a designer company's artistic vision takes precedence, leading a team of designers to develop collections that are not solely driven by commercial viability, but rather by a desire to demonstrate creative prowess.

## Co-creation in Design

In both the branded and designer space, co-creation in design is important, albeit with different nuances, applications and outcomes. A collaborative approach that facilitates the injection of innovation and creativity not only involves keeping the consumer at the heart of every design decision but may also involve the active participation of third parties in the actual design process. For example, brands may enlist the help of external stakeholders such as textile design agencies or freelance designers to bring a fresh perspective to design. Sometimes even the design resources of brand suppliers are used, either exclusively or collaboratively. Co-creation is mainly used to describe consumers becoming part of the design journey (see Chapter 4). For example, the Levi's Tailor Shop allows consumers to personalise their items with the use of various studs, buttons, badges, hems and pins. The expert tailors can even work closely with consumers to transform pieces into completely new items. The consumer particularly appreciates being part of the design journey, and this participatory experience enhances the customer experience, which leads to consumers forging a deeper emotional connection with the brand. When consumers are treated like active and valued contributors to the brand and feel that their opinions and preferences are heard, it strengthens consumer engagement and leads to increased brand loyalty (Kim et al., 2018).

Branded fashion often relies on collaborative initiatives such as consumer surveys, feedback sessions, product reviews and social media interactions to inform design decisions. User-generated content is fed directly into the design process, which in turn enables brands to create consumer-centric designs that align with their target audience. For example, a retailer can offer a direct feedback channel from the consumer to the design team through its feedback blackboard (see Figure 7.4). This channel provides an opportunity for the design team to hear first-hand from consumers, who in turn feel heard and connected to the brand. Through social media, consumers are directly involved in trend identification and validation, allowing brands to quickly respond to emerging trends and the fast-paced nature of the fashion industry. This involvement heightens consumers' sense of inclusivity and involvement.

Collaboration also presents itself in the branded space as design collaborations with renowned fashion designer brands. Since 2004, High Street fashion brand/

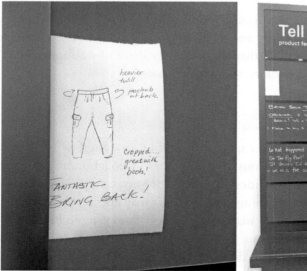

**FIGURE 7.4** Examples of in-store feedback boards. Photos by Fiona Bailey

retailer H&M has released many high-profile designer collection collaborations, including Karl Lagerfeld, Stella McCartney, Balmain, Jimmy Choo and most recently Paco Rabanne. These partnerships enable High Street brands to infuse their collections with a touch of luxury as well as bring fresh perspectives and cutting-edge styles that resonate with fashion-forward consumers. This not only keeps these brands relevant by elevating brand image (Michel and Willing, 2020), but it also enables designer brands to access a wider audience, bringing with it financial benefits, as well as raising brand awareness and desire. In the designer brand space, co-creation frequently takes on a more explorative approach, often exemplified by collaborations with coveted creatives across different industries, such as art, music, automobiles or even food. Supreme's collection with Tiffany & Co., Kith and Nobu, Frame Denim and the Ritz Paris, and Rhude and McLaren are some examples where brands share ideologies, inspirations, materials and communal design, to push collaborative projects beyond the norm. The late Virgil Abloh, who partnered with everyone from Nike and Serena Williams to Evian and Ikea, elevated the idea of collaboration beyond a marketing activity. Going beyond the need to address market trends or to solidify a brand's creative vision, he truly worked hard to change people's ideas about designer fashion and value, opening the market up to make it easier for consumers to access quality design. Often released as limited-edition collections, a sense of exclusivity and urgency is placed on collections, with consumers sometimes going to the extreme to secure prestigious pieces, not to mention the marketing campaigns that surround these collaborations, often generating widespread coverage that drives much-needed footfall to both bricks-and-mortar stores and online.

Co-creation is a direct response to over-production, in that it enables fashion brands to create pieces that align with actual demand, therefore fostering a more sustainable approach to the whole process. It also has the ability to bridge the gap between creators and consumers, and is a way to elevate the fashion industry's capacity for innovation. The team at Swedish design studio Streamateria state: "project collaboration and co-design is imperative. We as visionaries and designers rely on the knowledge of others - specialists, engineers, scientists, commercial companies and more" (Designtofade, 2024).

## Circular Design in Branded and Ready-to-wear Fashion

The global fashion industry accounts for around 10% of the global carbon emissions (United Nations Climate Change, 2018). This is about the same as the amount that France, Germany and the UK combined emit (McKinsey & Company, 2020). In addition, 87% of the textiles used to make clothing end up incinerated or in landfills (Ellen MacArthur Foundation, 2024). Fashion designers have seen the damage this industry has done to the planet and communities, and are therefore approaching the design process in a more sensitive and responsible way. The modern role of the designer is someone who looks beyond a beautiful garment and challenges themself to think not just about the after-life of clothing, but to design in ways that look to regenerate local ecosystems and communities. Known as circular design, this is an emerging practice which emphasises the principles of a circular economy: "an economic system designed to minimize waste, promote sustainability, and maximize the lifespan of products and materials" (Ellen MacArthur Foundation, 2024) (see Chapter 6). By considering the entire product life cycle – from concept, design and production to use, reuse and recycling – this approach contrasts with the traditional linear model, where garments are produced, used and then discarded. Strategic Design Manager and Editor at the Ellen MacArthur Foundation Elodie Rousselot stated: "Circularity is about designing for systems change, for a future where instead of being a source of global challenges like climate change or biodiversity loss the industry can become a solution to those issues" (Hahn, 2022).

Circular design aims to transform the fashion industry into a more regenerative and sustainable system, with fashion designers actively looking at methods to change the way they design products, as well as their business format (UNEP, 2023). Designing products with materials that can be easily recycled or repurposed, or creating products with modular components that can easily be replaced or upgraded, reduces waste and helps create a resilient fashion industry as well as assisting in regenerating the environment (see Chapter 6). Children's clothing brand Minories, from Swedish fashion retailer Kappahl, is designed for 100% circularity. Made from mono-materials, including seams and care labels, the collection is unisex to enable reuse between siblings and friends, and once worn out, every fibre is recyclable. Streamateria created another innovation that facilitates circularity. Launched on the principle of "design to die", the company brought to the market compostable fashion garments with a short lifespan, using 100% circular and print-on-demand materials made from cellulose and food waste. Once finished with, the material is mixed with food waste and biodegrades naturally, demonstrating zero tolerance to waste. In 2020, the company created the Design To Fade collaboration with PUMA innovation, a capsule collection of running vests that explored the potential of mass-customised, temporary garments and bio-functions. The life expectancy of these garments varies, as it depends on the interaction with the consumer's bodily functions; but hanging in the wardrobe, the garment can last for about six months (Design To Fade, 2024).

While circular design is a relatively recent approach in Western contexts, designers in China or Africa could affirm that this approach is a longstanding norm in their practices. When Rousselot carried out research, she found that transitioning from an exploitative to a mutually beneficial relationship with nature is often accompanied by "a rediscovery of indigenous knowledge and expertise" (Hahn, 2022). Circular design has also encouraged designers to forge better relationships with suppliers as well as build new relationships with industries such as waste and recycling. The Ellen MacArthur Foundation has consistently brought people and industries together to problem-solve, and in its 2023 *Circular Design for Fashion* book it features pioneering fashion designers and brands ranging from big conglomerates to independent labels which share their practical approach to design.

## Case Study: Tom's Trunks – Integrating Different Types of Innovation within a Niche Brand

*by Fiona Bailey*

Tom's Trunks is a niche online brand of unisex woven Kenyan loungewear offering sustainable, slow fashion which targets the younger Generation Z demographic. Tom's Trunks was founded in 2014 by Tom Holmes after a trip to Kenya inspired him to create product out of the traditional Kikoy cloth. This case study is based on an interview with Tom Holmes, discussing how innovation exists within different areas of his business. His insights are included throughout this case study, revealing how a successful niche brand innovates in several different areas. When asked what innovation means to Tom's Trunks, Tom described a method of reflecting on current processes to identify areas of weakness and opportunities for improvement: "For us, innovation is taking our current processes and looking critically at how we do them, challenging whether we are currently doing things in the most efficient way. Sometimes innovation doesn't mean changing things. It just means checking."

Not all innovation occurring within a business is driven internally. External stakeholders have a key part to play. To stay competitive and relevant, suppliers will present their innovations to fashion brands. Although innovation is often managed in-house, suppliers play

**FIGURE 7.5** Tom Holmes visiting a factory manufacturing Tom's Trunks. Photo with permission from Tom Holmes

a pivotal role in the process. Collaborative innovation can often produce the most creative results, as Tom reveals: "Innovation is mostly driven by me, but a lot of it is also driven by our suppliers. A lot of the time our suppliers will come to us and pitch ideas."

Sustainability is at the heart of Tom's Trunks brand values, and sustainable innovation is a key priority. Circularity is the end goal, and there are many initiatives in place within the pre- and post-consumer journey stages, as Tom explains:

> We try to innovate within logistics by looking at our circular ways. We're just releasing something called peer-to-peer returns. Rather than returning product back to the warehouse, you return it to a new customer. The customer uploads pictures into the returns platform and then sends to the new customer, saving carbon, energy and time. It also makes our business more efficient and it's better for the customer because they're getting a slightly cheaper product.

As part of the brand's circularity strategy, product repair is available as part of Tom's Trunks' service offering. This leads to increased customer loyalty and trust. If a product is in need of repair, Tom's Trunks will happily repair free of charge, either in-house or through an innovative new peer-to-peer repair service called SOJO, as Tom explains:

> If the product has any damage, we'll repair it for free in-house. We're also working with SOJO London, which is a really innovative company offering door-to-door alterations and repairs. It's like a dating app for people that are looking to get a repair done. Rather than sending the garment off somewhere, you send it to a SOJO repairer. For example, if you know how to repair denim jackets, you'd list yourself on SOJO under that category and state your fee. There's scalability through the SOJO platform – a lot of companies now are using SOJO for their own repairs.

A vital element of any circularity model is resale, whether operated in conjunction with a third-party platform such as eBay, Vinted or Depop or via the brand's website, managed wholly in-house. Tom's Trunks has implemented a customer resale facility on its website. As Tom states: "We let people sell their product back to us and buy it off them for a slightly reduced rate, giving them store credit to buy a new item. We'll then sell that item through our verified pre-loved store." Repurposing stock not fit for resale or repair is a strategy adopted by Tom's Trunks. This reduces waste and offers the consumer a diversified product offer, and Tom says: "If we don't think the product is repairable, we'll still offer a discount on a new pair, but we'll make it into something completely different, like a scrunchy or tote bag."

Product innovation is often the first type of innovation that comes to mind. Product teams are tasked to seek innovative improvements within a product's quality, appearance, performance and fit. It is crucial to consider all aspects of the product's design, evaluating the functionality of individual components, and the overall product performance and longevity. Tom reveals his strategy for product innovation:

For me it's all about the fibres we're using and the way we weave. We're looking at creating more interesting designs that aren't just prints or stripes. The big innovation we're looking at is trying to make products that last, a long, long time, looking at innovation in terms of how we can sew better so they'll last longer, how can we use less blended fabrics so you don't get the fabric wearing out as much. Innovation is how to make it last longer, be more comfortable, and ultimately just be stronger.

Finding new and innovative ways of connecting with the customer and showcasing the brand's offerings are essential for a brand like Tom's Trunks, whose core demographic is young Generation Z customers who value brand authenticity and transparency above all. Tom explains:

We're looking at moving and scaling our head office into a house where people will be able have drinks parties there. Customers can come experience the head office and the brand, making it much more experiential. Not only do you get that experience before you buy, once you've bought from us, you can become a part of the brand.

Creative and innovative customer engagement strategies that make the customer feel part of the brand are increasingly important when targeting the Generation Z demographic. Tom goes on to say:

Often, we find that our customers don't necessarily know what to style things with or how they can style one item completely differently each time they wear it. We're trying to really push that – we don't want people to buy loads and loads. We want people to buy one item and make the most of wearing it – and love it so it becomes a part of them. We don't believe that you buy a product from us once and that's it done. We want our customers to become part of our journey. It's not full stop, job done, the transaction's over. Really, for us it's just the start of the transaction.

Measurability within innovation is necessary to determine viability and success. In fashion brands, this may be through monitoring sales volume and rate of sale or customer engagement around the innovation on social media or on the website. It is essential for a business like Tom's Trunks, no matter how small or niche, to monitor innovation as a key performance indicator in terms of its return on investment to the business, as Tom explains:

We've not been that good at measuring how well our innovations work. The best way is seeing if it costs more money, or less money. Usually, it's based off a financial benchmark and then also an environmental benchmark, but the environmental benchmark is harder to quantify.

For a brand like Tom's Trunks, the measurability of success is not solely financial. Here, Tom discusses how environmental impact must also be considered:

Our peer-to-peer returns process is better environmentally because it uses less transport etc. But for production, it does get harder from a top line as we're making more product. Ultimately, we're growing as a business so it's harder to see where these efficiencies and innovations are coming in. But we do try to monitor it through tracking.

Innovation is not always disruptive. Sometimes innovation can take the form of smaller, incremental changes which collectively lead to a wider impact, as Tom explains: "We looked at a fabric innovation by changing the stripe design. This meant we wasted less fabric, really minute innovations, but we looked at how much we used before, how much we're using now and what the saving is." The traditional "'test-and-learn" innovation model is applicable within fashion brands. Test-and-learn can occur both prior to and at post-production stages. Brands will test new fits, fabrics or technical product innovations through user testing (such as wash-testing and wearer-trialling), gaining feedback and iterating the product according to the feedback. Trend, style, print, pattern and shape can be tested through releasing smaller trial quantities, testing the market and learning quickly from the data, as Tom explains:

A lot of what we're doing is testing. Trying new products, testing them - literally wearing it, seeing if it works better, how many washes it can go through. It is like a science experiment, at the end of the day, we'll record the data and see how it worked.

Whilst the benefits of successful innovation are clear, there exists an element of risk. Several factors can inhibit and constrain creativity and innovation within fashion businesses, and Tom says: "Sometimes the speed you're able to react is quite hard. Being able to take an idea and execute it while you've still got the day-to-day job and everything flying around you. That's a big challenge." Part of the risk of innovation involves significant investment in research and development. Smaller start-up brands like Tom's Trunks often rely on outside investment or grants to enable execution of innovation:

Innovation costs money, so you've got to make sure that you're not wasting time and money doing it. There are innovation grants, but to apply for those is time-consuming. You've got to have quite a big team to execute it and even just fill in the forms! But the grants are available.

Changing consumer perceptions around new sustainable business models can be challenging. However, Tom is confident that change is happening and consumers are becoming more responsible, demonstrating a shift in behaviour towards more sustainable practices. As he mentions:

A big challenge is changing consumers. It's very easy for you or I to say we'll just repair something, but to someone that's maybe not got time, or resources – they're not going to do it. And how do you get them to change? From a business perspective, it is hard to make customers take responsibility. It's definitely happening. Consumers are beginning to be much more responsible.

## Fabric Selection and the Production Process

Efficiency is paramount as designers balance creativity with the demands of mass production. The scale of production when it comes to branded ready-to-wear collections means that a streamlined design process must be employed. For example, when trying to align production costs to meet market expectations, designers sometimes have to consider using a less expensive fabric or even simplify the design by minimising details in order to meet market-driven retail recommended prices – e.g., remove unnecessary pockets or seams. Even at the higher-than-average prices that are typical in the branded market, there is demand for meticulous attention to cost-effectiveness, and sometimes this comes at the expense of design integrity. Collaboration and constant open communication with production teams is key, so building strong relationships with suppliers can help in arriving at innovative cost-saving solutions, especially through liaison with pattern-cutters and technologists who are significant in building in the quality standards which are of particular importance in the branded and ready-to-wear fashion sector.

In contrast, the production process for designer brands is a little less restrictive. With their focus on creativity, less pressures mean longer production timelines, which in turn means that the shift towards more seasonless collections and the renewed appreciation for craftmanship can be fully explored. The fashion industry as a whole has experienced significant changes since the COVID-19 pandemic began, with sustainability becoming a guiding principle in how designers approach the design process. Designer fashion brands have been more forward-thinking in embracing more enviro-friendly materials, given their access to funds and the freedom they have in the entire process. As designer and luxury fashion brands already carry a premium price, designers in this space can afford to not just look at fabrics that come via agriculture (e.g., cotton from crops), animals (e.g., leather from cowhides) or petrochemicals (e.g., polyester, nylon and acrylic derived from crude oil), but can work with a whole new generation of materials that have been produced using less resources from nature – biomaterials (raw materials that have been made in laboratories). Brands like Kering, Stella McCartney and Ganni are responsibly leading the way in their exploration and use of material innovations – e.g., mycelium leathers (leathers made from fungi). It takes time for designers to learn the unique new properties and benefits of these new materials, and not wanting to create another crisis in the long term (which is currently the case with the microfibre pollution crisis), adoption is gradual.

## Drivers of Innovation for Branded and Ready-to-wear Fashion

The drivers of innovation within a fashion organisation are multifaceted, involving various individuals and departments working collaboratively to propel the brand forward. Innovation is a collective effort that involves creative visionaries, technical experts, sustainability advocates and collaborative teams. Creative directors and design teams are at the forefront of innovation, as they drive the brand's aesthetic and conceptual evolution. When it comes to material innovations, teams responsible for product development and technical design play a crucial role in sourcing and experimenting with new materials and production techniques. Research and development teams analyse market trends, consumer behaviour and emerging technologies. Their insights inform strategic decisions, which in turn help brands to stay ahead by integrating cutting-edge elements and practices into their processes. With the increased focus on sustainability, dedicated sustainability teams can be employed to work across fashion departments in certain branded or designer companies, integrating responsible practices, materials, and processes into the design process. Together, these teams can drive innovation by exploring sustainable alternatives that align with the brand's ethos and values.

As previously mentioned, co-creation in design can drive different levels of innovation. Collaborations with third parties such as artists, tech companies or even other more experimental designers bring fresh perspectives and novel ideas. These partnerships foster cross-disciplinary innovation, and can lead to brands experimenting in areas and territories that were once unexplored. In what could be considered a crowded scene, innovation is one of the factors that drives partnerships such as Dior with Vespa, Thom Browne with Samsung, and Juventus with Palace. Apple merged cutting-edge technology with the craftsmanship and design expertise of luxury brand Hermès, whilst Adidas collaborated with environmental organisation Parley for the Oceans to create trainers made from recycled ocean plastic. It not only addressed environmental issues, but also showcased the innovative work of research and development teams within the fashion sector. Luxury brands like Louis Vuitton which partnered with tech giant Google to create the Tambour Horizon Light Up smartwatch, merged luxury fashion with wearable technology. Not only did it introduce a new revenue stream for both businesses, but it also showcased the potential of cross-sector partnerships in shaping innovative business models.

Leadership often sets the tone for fostering an innovative culture within an organisation. Encouraging risk-taking, embracing experimentation and supporting continuous learning are key elements that leaders can instil in their workforce to help drive innovation. Over the last ten years, the fashion industry has seen numerous managers build teams that include a mix of creatives, science and tech engineers, with inter-sectoral communities coming together to push boundaries and find more effective ways of working together to drive an entire industry forward. When teams with diverse expertise collaborate, it can lead to holistic solutions that consider both creative and practical aspects of design, and as a result provide solutions that keep brands at the forefront of industry innovation. Led by venture capitalists in the technology sector, material science lifestyle brand PANGAIA was born out of the need to speed up the adoption of technology-driven textiles within the fashion industry. In order to realise this vision, management had to create a team of experts that straddled product development and materials.

Digital transformation has accelerated since the start of the COVID pandemic, so by the sheer nature of digital and technical teams, they continue to leverage advancements to enhance the design process. From 3D printing and virtual reality to digitally inspired/virtual fashion shows and machine learning, the implementation of technology contributes to more efficient workflows and innovative presentation methods (see Chapter 3). Brands that can actively listen to their consumers can benefit from adapting and innovating designs and processes based on real-time feedback, thus ensuring relevance and consumer satisfaction. Here, recent technological innovations have enabled brands to embed responsive design into their offerings.

## The Role of Artificial Intelligence in the Design Process

To confidently steer through the uncertainties of the future, brands have to make strategic decisions; decisions that are clear, timely and inspiring. By harnessing the power of analytics, automation and artificial intelligence with human intuition and experience, it can help leaders resolve their most critical decisions, drive value, and achieve transformational success. The incorporation of AI into the fashion design process represents a paradigm shift where technology is used to complement and enhance human creativity. From trend analysis to virtual prototyping, customisation and beyond, AI-driven tools and technologies have become indispensable assets for fashion designers and brands seeking to innovate, stay competitive and meet the ever-evolving demands of the industry. As AI continues to evolve, its impact on fashion design is likely to expand, opening new possibilities for creativity, sustainability and personalised consumer experiences.

AI and computer visual technologies excel in colour and pattern recognition as well as automating processes, and therefore can play a pivotal role in trend analysis and forecasting. Machine learning algorithms can quickly analyse vast amounts of data from social media, fashion publications, and online platforms to identify emerging trends and patterns. Traditionally, this process would have required significant manual effort. Monitor Deloitte, a division of leading management consultant Deloitte which work with fashion and lifestyle brands to "identify transformative advantages and move faster with greater precision, to improve decision-making, and to create beneficial connections with customers" (Deloitte, 2023) stipulates that we are in era of "working with" AI. AI combined with human intuition and experience, empowers designers to make informed decisions.

When it comes to design inspiration, algorithms are adept at generating and facilitating the ideation phase of design. For instance, creative tools like generative adversarial networks can produce new data from existing data − creating design concepts by combining elements from existing styles to generate entirely new designs. Designers can leverage these AI-driven tools to spark creativity, explore unconventional ideas and overcome creative blocks. The collaborative interplay between human intuition and AI-generated suggestions often leads to innovative and unexpected design outcomes. However, *Business of Fashion* (2023) warns that AI can enhance creativity, but overreliance on technology trained to exclusively look at past designs can in fact hamper the creative process. Therefore, AI should merely be used as a source of inspiration, and not as a resource that will make the role of the designer redundant.

Predictive analytics can also help designers optimise material and fabric selection by considering factors such as the environmental impact, cost and performance of different materials. By analysing historical data, AI can predict the success of certain materials for a specific target consumer in a particular territory; again allowing designers to make more informed/data-driven decisions. AI may also contribute significantly to addressing the trend of customisation and personalisation in the fashion industry. By analysing customer data and preferences, AI algorithms can recommend personalised design and styling options based on a customer's past purchases, preferences and current trends, or even generate entirely bespoke designs tailored to individual tastes. This level of customisation enhances the customer experience by building a sense of exclusivity and engagement.

Within the fashion supply chain, AI can be instrumental in optimising efficiency and minimising waste. AI-powered virtual prototyping and 3D design tools have revolutionised the way fashion designers conceptualise and visualise their creations (see Chapter 3). These tools allow designers to create digital prototypes and simulations, enabling them to see how garments will look and move in a virtual space. This not only accelerates the design process, but contributes to less waste, as well as facilitating better collaboration amongst design teams and other stakeholders. Predictive analytics can also forecast demand, helping designers and brands to optimise production schedules and reduce over-production. Additionally, AI-driven systems can facilitate real-time monitoring of inventory levels, allowing for better demand–supply matching and preventing excess inventory. This not only aligns with sustainability goals, but can also contribute to cost savings for fashion brands.

## Innovative Business Models

Over the last decade, the fashion industry has witnessed a surge in innovative business models, driven by shifts in consumer behaviour, the changing global economic environment, technological advancements and sustainability concerns. Brands are looking for new engagement models, and although there is a heightened focus on selling direct to consumer (DTC), rising marketing costs mean that brands have to diversify their channel mix to include wholesale and third-party marketplaces alongside DTC. DTC models give brands larger profit margins, full control of the brand, and the ability to collect and analyse data in order to create personalised experiences, whereas wholesale and third-party marketplaces provide a wider reach to consumers and easier access to the brand.

The global second-hand fashion market is worth over $130 billion (*Business of Fashion Insights*, 2021), and in the luxury and designer brands sector, resale and rental services have played a big role in catering to consumers who seek variety without the long-term commitment of ownership. For example, launched in 2002 and bought by Richemont in 2018, Watchfinder & Co. established itself as the premier resource from which to buy and sell premium pre-owned watches, and in 2020 rental disruptor Rent the Runway saw its entrance into the growing resale market. So as not to leave their brands to chance, designer brands and retailers have also seen the importance of establishing their own resale strategies as a way to take control, closely manage their brands and deepen relationships with both new and existing consumers. Stella McCartney and Gucci (which launched Gucci Vault) have both collaborated with The RealReal as a way for their brands to promote responsible consumption and provide an environmentally conscious alternative.

Brands whose business models commit to putting sustainability (e.g., Mother of Pearl), personalisation and customisation (e.g., Levi's Tailor Shop), tech-driven retail (e.g., Amazon Fashion AI-powered recommendations) or collaborations and limited edition drops (e.g., Supreme) at the heart of their business were discussed previously in this chapter. However, in the branded sector, where companies are looking at ways to productively work with other brands in order to better engage consumers and add value, business models that are less reliant on holding large volumes of stock or are structured in a way that makes them more agile (and able to quickly respond to the changing consumer and/or marketplace), seem to be gaining traction. Subscription e-commerce is a business model whereby consumers receive branded products or services on a regular basis – typically monthly or quarterly. Due to its ability to offer convenience, personalisation and a predictable revenue stream for businesses, the global subscription e-commerce market which was worth US$193.6 billion in 2023, is set for continued growth (IMARCGroup, 2023). One of the better-known subscription services, Stitch Fix, is a personalised styling service where customers receive a curated selection of clothing items based on their style preferences and feedback.

In the beauty sector, companies such as Beauty Pie, which was founded by Marcia Kilgore, a beauty industry entrepreneur known for creating successful brands like Bliss and Soap & Glory, offer luxury beauty and skincare products at cost prices to their members. While subscription services present several advantages such as convenience, personalisation, customer loyalty and discoverability (enabling consumers to discover new products and brands they might not have encountered through traditional retail channels), businesses must carefully consider potential drawbacks such as customer churn, the need for ongoing customer engagement strategies, and inventory management challenges. In the third-party online space, drop-shipping is a popular business model as it allows retailers to offer a wide range of products without the need for holding physical inventory. It is a fulfilment method whereby retailers do not need to hold stock. Instead, when a store sells a product, it purchases the item from a third party (usually a wholesaler or manufacturer) and has it shipped directly to the consumer. This means that the retailer never sees or handles the product. While drop-shipping provides flexibility and lower upfront costs for entrepreneurs, it also comes with challenges, such as potential shipping delays, quality control issues and reliance on third-party suppliers. Exclusively online retailer Fashion Nova uses drop-shipping as part of its business model. Partnering with various suppliers to fulfil customer orders directly allows it to offer a vast and ever-changing inventory without the need for extensive warehousing. Using a drop-shipping model, Thread.com intelligently provided the perfect set of clothing recommendations based on what the consumer liked, sending personalised style ideas as well as styling inspiration. In November 2022, Marks & Spencer Plc bought this hybrid men's wear business's Intellectual Property, source codes and algorithms so as to further improve its own personalisation offering, earning more than £100 million in incremental revenue annually.

## Summary

This chapter has explored a variety of innovation sources and processes used in the development of fashion brands and designer ready-to-wear collections, discussing how the leadership and organisational structure of these differing market levels and recent global events have affected creative and innovative processes. Some of the key changes and drivers in this sector, including shifts towards sustainability and digitisation, have been examined. The design process, co-creation, fabric selection, the production process, potential uses for AI and innovative business models have also been discussed. The interviews with professionals in the branded and ready-to-wear sectors that follow provide personal insights into how creativity and innovation are applied at this market level.

### Interviews on Creativity and Innovation with Specialists in the Branded and Ready-to-wear Sectors

Gemma Shiel is CEO of Lazy Oaf, a London-based independent streetwear and lifestyle brand sold through its own website and a retail outlet near Carnaby Street. Gemma studied for a BA (Hons) Textile Design at Nottingham Trent University before founding Lazy Oaf in 2001, which launched as a branded label sold by retail companies.

*How do you incorporate creativity and innovation into the work that you do at Lazy Oaf?*

As a creative person and being creatively minded all my life, it was really important to create my own opportunity for a job and a way to make a living, using what I was best at, illustration and design. In my degree I specialised in screen printing, so I could bring illustration and screen printing together and create T-shirts for my mates. Creativity is my happy place and what gives me joy in everything that I do. Creativity is what we call the heartbeat of our brand, and without an element of play in the job, I wouldn't be doing it, so it has to be top priority. Being creative is essentially our purpose.

Running a business, being responsible for people's jobs and making products that are going to sell, there are lots of reasons to not make space and time for being creative, and you can be wrapped up in a process of looking at trends and designing what's popular. For me, doing that feels like it's not really stretching any creative muscles and not something that I would find enjoyable, so I think you have to make it a priority, for it to shine through. True creativity will outshine those commercial opportunities in authenticity, your own integrity and putting out the best version you can create. I personally find it more satisfying to know that I stretched my imagination to create something, and it makes us all excited and proud of what we've created.

For me, being able to retreat into my imagination is the way that I create. I draw and sketch and doodle, and I need to really immerse myself, put albums on that tell me stories. You need to get rid of some of the distractions sometimes to let your imagination work. I use Procreate on the iPad, and we sketch on body forms so that we can see the outfits coming together. We create faces and accessories that go with the outfit so that we can totally visualise the end result in sketch form, whereas when you go to the technical side and the CAD drawings, you lose it, it's a flat CAD drawing, and you can't completely visualise what it's going to look like at the other end.

You have your "bread and butter" products, and that allows you to make other [more creative] stuff. We have a "triangle" of product, with what we call like our "drivers" at the bottom, the stuff that sold really well, that is really important, so when we're building a connection [with customers], it makes sure that we've got something that fits into what

**FIGURE 7.6** Gemma Shiel, alongside Lazy Oaf products. Photos with permission from Gemma Shiel

people like, maybe a slight innovation. Then we have the next tier, which is what we're bringing in that feels new to the range. At the top is what we call "BOBs" which is "best of brands", so that's the innovation and creativity in our "hero" pieces. This triangle is the formation of how we consider product in a range. It's important that it is at an accessible level, and also considering that we don't make a lot of each item. It's important, though, to include something for £10, so if you're buying into the brand you can have a piece at an affordable price point, and it does tend to fall into that driver category. The newer level is going to be a mix of price points.

*Could you explain the different stages of the creative process for design at Lazy Oaf?*

At Lazy Oaf, I'm juggling different projects at different times, and so we could be working on the creative marketing alongside creative design on very different projects, all at different times. To describe the process, I get all of the creative people in my team to pitch and brainstorm concepts and stories for potential collections, and everybody comes at it from a different angle, which is brilliant. It's not exclusive to the designers, so the people that create our social media and work on the brand or do the copywriting all pitch in and we create mood boards or say "I just really like this idea" in a completely safe space. We're looking for things that just click as a group and generate that level of excitement. We can make jokes in our copy, or there are story arcs to take through to marketing, or you start to visualise what a campaign will be, and when you get all those magical bits coming together and everyone's bought in and excited, we can say, "Great, that's our Autumn story." Then we build up design concepts, take them away and put together a mood board.

For inspiration, if we're lucky we can go on a research trip if we've got the budget, or if not, we can go somewhere in London. Inspiration can come for me personally from what I'm watching on TV, the music we're listening to, and nostalgic stuff for me as a teenager or growing up and conversations that you overhear, sometimes great one-liners that we can then take through into T-shirt printing. It could also be a spark of some other content creation idea. We then also create a range plan, but I like to keep our inspiration really broad and start developing all of these ideas. Then we consider what products we need and start sketching and developing those designs, and it goes through and several processes of "What do we like, what does everybody else in the team think of the stuff that they do?", and we get them to drop little icons, make sure that we're getting feedback to sense-check "Are we all right and are we on the money? Is it doing what it needs to be doing? Is it offering something unique?"

Each product has to work so hard for us because we don't produce a lot. Sometimes it's generated in-house by me or we reach out to work with a creative community. We love working with artists to help bring our products to life. Lazy Oaf is known for its print and graphics and use of colour, so that's really integral. Then we go through a selection process and reduce our range down to what we feel really confident in, and then it goes into development, sampling etc. Then we repick up the creative baton when we're planning out how to launch it with the biggest impact that we can on what is quite often not the biggest buck, so that's also where we have to dig deep and get as creative as we can to stand out in a very crowded marketplace.

When I'm asking for people's ideas and story, that would probably be just outside 12 months in advance of launching the products at the moment, because we're operating as business-to-consumer, whereas previously when we were wholesaling [selling directly to retailers], our calendar would be probably about 14 to 18 months ahead, then we would start the design process, and shortly after the aim is to be designing and sketching and developing 9 to 12 months ahead from releasing that product. Depending on the scale of the collection, it could take us a week of research and development, a week of sketching, and then two weeks of putting together technical information packs and getting it ready to hand over to our product team. We would probably realistically have a four-week design window for designing our products.

*Where would you go to get these ideas?*

My favourite thing is to go to a different city, so I love going to Tokyo. It's my favourite city, and I always find it really inspiring. I like being taken out of my environment and looking at how other people are interpreting fashion, and I've always been a massive fan of Japanese youth fashion. I also find Seoul in Korea really inspiring. I love the shapes, and there is always a nice element of nostalgia in terms of characters, pop culture and nostalgia that I really love and connect with. It's an expensive trip, though, so I might go to the Japan Centre in London and raid all the magazines. Luckily, as we're in London we get access to exhibitions and amazing libraries that we can go and spend some time in. I spent a day just looking through books at the British Library recently because we were doing something that felt quite Gothic and we wanted some original imagery of ogres and gargoyles that we could sketch and look at on site. We got loads of great ideas from going there.

Personally, to get creative ideas, I have to almost declutter what I'm doing and try to make a dedicated amount of time to do that and prioritise it. It's really hard to go from an Excel sheet to suddenly "Now create this idea!" You have to allow yourself space, because creativity needs space and it needs oxygen, and you need to stare at a wall sometimes to let your mind reset and wander. That's really important to me, or you carve out that that time to get away from your screen, look at something different, that you're not looking at every day, go for a walk, get something you can physically hold, go and look at some vintage stuff, go to an exhibition, go to a museum, and give yourself some space and time and allow things to percolate. Also with creativity, I think you've got to take away the pressure of the end result, otherwise you'll never get to that end result. I think you need to allow yourself to play, to be truly creative, and it's also really nice to have someone to soundboard stuff, if you've got that opportunity, to have that reassurance and confidence to keep going. That's a really nice little ingredient to spur on a direction that you might be exploring.

*What would you say are the most important design innovations in the fashion industry from your perspective?*

There are several that come to mind. Re-looking at fabrics and what they're made of has been incredible. Digital printing for us has meant that we can like go really big and bold with our print and graphics, whereas previously it would have been quite inaccessible and really expensive to do that. Another really exciting one to me at the moment is that 3D-printing can play a role in being able to see an actual prototype of a sole or a shoe without having to go through a big expense and a big process that takes a really long time. We can now see a product that we're thinking of coming to life quite quickly.

*How would you define creativity and innovation based on your own experience and knowledge?*

…. It's really hard to be innovative, especially in the cyclical process of fashion, where we see things come in again and again. Now, with the rise of the internet, there are so many fashion designers creating clothing ,and innovation can be a really contentious issue. You can see that someone thinks something is innovative in 2024 because they've put a particular print on a T-shirt, but actually someone in 1964 got there first. You have to decide how to prioritise innovation, and you can sometimes get so preoccupied with it being fresh and new and doing something different that it inhibits what you're producing or executing. At the same time, it's got to be a driver for you to achieve and create something that feels new and exciting and that you need in your life. Innovation can also be a bit of a pressure sometimes, so I think you've got to find a bit of a balance.

*Who would you consider to be the most innovative and creative fashion retailers or brands from a design perspective?*

My instinctive answer is Martin Margiela. I loved how the recent collection reflected an almost AI-like world, but in a very human way, and it's really exciting to me to see a show that felt so theatrical and slightly odd, but brilliant at the same time, with people of all shapes and sizes and playing with the idea of femininity.

*Your brand is well known for its humour. How is that incorporated into the creative process?*

Lazy Oaf sense of humour is my sense of humour and it's one of our biggest priorities to make sure that we've always had a tone of voice and a sense of humour. It's what has given us a bit of a distinction within our marketplace. I definitely think that fashion can become quite pretentious quite quickly and it's the human element that makes us grounded, so I like to bring through that thread of humour because it's also a great leveller. I want people to smile and giggle when they see our stuff or connect with it, and I think that's been a massive key to us growing the community that we have. If you can't have a giggle at work, then what are we doing here? It runs through our whole team and what we do.
https://www.lazyoaf.com/

*Interview by Helen Goworek and Christina Goworek*

**FIGURE 7.7** Craig Smith. Photo with permission from Craig Smith

**Craig Smith is an experienced leader in innovation, having held senior positions at PANGAIA, Speedo, lululemon and Adidas. Craig holds a master's degree in Science and Engineering of Materials from Birmingham University, UK.**

*How would you define innovation?*

Innovation is a term that has become ubiquitous within business, and often tends to have an air of mystery around it, but in essence is a form of problem-solving. Innovation or innovative thinking can be utilised in any form of business, and is intended to lead to new products, processes, services or the improvements in those that already exist within a company. Innovation should be seen as a spectrum where solutions can be incredibly complex, leading to disruptive solutions, or more simplistic, leading to incremental improvements. The type of innovation that is pursued is contingent on the business appetite for it, the resources that are allocated to it and the patience that exists to create change.

*Can you give me an example of an important recent sustainable innovation in fashion?*

FLWRDWN™ is a great example from PANGAIA (a down-style filling made using a combination of wildflowers, a bio- polymer and aerogel which is cruelty-free, warm and breathable). Originally, its feasibility was tested through the PANGAIA brand and then subsequently offered out to business-to-business. Brands like H&M and COS have used FLWRDWN™ in small campaigns. There is also a huge amount of work and solutions within the leather alternative space, from lab-grown to mycelium to a range of natural inputs used to create alternatives to conventional leather. However, like all next-generation materials, they all require support to develop, from funding to pioneering brands that are willing to work with these new materials, and generally patience, as these are new material solutions that are being compared to or trying to replace materials that have been used for hundreds if not thousands of years.

*How do creatives work alongside scientists to generate innovation?*

When building teams, particularly more recently within a "fashion world", I've tried to create multi-disciplinary teams where creatives are working closely with scientists to create this collision of perspectives which is more of the norm within R&D teams or innovation teams in the sports industry. This is intended to create a more rounded view of innovation that hopefully creates a better end value proposition. The conventional roles that were previously set as a designer and product developer are becoming much more blurred. You'll find product engineers, design researchers with more of a mix of backgrounds that can speak to both the technical and the creative side of things, which helps enable the transition and development of innovation.

*How do you recruit people who have skill sets in both creativity and science?*

The people who do both are very difficult to find. There tends to be a separation in camps between creative and technical, but hopefully you can find an individual who then straddles both disciplines. Those roles tend to be more senior, where these individuals have built up experience in a range of different positions and businesses, but with changes in our approach to teaching and higher education courses evolving all the time, we'll see more of these individuals emerging.

*How do you encourage innovative thinking?*

By breaking down the stigma attached to innovation, you'll tend to see more engagement with it. By sharing practices and approaches to problem-solving that can be used across a range of business functions, this can help unlock innovation as a business practice. This is also driven by mindset and giving teams the agility, and most importantly the opportunity to pursue challenges or problem-solving within their area is critical to enabling innovation. This could be encouraged by asking teams to share learnings more broadly within a business or facilitating events like hackathons for random idea generation. From a product perspective, taking the user-centred design approach and then using innovation to come up with a solution, testing it on the user, iterating it and re-testing it is a great place to start.

*Who do you consider to be the most innovative and creative fashion retailers or brands, and why?*

Innovation is such a broad spectrum, and brands are difficult to compare as they are all approaching it quite differently. Of course, I am a little biased on this one, but I think the business model for PANGAIA is innovative in terms of how it was set up to try and address the innovation scaling issue. Ganni and Stella McCartney are working very closely with a large range of innovators, and launched a lot of interesting product collections with great technologies. Patagonia have, of course, been pioneers in terms of their over-arching philosophy centred around sustainability. Finally, from a technology perspective, I like the focus that lululemon have been putting on new sustainable innovation, and I have admiration for Vollebak for their clothes of the future.

*In your experience, how is the process of innovation managed differently within different fashion retailers or brands?*

From my experience, the sporting goods industry has much more patience and a certain propensity for the risk associated with innovation, but this has been integrated into the product creation process for a considerable timeframe now. Generally, there are much larger teams here due to the inherent focus on innovation, but they also have a more aligned/integrated model into product. Fashion is catching up, though, and you can see much more expertise being pulled directly in brands more recently, and a greater appetite for creating/adopting unique technologies.

*How would you sum up the creative and innovative work that you have been involved with in your career?*

During my career, I've been very fortunate to work with some of the most talented engineers, scientists and creatives in the industry whilst developing/commercialising some truly ground-breaking technologies. During this period, I've picked up so many different learnings and nuggets of knowledge, so it would be difficult to summarise that all here. However, if I were to take two to three key broader themes it would be to: (1) test and validate as much as possible, particularly in a true use scenario (people tend to do unexpected things with product); (2) facilitate relationships, particularly with supply chain partners (these individuals/entities are your greatest allies in innovation); (3) don't let perfect stand in the way of good, as it can be tempting to keep tinkering and developing, but you'll either lose your momentum or someone will beat you to it!

*Interview by Fiona Bailey*

**Harriet Eccleston is an award-winning fashion designer with her own label, crafted In Tthe UK, which has been shown on the catwalk in London, Paris and Moscow. After graduating from Northumbria University, UK, Harriet worked for Paul Smith and other companies before launching her first fashion collection in 2019.**

*How would you sum up the creative and innovative aspects of the work that you do?*

I like to think of myself as a responsible women's wear designer, so everything that I create is done in a way that is conscious of the people who are going to wear the garments, as well as everybody who is involved in the whole process of it being created. It's all about keeping the circle of creation as local as possible, and everything's traceable, from the cotton onwards. I know who picked the cotton from which part of the field, who cleaned it, spun it, dyed it, wove it, and then the garments are crafted in my studio. The idea is that they are going to be worn and loved for many years to come, and as soon as they are done, they're all natural fibres, so they go back into the ground where they came from. I knew that's what I wanted to achieve, and I was very fortunate to find a company about an hour away from where my studio was based at the time renovated and restored the old cotton mills near

**FIGURE 7.8** Harriet Eccleston alongside one of her adaptive designs, and her family's shop in the 19th century. Photos with permission from Harriet Eccleston

Manchester. They produce British cotton fabric, and the raw cotton is grown in California then shipped over in huge quantities in its raw state, so it's a lot more eco-friendly with a lot less pollution than flying over small quantities when you need it. The rest of the process is completed in the UK, so apart from that shipping, the rest of the process is done in the UK, in the Midlands. I learnt to be creative from both grandparents when I was tiny, and I think it's really interesting to look back on your life and see how you've been inspired over a long time to get to what you do today, and how that plays a part in your creativity.

*What do you think are the most important recent innovations in the fashion industry from your perspective?*

I think it is a really exciting time at the moment, and a lot of that is coming from people being aware, whether it's consumer or designer, of the impact that fashion has on the environment. The digital side, like 3D designing, is not something that I do, but it's something that I have worked with. I had a 3D designer produce some models when I was creating an adaptive fashion collection. She produced a 3D model so that we could see how my designs fit on the model before I even put pencil to paper to create the patterns. I think the amount of waste in sampling is crazy, whether that's paper or fabric, and the cost of that on the environment is vast, so I think 3D design and being able to see your garments move before they are physical products is brilliant, and it's really exciting to see that develop.

*How would you describe the process of innovation in your company?*

My family had a men's wear shop in the late 1800s/early 1900s (shown in Figure 7.8), so that heritage, craftsmanship, the way that fashion, the clothes and design were at that time is poles apart from how it is now that consumerism is taking over. At that time, if it wasn't you making your clothes, it was a family member or somebody down the street. I'm not necessarily trying to get back to that point, but to make people more aware of where their clothes come from. That's the inspiration behind the business and the clothes we produce, as well as personal and emotional connections to my family members who were in the shop at the time. I'm influenced by stories passed down to me of what was happening at the time, whether it's politics or just general everyday life, whether it's the emotional side or the feel of the men's wear. I'm a women's wear business, but the garments are androgynous in style. I am often inspired by seeing a photograph or hearing about a story. I was sent a receipt by a family member connected to Emily Davison and the suffragettes which then sparked researching more into that avenue and inspired a whole range of pieces. I've used the archives just outside Newcastle as well to do a lot of digging, and I like to get all the information and any photographs, then sit down with sheets of paper and just sketch. I think for me the thing that really helps in the design process is when I start to get things onto the mannequin, onto the figure, and then you can really see them come to life. My background is in pattern-cutting, so I'm very technically minded, and a lot of the ideas and details happen when you're pattern-cutting.

My journey after finishing university was a bit crazy. I was one of the students picked to have my clothes on the catwalk at *Graduate Fashion Week* [in London], and I was spotted by a stylist, and my collection was later featured and published in some magazines. In my placement year, I worked at Paul Smith and went back to work as a pattern-cutter and grader once I graduated. While I was doing that, I entered the Midlands Fashion Awards, and I was spotted by a fashion scout. I knew I wanted to have my own business, and it felt like it was now or never while there was a little bit of publicity, so I jumped and did it and started working from home for myself as well as doing some freelance work. When I launched the following year, I was selected for something called *Global Talents,*, which was in Russia. I showed my collection on the catwalk at *Mercedes Benz Fashion Week* in Moscow, and it just went from there. I was on the hamster wheel of fashion – of a new collection, new season showing, and then a new collection, new season showing etc. I knew that wasn't what I wanted to do at all, but it felt like that was what was expected. I came back from *Paris Fashion Week* a year later, and we went into lockdown, and it was a good pause to say, "No, I'm not doing that," and I think a lot of people also changed their mindset at that time. I was able to really work on the business that I wanted to have, as opposed to the business that it had fallen into.

*How did you become involved in adaptive fashion?*

I became involved through Faduma's Fellowship. Faduma is a bubbly character who had become paralysed from the neck down in 2011. She loved fashion, but could no longer wear her clothes and didn't feel like there was anything to express her personality, so she teamed up with Oxford Fashion Studio and they launched Faduma's Fellowship. I saw this opportunity when they were looking for a designer, and I thought, "Well, my background's in pattern-cutting, I'm quite technically minded, and this sounds like a brilliant challenge," but then I thought, "I have no experience in adaptive fashion," and that was a shocking realisation, considering that I'd gone through four years at a brilliant university and worked at three fashion houses, but nobody had ever raised it. That's such a large proportion of the population that can't wear the clothes that were being designed, so I felt like I needed to go for it and see what I could do. I teamed up with two graduates from Northumbria University

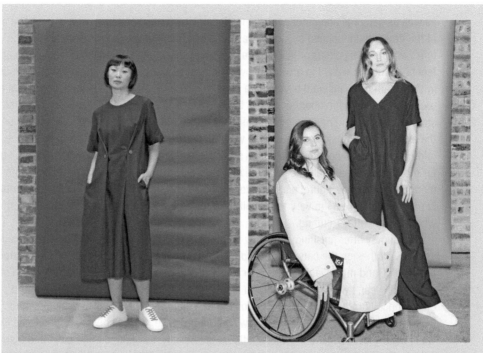

**FIGURE 7.9** Adaptive fashion designs from Harriet Eccleston's Faduma's Fellowship collection. Photos by Oxford Fashion Studio with permission from Harriet Eccleston

from the fashion communication degree. For their final project, they'd researched the lack of adaptive fashion and problems that people face, so they were able to provide me with what was missing the mark in fashion and what a lot of the problems were. Then I was able to come up with solutions for how we could get these garments to fit properly. We won the award and designed a 12-look collection which showed at *London Fashion Week* in 2021, and we were completely overwhelmed at the amazing reaction. I met Victoria Jenkins from Unhidden when I was working, we did pop-ups with her, and it was brilliant. It feels like there's a lot more movement happening with that sector, which is incredible, and it's really started getting the light shone on it, there are exciting things happening, but it shouldn't have taken this long. I've been back a couple of times to Northumbria, and it's brilliant to see students creating adaptive fashion final collections and having these conversations, because it just takes one person in a room to say, "Hang on, why aren't we designing fashion for everybody?" It seems simple, small changes can make a huge difference to a lot of people.

*Do you think there are any particular brands or fashion retailers that are especially innovative?*

I'm enjoying seeing brands that are being a lot more aware of how they're producing garments, and I think Amy Powney at Mother of Pearl is doing incredible work there. It's really inspirational to see what she's doing because she talks about a lot of the things that I was feeling like when I launched, that no one was listening and people are tied into the seasons, they're more focused on the price points than they are about how the garments that they're wearing or buying have affected the planet and the people on it.

*Do you collaborate with suppliers in creating innovation in any way and do they supply ideas or fabrics that have helped to push innovations forward?*

I've had the privilege of working with other creatives, but I recently met a brilliant company which produces eco-leather products made from apple waste, the by-product of juices, food production etc. We're hoping to collaborate next year to try, and I haven't worked in leather yet so am really excited for it. I'm very cotton- and wool-focused, but it's really interesting to see the different sustainable products and materials that are out there.
https://www.harrieteccleston.co.uk/

*Interview by Helen Goworek*

**Yiva Wu is a designer for the innovative sustainable ready-to-wear brand Rhyzem, blending traditional aesthetics with biotechnology. Yiva graduated with a BA (Hons) Fashion form Beijing Institute of Fashion Technology, then completed an MA at London College of Fashion in 2022 before launching Rhyzem at *London Fashion Week* with fellow designer Boqun Huang.**

*How would you define creativity and innovation based on your own experience and knowledge?*

I really like to start my design with draping with the fabric I'm into and try to figure out what kind of garment would this piece of fabric end up with, and the best thing is to try to make this fabric "mine" by draping it into the shape or curve I like. I always define creativity and

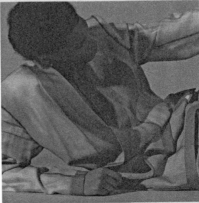

**FIGURE 7.10** Yiva Wu alongside an image from the Rhyzem collection lookbook. Photos with permission from Yiva Wu

innovation in fashion as telling a story through your own fashion language. I don't think creativity and innovation is only about inventing something extremely new or creating something that's never seen before in this entire world, I always believe that a good designer with creativity and innovation is someone who could use regular things to create their own system, dissolving inherent rules and thinking in design.

*Please could you explain the process of design and innovation in your company – e.g., the stages and procedures you go through, as well as the inspiration and thinking behind your creative process?*

In my last collection, I attempted to express Deleuze's theory of the organless body through pattern, I deconstructed the rules of style inherent in the men's wear system by connecting different parts of the garment through pleats. At the same time, I photographed different materials such as yarns and knits into prints. By dividing the same garment structure into draped, plain and printed versions, I can reduce waste in the development process and achieve a sustainable design system by transforming styles.

*What are the most important recent design or technological innovations in the fashion industry in your opinion?*

I think it would be the combination of some traditional craftsmanship and fashion creative ideas. It's really good to see that craftsmanship is used in nowadays fashion and the heritage in continuous innovation.

*Who do you consider to be the most innovative and creative current fashion brands from a design or technological perspective, and why?*

I would always say Issey Miyake, the great designer [who] created so many innovative ways of thinking in fashion design. In the design of Issey Miyake, techniques, textiles and pattern-cutting are always breaking boundaries of typical thinking of those materials and the human body as fashion.

https://londonfashionweek.co.uk/designers/rhyzem

*Interview by Helen Goworek*

# References

Business of Fashion Insights (2021) 'The Future of Fashion Resale', *BoF Insights Lab*, available online at: https://insights.businessoffashion.com/products/the-future-of-fashion-resale-publication

Business of Fashion (2023) *The Year Ahead: How Gen AI Is Reshaping Fashion's Creativity*, available online at: https://www.businessoffashion.com/articles/technology/the-state-of-fashion-2024-report-generative-ai-artificial-intelligence-technology-creativity/

Deloitte.com (2023) *Artificial Intelligence and Data*, available online at: https://www.deloitte.com/global/en/services/consulting/services/artificial-intelligence-and-data.html

Designtofade (2024) *Design to Fade PUMA*, available online at: https://designtofade.puma.com /project/streamateria

Ellen MacArthur Foundation (2024) *What Is a Circular Economy?*, available online at: https:// www.ellenmacarthurfoundation.org/topics/circular-economy-introduction/overview

Hahn, J. (2022) *Six Fashion Brands Pushing Circular Design Beyond Recycling*, available at: https:// www.dezeen.com/2022/01/14/circular-design-for-fashion-ellen-macarthur-book/

IMARCGroup.com (2023) *Subscription Box Market Size, Share, Industry Growth 2024–2032*, available at: https://www.imarcgroup.com/subscription-box-market

Kim, J., Park, J. and Glovinsky, P.L. (2018) 'Customer involvement, fashion consciousness, and loyalty for fast-fashion retailers', *Journal of Fashion Marketing and Management: An International Journal*, 22(3), 301–316.

McKinsey & Company.com (2020) *How the Fashion Industry can Reduce Its Carbon Footprint*, available at: https://www.mckinsey.com/industries/retail/our-insights/fashion-on-climate

Michel, G. and Willing, R. (2020) *The Art of Successful Brand Collaborations: Partnerships with Artists, Designers, Museums, Territories, Sports, Celebrities, Science, Good Cause… and More*. London: Routledge.

UNEP.com (2023) *Sustainability and Circularity in the Textile Value Chain: A Global Roadmap*, available online at: https://www.unep.org/resources/publication/sustainability-and -circularity-textile-value-chain-global-roadmap

United Nations Climate Change (2018) *Milestone Fashion Industry Charter for Climate Action Launched*, available online at: https://unfccc.int/news/milestone-fashion-industry-charter -for-climate-action-launched

# 8

# Creativity and Innovation in the Mass Market Fashion Business

*Fiona Bailey*

## Introduction

Innovation can take different forms, depending on the type and nature of the fashion company. A fashion business positioned within the mass market must consider innovations with mass appeal. High Street brands and retailers producing goods in large quantities for mass market consumption will have a different perception of creativity and innovation than retailers or brands occupying a higher-end market space. This chapter will discuss the key differences between the creative and innovative processes within the two sectors. Drivers of innovation and creativity as well as common constraints on innovation will also be explored. The mass market is characterised as fast-paced, highly competitive and primarily driven by profit. Mass market fashion retailers are concerned with the interpretation of affordable and accessible trends inspired by higher-end fashion brands and designers. Posner (2015:15) contextualises mass market fashion as "high-street multiples or fashion retail chains such as … H&M or Zara, available on High Streets in most major cities or towns, or internationally". Identifiable features of mass market fashion are high volumes and low price points, and it is considered the largest market segment in terms of both production volumes and sales (Posner, 2015).

## Mass Market Retailing

Profit margin[1] targets are front and centre in every mass market retailer's strategy. These "non-negotiables" lead to constraints within creativity and innovation. This results in a trade-off between achieving the required level of profit margin and creating the "next best thing" or runaway best seller. However, creative and innovative thinking can overcome these "profits over aesthetics" constraints to produce novel, technologically advanced and innovative products despite the restrictions that mass

DOI: 10.4324/9781003332749-8

market fashion may impose. Problem-solving mindsets are hugely valuable within this sector in particular. Examples of how innovation constraints can be overcome are included later in the chapter. Arguably, there is a greater level of competition between mass market retailers than within luxury brands due to the sheer volume of competitors. Accessibility and affordability of product only add to the level of consumer choice. Unlike luxury and high-end brands, mass market fashion may have limitations on research and development budgets. However, there may still be the same expectation from consumers that these retailers will continue to offer innovative product "newness" despite the lower price points.

Consumers look to mass market retailers to buy everyday essentials such as underwear, therefore competing solely on price is difficult as all retailers are likely to produce similar offerings. Innovation can become the differentiating factor through superior design. This could be through upgrading fabric, updating the fit, utilising new techniques such as seamless technology or any other quality improvement. In turn, this becomes a source of competitive advantage for the brand or retailer, and innovation is an important and fundamental way to achieve this. Munasinghe et al. (2022) describe mass market retailers as having a core range of products on offer continuously all year round and a "new" product offer which includes more trend-led products. This is true for most mass market retailers, although product innovation should not solely focus on one area or the other. It is equally important to innovate the core, essential products as it is the new trends. Generally, core products are incrementally innovated, rather than completely redesigned. Innovation in core ranges can come from a number of areas, such as improving and upgrading fabric performance (e.g., moisture-wicking activewear), improving the fit (e.g., increased stretch in jeans), solving a problem (e.g., crease-free shirts and stain-resistant school wear) and increasing inclusivity (e.g., skin-coloured underwear). Certain mass market retailers offer a more expensive range than their average products, usually with a sub-brand label, such as Autograph at Marks & Spencer, or a more trend-led range than their core products, such as AND/OR at John Lewis. This type of range will still be exclusive to the retailer that develops it, but may offer some more scope for innovation for the designers in terms of quality of fabrics used or the inclusion of additional design details, so in these respects could be similar to designing for a branded company.

## The Design Process

McKelvey and Munslow (2012:79) describe the design process as "a complex process to unravel due to changing contexts and a myriad of individual approaches". However, the design process for mass market fashion has many similarities with the branded and ready-to-wear fashion sector (Munasinghe et al., 2022), although there are some notable differences. The mass market design process generally follows a

**FIGURE 8.1** Mass market fashion design and innovation process diagram.

linear process of research, strategy, design, evaluation, creation and launch to market. The process is outlined in Figure 8.1, with a more detailed breakdown of the stages involved shown inFigure 8.2.

## Research

The research stage of Figure 8.2 is the starting point for the mass market design process, and although different mass market brands and retailers will have their own methods of research, this is nearly always the designer's role. Smaller retailers or brands may rely on suppliers bringing research and trend insights to them (e.g., in meetings about product development), especially if they do not have their own design team.

### Comp Shops

It is common practice for mass market retailers to conduct "competitor shops" (otherwise known as comp shops) within each other's stores and online (see Chapter 2). A key requirement of the buyer's role is to be fully aware of the market and competitors' product, price and value offerings, benchmarking against their own. This process is conducted regularly to help forecast and plan range requirements, but also retrospectively to understand gaps within the range and missed opportunities.

### Bought Samples

Typically, within the mass market research stage, garment samples are often bought from both competitors' and aspirational brands. These are bought by the retailer's teams for fabric, colour, shape and style inspiration, and are referred to within the industry as "bought samples". Swatches of fabric from the garment are cut and

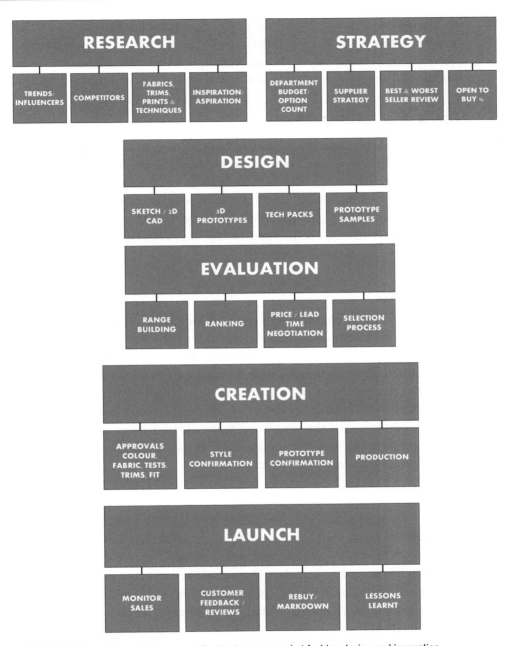

**FIGURE 8.2** A breakdown of stages contributing to mass market fashion design and innovation.

sent to suppliers or agents to source similar fabrics. At this point, a buyer will normally indicate the target selling price of the garment, to help assist in the sourcing process. It is hugely frustrating for a designer or buyer to be shown a beautiful, innovative fabric, only to be told it does not fit within the price and profit margin constraints. Most mass market retailers will allocate a "bought sample" budget which is apportioned between the various product departments. Bought samples are often "reverse-engineered", whereby the samples are deconstructed to identify pattern pieces, manufacturing methods and techniques. These are often used to brief the suppliers for inspiration or technical information on new product developments.

## Trend Research for the Mass Market

Trend research is similar in process to branded and ready-to-wear fashion. Street style, inspiration shopping research, trend research on platforms such as WGSN (see chapter 5), trend agencies and competitor insights are all used to inform the direction of the range. Unlike branded and designer companies who particularly value originality in design, social media is a huge part of trend research for the mass market, with Pinterest, Tik Tok and Instagram, generating almost unlimited ideas for creativity, innovation and trends.

## Fabric Trends

Trend research may also take the form of looking at new and innovative fabric developments. It is common for a creative idea to be sparked from a swatch of fabric alone. Designers may attend fabric trade fairs (like the *London Textile Fair*, or *Première Vision Paris*) and see new fabrics which take their interest (see Chapters 2 and 5). Alternatively, suppliers often visit retailers' head offices to meet with product teams and bring with them swatches and examples of new fabric innovations they believe will be a key trend for the upcoming season. Designer collections and brands are likely to have more budget to create bespoke fabrics, and are less reliant on their garment suppliers' own developments.

## Strategy

In addition to trend research, designers are given data by the buyer (who selects a mass market retailer's products) and merchandiser (who is responsible for liaising with suppliers to order the selected products and manage progress with suppliers and internal colleagues) which act as parameters for design. This is important in mass market retailing because unlike designer brands, mass market designers do not have as much free rein in the design process. The department and range strategies are influenced by the overall retailer strategy and are informed by data insights provided by the retail merchandiser. These include previous best and worst sellers, budget allocation and option count. The buyer will layer on information about supplier strategy, competitor analysis, pricing architecture, missed opportunities and the percentage of newness (innovation) versus core product the range should consist of. Additionally, the balance of the range is carefully considered in terms of attributes including shape, colour, style, sleeve length, leg length, neckline, fabric and fit. This is not an exhaustive list, and attributes vary from retailer to retailer.

This range strategy allows the designer to understand what the season's "must-haves" are. There is always a percentage of the range designers must redesign, following strict criteria. However, with new, trend-led styles, they will have more creative freedom to innovate. Ultimately, it is the job of the designer to take these insights and the latest trend research and skilfully balance the range to meet all criteria. Core product may have to be "moved on", meaning updated and innovated in terms of fabrics, fit or engineering into a lower price point to achieve a higher profit margin. It is within this area where mass market designers have to factor in more variables into their range designs than higher-end, branded fashion designers, who will have more creative freedom over the range. As shown in Figures 8.1 and 8.2, research and strategy sit alongside each other to give a holistic view of trends, customer and competitor insights and range parameters, allowing the design teams to proceed to design with a high level of informed knowledge. In a similar way to branded collections, mass market retailers tend to have their own signature style, which ensures that consumers know what type of garments to expect from these labels. For example, Hash Ladha, CEO of own-label retailer Jigsaw, at the upper end of the mass market, stated in 2023 that its new Design Director, Julia Reimann, "will bring a beautiful feminine handwriting to the collection and will continue to elevate our proposition of timeless design, uncompromising quality with an unexpected twist" (Weston, 2024).

## Design/design Development

This is the part of the design process where designers will come up with creative and innovative new product ideas based on the information they have available to them. This stage may vary within different mass market retailers, as some retailers have their own in-house design teams and some are fully reliant on suppliers' designs. Essentially, this is the design part of the process, where the designer puts pen to paper (or pen to tablet if designing digitally). Some designers may sketch out initial concepts on paper or via CAD packages such as Adobe Photoshop® or Illustrator®. Many designers now work on innovative 3D design software such as CLO3D, Adobe Substance 3D, Romans CAD, Tuka3D and Browzwear, which (unlike 2D software) shows the garment on a 3D-effect avatar from any angle (see Chapter 3). Designers will work with buyers to decide which of the designs should be made into sample garments. Often, when working with 3D design packages, the need for a physical garment sample is eliminated until the style is fully selected, however it is worth noting that not all mass market retailers work this way, with many of them only just introducing this technology at the time of writing this book (see Chapter 3). In mass market retailing, speed is key, and 3D sampling allows the whole process

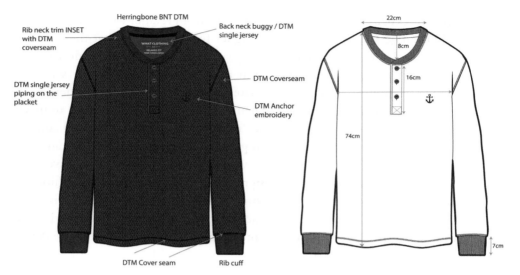

Herringbone BNT DTM

Rib neck trim INSET
with DTM
coverseam

Back neck buggy / DTM
single jersey

DTM single jersey
piping on the
placket

DTM Coverseam

DTM Anchor
embroidery

DTM Cover seam

Rib cuff

22cm

8cm

16cm

74cm

7cm

**FIGURE 8.3** Working drawings in a tech pack of information required to create a mass market sample garment. Images with permission from Helen Tarratt

to be sped up. However, if physical garment samples are needed, the designer will produce a "tech pack" with measurements and specifications for fabric, fit etc which will be sent to the supplier (see Figure 8.3). The first prototype sample will be made, usually in the specified fabric, but not always in the correct colour – depending on availability of the sample fabric. This garment sample should be made according to the requested pattern, and therefore should be suitable for fitting either on a size-specific mannequin or a human model of a specific clothing size.

## Evaluation

This is also known as the selection stage, where the garment goes through a selection process with senior decision-makers. Prior to selection, there is a "range-building" process which takes account of the parameters outlined within the insights stage. Prior to presenting the products to management and directors, the buy quantity needs to be indicated. This is done through a ranking process whereby the range is sorted from predicted best to worst seller and the quantities the retailer will buy are attributed to each style accordingly. Depending on the mass market retailer and the required speed to market, the selection process could take the form of one selection meeting or more. Historically, several selection meetings took place before orders were confirmed, but with the increased speed and competition, especially within fast fashion retailers, this stage of the process has been expedited to happen as quickly as possible. In many mass market retailers, the most innovative product is

**FIGURE 8.4** Mass market retailers place some of their most innovative products in store windows or on mannequins inside retail outlets to attract consumers' interest. Photos by Helen Goworek

required to be ranked at the top of the range, meaning the retailer predicts that this style will be the best seller within the range. As a result, the innovative styles will be bought in the larger quantities, and if the retailer has bricks and mortar stores, every store should expect to get stock of these products. The retailer may even go as far as promoting these products in its shop windows and on the landing pages of its website in order to show customers and competitors that it values innovation, trends and newness (see Figure 8.4).

## Creation

Similarly to higher-end brands, the buyer confirms the final styling details and negotiates the garment price with the supplier. Comments about the fit of the garment are sent to allow the factory to make a second prototype sample. Merchandisers will "book" the styles with the suppliers, giving them quantities of each style they'd like to order, and negotiating production dates. Designers will not ordinarily be involved in price negotiations or booking the styles, but they may wish to be involved with the fit process to ensure that the aesthetic of the garment remains faithful to their original design concept and idea. A final fit prototype sample may be made, and when approved, this "sealing sample" becomes the standard for production (see Chapter 4). Some mass market retailers speed this process up by giving the suppliers autonomy to approve the prototypes themselves. When supplier autonomy was introduced in the early 2000s, it was seen as a hugely innovative step in the supply chain process, but to this day many retailers are still reluctant to relinquish control of the approval process to even the most trusted suppliers. It may be seen as a trade-off between speeding up the processes and assessing the risk of the supplier making the wrong decision. It's worth noting that some retailers work entirely digitally with

3D CAD designs and may skip the garment fitting stage by conducting a virtual 3D fitting process using the design software and proceeding to production without the need for a physical garment sample.

## Launch

Once the style has been manufactured and received into the retailer's warehouse, it will go on sale through the website, in-store or both. The buying and merchandising team will closely monitor sales to gauge product popularity, especially for an innovative new style. It is essential that any promising styles are acted upon quickly and further quantities are bought. Garment returns and customer feedback are monitored to inform the team of the customer response. This is where the designer learns whether the innovation has been well received or not. The customer feedback, whether positive or negative, is invaluable in allowing the designer to iterate the next collection through data-driven insights. Negative feedback in particular allows designers to innovate based on "problem-solving design", find out what the customer's pain points are within the garment, and alleviate these through empathy and innovation. This stage is also called "the iterative process", "the feedback loop" or "the test-and-learn cycle".

### Case Study: The Role of the Garment Technologist in Product Innovation

It is not just the designers and buyers who face challenges and constraints when trying to innovate product ranges. Jessica Apps, an experienced Senior Garment Technologist at a major High Street retailer, discusses some of the issues she and her team have faced when developing clothing ranges.

Cost – Often the initial garment costing will necessitate changes to fit, styling or fabric. In mass market product development, cost and profit margin are the main factors in product development and dictate many of our decisions. For example, the hem circumference of the garment may be reduced to save fabric, and therefore save cost which then allows us to hit our target profit margin. Styling changes (for example, functional pockets changed to mock pockets, design details removed or simplified) can be made to help reduce cost. Also, if the initial fabric cost is too high, a cheaper alternative can be sought.

Image representation/photo shoot image – We have had a couple of instances where the production garment sample just doesn't look as good as the photo shoot sample. This has resulted in the garment needing a redesign to look more like the photo shoot image, or a reshoot. We have a dress currently in the range – an elasticated waist shirt dress, but the bulk fabric is heavier than the initial sample and we can't replicate what they used for the photo shoot – the dress doesn't hang as well and pulls the waist down. This has resulted in a complete redesign and reshape, and a change to a different shirt pattern block with drawstring waist. The style just hasn't worked using bulk fabrics. We have changed the styling to a proven shirt pattern block as we feel more confident that the customer will like the shape.

**FIGURE 8.5** Jessica Apps. Photo with permission from Jessica Apps

**Returns** – We will always monitor the rate of returns (sending back to the retailer) of a product and the cost to the business of those returns. We also look at the customer feedback to identify and address any potential fit issues with the products. Sometimes high-returning garments can be attributed to the representation of the garment image online. If the customer receives a product that doesn't look like the website image, this can result in high returns. All these factors can really affect the further development of the ranges and the repeat buy quantities the team places with the suppliers. We know that a short dress at 88 cm will return higher than a dress at 90 cm – this has helped to give us minimum measurements for our garments. Consideration of returns percentages and customer feedback helps to improve the garments for future ranges.

**Fit innovation** – We can implement changes to the make and construction of the garments to improve the product. We recently introduced an adjustable hem to school wear trousers, which allows the customer to remove a line of stitching to make the trouser longer, giving more longevity of wear and value for money for the customer. Something else we do is to assess the style suitability for the planned age range, for example, we had a girl's dress with a cut-out panel at the waist – but this design is not suitable for all ages, so age 12–18 months was changed to be a standard dress without the cut-out panel, and age 3 years and above has the cut-out panel at the side waist.

**Customer profile** – It's really important we know our customer profiles and understand the age ranges, likes, habits and needs of our customers. This allows us to design with empathy (putting the customer and their wants and needs at the heart of our decisions). This is a major factor in how the ranges are designed and how we design the garment fit for our customers.

> **Brand DNA** – This is something we look at quite a lot. We are developing product for a number of brands, and it is important that we represent the brand that we are designing for. Is the look of the brand bold and bright, or feminine and nostalgic? It is important that we ensure that the fit and look of the garment represents the brand DNA.
>
> **Sizing** – Dual sizing (offering the range in sizes small, medium and large) can be more cost-efficient than single sizing (10, 12, 14 etc) as there are less sizes for the factory to cut. This results in a more efficient lay-planning (where the pieces of the garment pattern are laid on to the fabric to maximise fabric usage and minimise wastage). However, the way the garment fits needs to be carefully considered here – will the medium garment fit both a 12 and a size 14 correctly? If not, design details need to be reconsidered, such as the fabric, styling details and construction (e.g., elasticated waist detail to help the garment fit well for both sizes). The size offer can affect customer demand and also the percentage of garments that are returned. So, whilst minimising the number of sizes we offer can help to maximise efficiency and profitability from a manufacturing point of view, we have to consider what size ranges we offer to meet customer demand and ensure the garments fit as well as they can for every customer.

## Drivers of Innovation in the Mass Market

There are several drivers of innovation. Current trends and a demand for novelty and newness are key drivers, as well as getting and staying ahead of the competition through the continual generation of innovative ideas. Tidd and Bessant (2015:122) state that "innovative ideas can come from a wide range of sources and situations: from inspiration, transfer from another context, from listening to customer needs, from frontier research or by combining existing ideas into something new".

### Trends

Chapter 5 discusses how trends are pivotal to the creativity and innovative process as a whole; however, it should be noted that new trends are one of the key drivers of innovation within the mass market fashion industry. "Trends create opportunities or needs for innovation. For instance, new customer demands create opportunities for innovators to spot and act upon by generating ideas and new products", according to van den Ende (2021:31). Trends can fall within the categories of macro or micro trends. Macro trends concern society as a whole, and are defined by van den Ende (2021:36) as "a long-term change process in society or the economy that affects a large part of the population". For example, during the global COVID pandemic, when the UK were locked down in their homes, online shopping became the only way consumers were able to buy clothing, and loungewear became a huge trend. Fashion consumers got used to a level of comfort within their clothes, preferring softer, stretchier styles to denim and formalwear. Subsequently, this resulted in fashion designers focusing on elements of comfort within their ranges, and jeans, trousers and shorts were incrementally innovated. Elasticated drawcord waists were added to garments to allow for comfort, at the request and expectation of consumers who had got used to a non-restrictive waistband with their loungewear. In contrast, micro trends are short-lived fashion trends which are adopted by a specific market or demographic. Micro trends are a powerful driver of innovation, as discussed in depth in Chapter 4.

## Competitive Advantage

Competitive advantage relates to the reason why a consumer selects one brand over another (Porter, 1985). There are many factors at play within competitive advantage – e.g., the in-store experience, online user experience, product offer, quality, value and range offered. Within all of these areas, innovation is key to meet the ever-evolving demands of the consumer. Consumers within the mass market level are constantly looking for viable new offerings from businesses to excite and delight them, and to provide a novelty value which causes them to purchase. Being "first to market" with a new innovation allows for increased sales and marketability. However, in the competitive landscape of mass market retailing, the innovative product or idea does not hold uniqueness and novelty for long. The innovator will always have an imitator quick to copy and bring to market a competing version, often at a better price.

## Intuition

Many experienced buyers and designers in the mass market fashion industry rely on intuition or "gut instinct" to drive successful innovation. Samier (2019:2) defines intuition as

> a process, an apperception and an immediate type of knowledge that does not belong to either a cognitive process or an intellectual reflection … and a type of immediate knowledge that does not derive from a rational process or logical thinking.

It is a commonly held belief that intuition cannot be taught; however, Samier (2019:10) believes that "everyone can intuit, even those who still think they cannot". Within the context of the mass market fashion industry, it is clear that increasing industry knowledge and experience can make intuition towards what makes a successful product innovation, even stronger. It is this intuition, or innate knowledge of consumers and what they need, want – and most importantly, are likely to buy

– which leads product teams to successfully innovate products that go on to become best-sellers. According to Brown (2019:3), "being intuitive in the application of design leads to more relevant experiences that connect emotionally to people and gain greater loyalty from customers".

## Supplier-driven Innovation

As Ridley (2021:255) states: "innovation always requires collaboration and sharing". Supplier-driven innovations contribute significantly to the fashion industry's evolution, providing brands with new materials, technologies and sustainable practices to incorporate into their designs and production processes. Many product innovations sold by mass market retailers originate from their suppliers. It is essential that product teams from mass market retailers visit the suppliers, ideally at their factories to see first-hand what innovations the suppliers may be working on. Suppliers are in a privileged position to see a holistic view of the marketplace and will generally be working with several well-known mass market retailers at any one time. This gives them a unique overview of key trends, sales data and where best to invest their time and efforts within innovation.

Suppliers have a keen interest in monitoring the performance of the products they supply to mass market retailers. Suppliers can actively observe customer feedback on social media and online reviews to gauge customer reactions. Positive sales and feedback allow suppliers to maintain strong prices for their innovations, based on the fact the brand or retailer may want to negotiate exclusivity. By granting exclusivity of the innovation to one retailer, the supplier would be in a good position to achieve a higher profit margin or higher minimum quantities, depending on the cost of innovation and the return on investment sought. From a retailer's point of view, a new innovation from a trusted and known supplier is a win–win. The retailer may buy a higher quantity of garments up front than it may otherwise do, or pay slightly more to secure the exclusive rights to sell the innovation and thus prevent its competitors from accessing the innovation. Examples might be a new type of sole for trainers, or a recycled sustainable fabric.

The ideal situation for a supplier would be to sell iterations of the same innovation to different retailers, without a conflict of interest. However, one of the main benefits of innovation for the consumer is the fact it is new and never seen before, so there is a real risk the market could be saturated very quickly with the product. This is a trade-off suppliers must discuss with their retailers. One way to ensure exclusivity of innovation when the original design is owned by the supplier is for the buyer to negotiate an "assignment of design rights" to the retailer. This is normally done when the retailer can offer to buy quantities which are large enough for the supplier to make a substantial profit.

## Constraints on Creativity and Innovation within the Mass Market

Chapter 7 demonstrated ways in which creativity and innovation can flourish in brands and ready-to-wear businesses. In comparison, the mass market fashion industry, by its very nature, faces several constraints that can impact upon the innovation process. Selling price and margin can form an immovable barrier to innovation, or at least restrictive boundaries within which to innovate (see Chapter 4). Likewise, commercial and market constraints must be taken into account (McKelvey & Munslow, 2012). Boundaries to creativity and innovation within the mass market are largely financial, technical, temporal and visual (see Chapter 4, Figure 4.3), such as limited capabilities of the supply chain, sustainability considerations, lack of investment, timing and an unwillingness to take risks. Similarly, the business may have had a bad experience in the past of launching an innovation to great expense, only for it to fail to sell, or be copied by a competitor. Lastly, the culture of the business and whether it fosters a sense of creativity and innovation within its staff is also a crucial factor in how creative and innovative a mass market brand or retailer can be.

According to Munasinghe et al. (2022), the mass market design process is restricted by short lead times and low price points, therefore the development of entirely new concepts is limited. Every fashion mass market business will face the same issues, and it can be frustrating for product teams to feel that their creativity and innovation has to be constrained to meet the various pressures of the business model. However, when facing constraints, creativity and innovative thinking are skills which are needed in abundance. Questions such as "How can we find new ways of doing things?", "How can we find solutions to the problems?" and "How can we make this item cost less whilst maintaining the look, feel and quality?" all require innovative thinking and creative problem-solving. This is why many designers, product developers and buyers within the mass market industry are adept at quickly generating new, problem-solving creative ideas daily. Overcoming these constraints requires a strategic approach that balances the need for efficiency with the pursuit of innovation. Successful mass market fashion brands often find ways to integrate innovation into their processes while navigating these challenges. Some of the constraints faced by mass market retail product teams are identified below, as well as some examples of how problems may be overcome using creative thinking.

### Team Dynamics

The buying team within a mass market retailer is generally made up of a buyer, merchandiser, designer and garment technologist and their respective assistants and trainees/administrators. Certain retailers also employ fabric technologists who work across several product teams. The power associated with each individual team member goes a long way to predicting the level of creativity and innovation within the team. In teams where the buyer is charged with developing the overall product and department strategy – i.e., making the important product decisions and "leading the charge" – this may constrain innovation and creativity from the designer.

## Production Lead Times

Mass market fashion brands, and especially fast fashion brands, often operate on tight production schedules and short lead times. To gain competitive advantage within fast fashion, it is often the brand which is first to market with a product which wins the most sales. The speed of production is often a constraint on creativity and innovation, as the time available for research, inspiration, creative development and thorough consideration of innovation is limited. The industry's focus on rapid turnover of inventory and frequent product releases may hinder the adoption of slower, more thoughtful innovative processes. Mass market brands often produce large quantities to meet consumer demand. This can limit the ability to experiment with smaller-scale or niche innovations due to the need for standardised, scalable production.

## Limited Differentiation

Mass market brands often face challenges in differentiating their products in a crowded market. This limitation can affect the extent to which they can experiment with unique or groundbreaking designs. It is common for mass market brands to offer similar products to their competitors as a result of their respective design teams looking for inspiration in the same places. For example, many swimwear design teams will use the same trend insights from WGSN and may attend the same trade fairs. They may also conduct their inspiration travel to the same countries and follow the same influential designer brands. This results in their product trend inspiration being very similar. The retailers may also use the same factories as their competitors, thereby seeing competitors' samples at development stage. These factors combined result in a somewhat homogenous approach to the final product offered within the store.

## Customer Expectations

Mass market brands may be constrained by consumer expectations for low prices. This can limit their ability to invest in premium materials, innovative technologies or sustainable practices without risking price competitiveness. This is especially true for value-driven brands, such as supermarket own-brand fashions or retailers such as Primark. Customers who shop at the lower end of the mass market may prioritise price above all. Additionally, more basic items such as T-shirts and vests are designed to be manufactured in the quickest way possible, driving efficiencies and achieving the high throughput required by the buyer or merchandiser. This prioritisation of efficient manufacturing can be to the detriment of improved fabrics or design details.

## Fast Fashion

Likewise, the fast fashion consumer is likely to prioritise the importance of speed to market of the latest trends, over creativity, innovation and quality. The fast fashion model, which emphasises quick turnover of styles, can constrain the ability to invest in innovative high-quality materials or engage in slower, more considered design details and production processes.

## Sustainability

The sustainability-driven consumer will prioritise sustainable fabrics and practices, including transparency and provenance of the garment. While sustainability is gaining importance, mass market brands may find it challenging to adopt sustainable practices across their entire supply chain[2] without significant investments and potential increases in production costs. Many mass market brands are working to improve sustainability throughout the supply chain, but this may involve careful redesign of well-established practices. Sustainable innovation is important for the future of mass market fashion businesses; however, implementing these practices requires knowledge, time, expense and commitment on the part of the retailer to make these changes (see Chapter 6).

## Previous Experiences

Innovation within mass market fashion retailing requires some level of risk. Decision-makers have to be comfortable with the risk of introducing new products into the existing offer. It is the job of the designer and buyer to jointly sell the vision of newness and range innovation. However, this requires a level of financial investment into the untried and untested products. Mass market brands may be risk-averse due to the potential financial implications of previous unsuccessful innovations. When the overarching key performance indicator of a department is profitability, it can be hard to persuade senior leaders and decision-makers to trust the instincts of the designers and buyers. Ironically, risk aversion leads to stifling creativity, and limiting innovation and experimentation is a certain route to staidness and failure.

## Trend Shifts

Within any multi-product fashion retailer, certain product types will be on-trend or off-trend at any point in time (see Chapter 5). On-trend product areas (e.g., outerwear, swimwear) will be allocated more buying budget by the retailer's management or finance team to expand its ranges and buy deeper levels of stock. Conversely, off-trend areas may have to relinquish their budgets to these on-trend areas, limiting their option count and the depth of their buys. Testing new and innovative concepts within off-trend product areas can be challenging due to sales trends and the customer being less receptive to these product types at a particular time. Timing is hugely important when releasing innovative products. Testing the customer's reaction to the product is crucial. If the desired sales are not achieved, but the product teams still feel strongly in favour the product concept and design, re-launching the product at a later date in order to re-test the market is essential. In these circumstances, a mass market brand may be hesitant to risk large-scale pro-duction on unproven innovations, so testing and re-testing to prove the customer demand is there is crucial.

## Solutions to Innovation Constraints

Where innovation exists to improve product design, cost and margin pressures can often undo any improvements in order to achieve profitability. However, mass mar-ket fashion buyers, designers and product developers face this challenge daily, and must become adept at using problem-solving innovation to reduce the cost of the garment and meet the all-important margin targets.

Some examples of this are discussed below:

## Fabric

The designer may specify a new innovative fabric within a design, but if this is unaffordable, then an alternative needs to be sought. It is worth asking the fabric supplier if any other retailers or brands are using this fabric, and "piggy-backing" on to their order to achieve economies of scale and reduced cost. The weight of the fabric plays a part in the price, and in general, the heavier the fabric, the costlier it is. Reducing the weight (gsm or grams per square metre) can have a significant impact on price, whilst still maintaining other innovative features.

## Fit

The fit of the garment is determined by the pattern specified by the designer (often referred to as the "block" of the garment). Innovation in fit can take the form of seamless garments, new pattern developments, new ways of incorporating pockets or zips etc. Changing the fit of a garment to meet cost and margin pressures is not always welcomed by the design team. However, it is the combined responsibility of the buyer, designer (and if the retailer employs them, garment technologists) to find innovative ways to change the pattern or sewing technique to reduce costs whilst still maintaining the overall fit and aesthetic of the garment. Advice from the supplier almost always proves to be invaluable here.

## Design Details

Design details on a garment can consist of stitch techniques, seaming, pockets, zips, embroidery, print, sequining, badging, appliqués or a combination of these (see Figure 8.6 and Chapter 2). Embellishments on garments which were traditionally done by hand can be innovated through automated digital processes which give a similar effect whilst reducing cost. New digital print techniques can offer unlimited options for printing whilst reducing waste and costs. This is an example of where new innovations, whilst costly to implement, provide cheaper solutions in the long term and reasons why suppliers should be encouraged to seek new technology and buyers should be aware of new technology within the market.

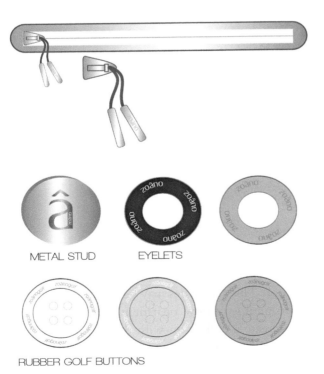

FIGURE 8.6 Design details for fastenings by Purdy Creative. Photo with permission from Karen Purdy

## Co-creation in Design

Whilst designers are crucial to the creative design process in mass market retailing, they are not the only source of design input. Co-creation (see Chapter 4) allows for a more diverse offer, and the sharing of ideas, frequently involving consumer input, often generates a higher level of creative output and synergy than if a designer is left to ideate in isolation.

## Designer Brand Collaboration

As a tried and tested route to success, mass market brands such as H&M and Uniqlo are well known for their designer collaborations. These collaborations succeed by maximising the strengths of both parties involved. They bring high-end design aesthetics to the mass market. Stock is limited-edition, and this forced scarcity generates excitement and hype, often resulting in heightened brand awareness, higher footfall into store, and increased sales for both the High Street brand and the designer brand. It is not uncommon for such hype to be generated in advance of these collections that consumers queue up at the physical retail store to be amongst the first to buy. Often, with more premium and high-profile designer collaborations stock sells out almost instantaneously. This results in a strong re-sale demand on sites like Depop, Vinted and eBay, where the product can fetch a price well in excess of the original sale price. Examples of successful High Street and designer collaborations include:

H&M × Karl Lagerfeld (2004)

H&M × Balmain (2015)

H&M × Erdem (2017)

H&M × Moschino (2018)

H&M × Giambattista Valli (2019)

H&M × Simone Rocha (2021)

Zara × JW Anderson (2017)

Uniqlo × Anya Hindmarch (2023)

## Celebrity Collaborations

Mass market retailers may also collaborate with celebrities with whom they feel their customers have an affiliation. The celebrities may be used to wearing designer clothes and have a good understanding of how a garment should fit and feel when worn. The celebrities may co-create a collection with the retailer based on items within their own wardrobe, as well as forthcoming trends. The endorsement of the celebrity is often enough to generate press and PR around the collections, and it is not uncommon for celebrity collaborations to run for several seasons, if not years.

## Beyonce × Ivy Park for Topshop

Beyoncé's Ivy Park is a street-inspired leisurewear range, highly successful with a younger demographic. The price points were slightly higher than Topshop's standard pricing architecture, but the consumer was happy to pay the higher price point because of the Ivy Park branding and the celebrity endorsement.

## Kate Moss × Topshop

Kate Moss was arguably one of the first celebrities to collaborate with a High Street brand. Her collections for Topshop featured her signature rock-chick style and were highly successful, generating hype around the retailer and an upsurge in profits at that time.

## Rihanna × Primark

Rihanna has had successful collaborations with River Island and Primark, bringing her edgy, street-inspired styling to a range of products, including dresses, jersey tops and jeans. Rihanna's collection with Primark is positioned at the front of Primark stores to catch customers' attention as they walk in and out of the stores.

## Summary

This chapter has explored the key differentiators between ready-to-wear or branded fashion and mass market fashion. The drivers of innovation have been discussed, such as competitive advantage, intuition, sustainability, co-creation, technology and supplier-driven innovation. The key constraints on innovation have been explored, including margin and cost targets, time pressures and manufacturing capabilities. Constraints on creativity and innovation within the mass market include team dynamics, production lead times, limited differentiation, customer expectations, fast fashion, sustainability, previous experience and trend shifts. However, creative thinking and innovation can overcome many of these constraints, allowing for even the most basic core products to be innovated through creative problem-solving. Solutions to innovation constraints can be found in terms of the effective development of fabric, fit, design details, co-creation, and collaborations with other brands or celebrities. Successful innovation often involves a combination of technology adoption, sustainability initiatives and strategies that resonate with the diverse and evolving preferences of mass market consumers. By adopting these innovative strategies, mass market fashion brands can differentiate themselves from the competition, meet consumer expectations and navigate the dynamic landscape of the mass market fashion industry. The following interviews offer insights into the ways in which creativity and innovation operate in practice in mass market companies.

**FIGURE 8.7**  Richard Price. Photo with permission from Richard Price

## Interviews on Creativity and Innovation with Mass Market Fashion Specialists

**Richard Price is Managing Director of Clothing, Home and Beauty at Marks & Spencer (M&S). Richard graduated with a BA (Hons) Business Studies at the University of Wolverhampton, UK before embarking on his retail career at Next.**

*How important is innovation within Marks & Spencer?*

I think innovation takes many forms and M&S has always prided itself on product innovation, particularly from a technical perspective. We were the first to market with machine-washable lambswool, miracle linen, which is a crease-resistant linen, and many others. Having products that provide solutions for customers through innovation is really, really important ,and we've always been known for our quality, value for money and our cost per wear. What we're doing at the moment is looking to be more innovative in terms of creating more stylish, more desirable product. The other aspect of innovation is trend and creating innovative solutions, outfits and end uses for customers to buy into our products in a way that we probably haven't done before.

We are still looking at technical innovation, particularly in areas like home and bedding. We have solutions for menopause, such as cooling, wicking and moisture-removing fabrics across a number of categories for home, towels and sportswear. We're having a bit of a refocus on innovation from a garment perspective, particularly in areas like lingerie ,where we're market leaders and continually innovating to create helpful solutions for customers, whether that's wireless bras that behave like wired bras, solutions for post-surgery ... the list goes on. We're always looking at both garment and fabric innovation and creating a USP that attracts customers to M&S products. In such a competitive environment, we're looking to create a point of difference from the competition. We've realised and seen from the past couple of years we definitely want to be more fashion-conscious, but definitely in a way that's right for our customer. We're looking at innovation in a massive way in terms of how we incorporate tech, things like digital bra fitting and digital product creation, and how we incorporate that into our critical path. We're working with suppliers to create a sample-less process, or certainly a much-reduced dependence on sampling, which is going to save us millions and make us quicker. The other element is using AI and machine learning to start to predict what your best sellers are going to be and what your range architecture should be, such as what stock to send to what stores.

*How are you using machine learning and AI in other areas of the business?*

We bought the business Thread a year ago, and what they're doing is looking at using data and AI to generate output solutions and matching outfits with customer behaviour. It's a combination of understanding your size, shape, and looking at your purchasing profile, giving recommendations and outfit-building based on your purchasing habits. This technology provides full outfit solutions, based on knowing what you like, where you like to shop and knowing what size you are. Based on this information, we can give our customers more personalised style and "ways to wear it" recommendations. There's a human logic to it, too. It's based around how most people will match colours, and as it gets more sophisticated, it will learn more and more and start to do that for itself, but when you're starting off, you've got to guide it.

*How important is empathy in design when you are looking at innovation and how do you market that to your customer?*

I think it's really important to understand and be empathetic to your customer. One of the things that's been our downfall in the past is trying to be all things to all people and serving up things that the M&S customer thinks is not for them. One of our biggest challenges as we've gone on a journey of improving our style credentials and modernising the business is offering the customers the right solution. From a customer's viewpoint, they're being offered solutions which they're never going to wear, so they are thinking, "Don't offer it to me." One of our newest pieces of innovation which we're looking at, but haven't implemented yet is digital fitting. It gives you a digital profile based on a reading of your figure, it's not measurement-driven, it's all based on data points and trying to match that with a style that will best suit you. We want to serve up recommendations to our customer that we know will fit them. This is where you've got to be empathetic and know your customer, and we will be testing this in a live environment. There's a statistic which states around two-thirds of all women are wearing the wrong bra size on a daily basis, and that's why we push bra fitting so heavily. We get letters to say, "Oh my gosh, you've transformed my life because I didn't realise for 15 years, I was wearing a bra three sizes too small, and it makes me makes my back pain go away and my posture better.

*How important is it that your teams are protecting new innovations from infringement by competitors?*

Without a doubt, if it's protectable and it's our IP, then we will seek to protect it. In terms of new fabrications, if we've absolutely created and developed them with the mills, then we'll seek to protect it.

*What examples of creative innovation are there in the business?*

The latest piece of tech which we're looking at is where you can design by speech. For example, you might say, "I'd like an evening bag with a long handle and metal fastenings," and it basically designs it for you based on what you told it. It's AI-driven. So you could design a skirt and then ask for it to be 2 inches longer, and it does it. You give it an instruction, for example, "Make that pleat 1 cm wider," so you don't have to physically do anything. You tell it, and then it creates a digital solution on an avatar that you can then say, "I want to create a sample of that."

*Do the majority of your innovations come organically from your product teams, or are they driven by supplier innovations, or a mixture of both?*

I think it's a mixture of both. We often present suppliers with the problem-state, and they'll go away and come back with a solution. Some of our fabric techs are a bit more technical than others, and they'll come up with the ideas themselves and get the mills to execute them, particularly things like products that hold you in or technology that's firming and shaping. It's not new technology – the moisture wicking has been around for decades, but it just gets more and more sophisticated through innovation.

*What sustainable innovations are you working on at the moment?*

Innovation in sustainability is massive in terms of environmental impact, recycling regeneration and using less water. That's probably where most people's innovation at the moment is going. We've said we're going to be carbon-neutral by 2040, so we're looking at how we can grow cotton without water. How can we make jeans without water? How can we use lasering? How can we dye without chemicals? The list is endless. Understanding the impact of innovation on manufacturing to save the planet is probably the single biggest source of innovation that's happening at the moment. The other element of it is traceability and technology to prove provenance. You can now test the DNA of cotton to see where it was made. We test 100 garments periodically, and we can see that our supply base is compliant and not using cotton from areas that have not been approved by us.

*How important is it to communicate what you're doing to the customer in terms of sustainable innovation? How interested are they, and do you monitor this via your website?*

We do. We are living in a world where second-hand is much more acceptable, and Vinted is phenomenal in terms of its growth. We see that as an opportunity because we're trying to innovate to make products more durable and last longer. There's a marketing piece, in that you buy M&S kid's wear and it might be a bit more expensive, but it is still exceptional value because the quality means you can hand it down to the next generation or you can sell it on.

*How would you define innovation in fashion?*

Innovation is creating something that nobody else has thought of that is new and ground-breaking and makes a difference. There's no point in doing innovation for innovation's sake. It has to have positive impact on the desirability or sustainability or longevity of a product or service. The important thing is it has to provide a solution or make a product better, more durable, cheaper or less harmful to the environment. It has to have a purpose.

**Abigail Bourne is Senior Buyer in women's wear at Joules, covering outerwear, knitwear, jersey, fleece, sweatshirts and nightwear. Abigail studied for a BA (Hons) in Fashion Marketing at the University of Central Lancashire, UK before working in buying at Next then Joules, as well as being a guest lecturer in Fashion Marketing.**

*What are Joules's priorities in terms of innovation – for example, fabric, sustainability, fit, shape trend etc.?*

Joules is very much known for its lifestyle product, so innovation is making sure that we are creating that lifestyle brand. For example, in fleece, because we're an outdoors brand, we're looking at getting Polartec® fabric in the range. That's innovation within the fabric, and although it's still very early stages, we're currently looking at what competitors are doing, such as the more technical outdoor brands. As a brand, we're really known for our rainwear, and we're constantly innovating fabrics in terms of the finish and performance, making sure that the factories that we work with are credible in terms of what we need. Can they do the taped seams? Can they offer the performance that we require because that's quite a big

**FIGURE 8.8** Abigail Bourne at Joules. Photo with permission from Abigail Bourne

marketing piece for us. The Right As Rain trademark is really prominent and definitely a big brand identity that we want to push and be known as that "stay warm, stay dry" brand.

*Joules has trademarked Right As Rain. Is that innovative in itself?*

Yes, definitely. We do quite a lot of trademarking actually, and now that we're part-owned by Next, we work with the legal team in terms of what we can trademark. We're looking at whether we can trademark a fabric as well. We have previously sold a dry wax jacket product, but because it's not waterproof, the customer doesn't buy into it as much. We're trying to create a fabric that is wax-look, but create the end-use aesthetic of a traditional wax jacket that has all the 'Right As Rain' credentials that we're known for.

*Would you say that innovation is led by the product teams or the suppliers, or is it a collaboration between the two?*

I'd say it comes more from the product teams in terms of our requests, and then the suppliers work alongside us to see what's possible. On jersey [department], we're doing a performance equestrian range, and we've worked with our supplier to get a fabric that is sweat-wicking and breathable. Then we'll look at engineering the garment, so the seams aren't poking out on the inside. It's all about comfort. So innovation is driven by Joules, but working closely with the supplier to make sure that we can get it right.

*What do you find are the biggest constraints to innovation, and how do you overcome these?*

It's all about perception of value. For example, with the Right As Rain product, we consider whether having a fully waterproof fabric and fully taped seams adds value to the garment so that the customers are willing to pay more for it. We really need to look at the cost of every function of the garment that makes it "performance". We need to question, "Is it worth it? With the Right As Rain product, it is worth it. The customer can see the value. A lot of brands might do "critically taped" seams, where it's just taped on the shoulder, whereas we do fully taped seams, and the cost differences may be a dollar, which puts £5 to £10 on your retail sell price. But for us, that's definitely worth doing because it's what the customer expects and we want to have a fully functional product.

*In terms of creativity and idea generation, how do you stay fresh and ensure that you're innovative in your role?*

We have got an amazing design team and founder, Tom. The way his mind works is very unique. He's one of a kind because he's constantly thinking of the next thing and his awareness of the market is second to none in terms of where we sit as a lifestyle brand. A lot of ideas are generated from Tom, and our job is to constantly be aware of what's going on and constantly research. The designers are amazing at this, but we also have an input as product teams. For example, is there a new fabric that someone else is doing that we want to tap into? It's about market awareness and research, generating ideas from a performance point of view by looking at technical brands for outerwear, but then making it very much our aesthetic, thinking about how we can combine technical elements but keep it Joules and keep the brand identity. That's the same across the board for all our categories. Knitwear has had the biggest innovation in product design over the last couple of seasons. We'd gone into quite a safe place with it and it wasn't selling as well, whereas now we've gone down a much more heritage route, which is selling really well. We've got beautiful quality fabrics, and we work really closely with key suppliers bringing in new yarns.

*How is innovation different at Joules to other High Street retailers?*

I think there's innovation to be found in lots of different ways from a technical element, but then also from innovation in design and keeping it fresh. What's different about Joules, having worked at other High Street retailers, is that it's a bit more playful, a bit more tongue-in-cheek. You can have more fun, and it's a brand that doesn't necessarily take itself too seriously. Tom instils that in everybody. We've got some really unique slogans coming out on knitwear, and we've got some really nice characters, too. We've got a fox that's just landed on the website – Jonty fox. It's just a lot more playful.

*What excites you about the creativity and innovation process?*

I think it's always nice to find something new. As creatives and buyers and product people, that's what we're always striving for. What's going to be exciting? What's going to be the next big thing? Ultimately, we're all there to appease the customer and to make sure you've got the product that she wants to buy and make money for the business. When you know you're onto a winner as a buyer, that's the most exciting element. When you get a new product in, you know you've nailed the price point, you know the quality is bang on, you know that it's something she's not seen before. It's still really exciting. I think you still get a buzz from that, no matter how many years you've done it.

**Bradley Lane is an e-commerce and omnichannel retail consultant, helping small and medium-sized businesses to expand their online presence. Bradley previously worked for House of Fraser and Selfridges, as well as formerly being Senior Digital Leader at John Lewis.**

*I'd like to start by asking you how you would sum up the creative and innovative work that you have been involved with in your career.*

I'd sum this up as "being on a journey, testing and learning as time goes on". For me, regardless of which role I've had, I've always tried to bring creativity and innovation to the front. In my buying days, this was through brand acquisition and own brand development, to appeal to new customers. In my digital career, it's had everything to do with trying out new technology solutions to make the end-to-end journey for a customer online easier and less sticky.

**FIGURE 8.9** Bradley Lane. Photo with permission from Bradley Lane

*What are the most important recent technological innovations in digital retailing from your perspective?*

The landscape of digital retailing has been evolving rapidly, introducing several impactful technological innovations. Some of the most significant recent advancements include:

- AI-powered personalisation: AI algorithms analyse customer data to offer personalised recommendations, create tailored shopping experiences, and predict consumer behaviour, which then enhances customer satisfaction and engagement.
- Augmented reality (AR) and virtual reality (VR): These technologies allow customers to virtually try products before purchasing, leading to a more immersive shopping experience. AR and VR have been particularly influential in the fashion and cosmetics industries.
- Voice commerce: The rise of smart assistants (like Amazon's Alexa, Google Assistant, and Apple's Siri) has facilitated voice-based shopping, allowing customers to browse and purchase products using voice commands.
- Mobile commerce and wallets: The importance of smartphones has boosted mobile shopping, leading to the integration of mobile wallets and payment systems, simplifying the checkout process and in turn enhancing convenience for customers.
- Omnichannel retailing: Retailers are increasingly integrating various channels seamlessly – online, mobile, and brick-and-mortar stores – to provide a unified shopping experience. It's about making everything as seamless as possible for the customer at the end of the day.
- Automated customer service: Chatbots and AI-powered customer service tools assist shoppers, answer queries, and provide support 24/7, improving the overall customer experience, though in my opinion there is still much more work to be done in this space.

*How would you describe the process of innovation within John Lewis and in the sector overall?*

John Lewis went through a period of leading in this space, but then a significant re-platform occurred and the cost of this placed significant pressure on the business, so much so that the competition started to move ahead of them. As a digital team, we were challenged to innovate, digest customer feedback and test and learn everything and get under the skin of data to make better-informed decisions. Of course, there was an official process, but I would try to go around the process if it was a small business investment that I quickly wanted to get feedback on. In difficult and challenging times, you'll be amazed at what you can pull off. We would always ask the teams for their input to feel part of the journey, the tech roll-out or for ideas to innovate better as a brand.

*When dealing with clients, how do you help them create and use innovations within their business? Is it an iterative process?*

Yes, it's an iterative process. I usually start at the beginning as part of my client onboarding, I'll ask a client what their ambition is, what they have done so far, and what they wish to try in the future. I see my role, in some ways, as joining up the pieces, helping clients to get the best deal at a fair price and not to get tied into a lengthy contract. Innovation comes in all shapes and sizes, for one client it's integrating a sizing tool to allow customers to make better decisions, whilst reducing unnecessary returns, for another client it could be testing a new piece of technology that enables them to launch newness quicker and through a selection of images opposed to the traditional "one image" that tends to impact conversion and increase a website's returns.

*How would you define creativity and innovation based on your own experience and knowledge?*

Creativity for me is about generating ideas, concepts or solutions that assist the customer/user. You can achieve this by using your past knowledge, experiences and your creative imagination. To be creative, you need to try to think outside of the box, finding innovative ways to solve problems or do things differently. Innovation is about applying creative ideas or solutions that bring about meaningful change or improvement.

*Who do you consider to be the most innovative and creative fashion retailers or brands from a digital perspective?*

Nike in terms of innovation with technology and design, Stella McCartney for the progress made with sustainability, Next for having become a platform for hosting brands and acquiring brands that are or have gone through difficulty, and Sephora for integrating AI into the customer experience.

## Notes

1 Profit margin is the difference between the cost of making the garment and the selling price of the garment, which is often expressed as a percentage.
2 The supply chain refers to all the processes involved in creating the finished garment, from the starting point of fibres and fabrics through to the manufacturer making the finished article.

## References

Brown, T. (2019) *Change by Design, Revised and Updated: How Design Thinking Transforms Organizations and Inspires Innovation*. New York: HarperCollins Publishers.

McKelvey, K. and Munslow, J. (2012) *Fashion Design: Process, Innovation and Practice*. Chichester: John Wiley & Sons.

Munasinghe, P.D., Dissanayake, D.G.K. and Druckman, A. (2022) 'An investigation of the mass market fashion design process', *Research Journal of Textile and Apparel*, 26(4), 323–342.

Porter, M. E. (1985) *The Competitive Advantage: Creating and Sustaining Superior Performance*. New York: Free Press.

Posner, H. (2015) *Marketing Fashion Second Edition: Strategy, Branding and Promotion*. London: Laurence King Publishing.

Ridley, M. (2021) *How Innovation Works*. London: HarperCollins Publishers.

Samier, H. (2019) *Intuition, Creativity, Innovation*. London: ISTE/Hoboken, NJ: John Wiley & Sons.

Tidd, J. and Bessant, J. (2015) *Innovation and Entrepreneurship*. Chichester: Wiley.

van den Ende, J. (2021) *Innovation Management*. London: Red Globe Press/Macmillan International Higher Education.

Weston, J. (2024) 'Jigsaw announces raft of promotions', *Drapers* 5th March 2024, available online at: https://www.drapersonline.com/news/jigsaw-announces-raft-of-promotions

# Index

9781032365800